Small Talk

For our children – Jess, Minnie and Monty

Small Talk

Simple ways to boost your child's speech
and language development from birth

Nicola Lathey

Top speech and language therapist
and **Tracey Blake**

MACMILLAN

First published 2013 by Macmillan
an imprint of Pan Macmillan, a division of Macmillan Publishers Limited
Pan Macmillan, 20 New Wharf Road, London N1 9RR
Basingstoke and Oxford
Associated companies throughout the world
www.panmacmillan.com

ISBN 978-0-230-76643-3

1 3 5 7 9 8 6 4 2

A CIP catalogue record for this book is available from the British Library.

Designed and typeset by seagulls.net

Printed by and bound by CPI Group (UK) Ltd, Croydon, CR0 4YY

Visit **www.panmacmillan.com** to read more about all our books and to buy them.
You will also find features, author interviews and news of any author events, and you
can sign up for e-newsletters so that you're always first to hear about our new releases.

Contents

Foreword

My name is Nicola Lathey and, for the past 14 years, I've been fortunate enough to have my dream job – I am a children's speech and language therapist. My work has taken me to child development centres as far afield as Australia, Sri Lanka and Vietnam, but now I am based in Oxford where I split my time between NHS work and my own private practice, The Owl Centre.

I specialize in working with children under the age of five and have helped patients with all sorts of speech, language and communication problems – from babies who aren't yet babbling, to toddlers who are more interested in Thomas the Tank Engine than talking, to children whose speech has been severely affected by their dummy addiction. I have helped children with a huge range of issues over the years and, in this book, I share my expertise, tips and tricks with you. *Small Talk* is all about boosting your baby's speech and language skills – and you both having fun whilst doing it.

Many times, I've had the privilege to witness the special moment when a child seemingly so effortlessly utters their first word – and the parents shed a tear that all their coochy-coos, peek-a-boos and constant repetition have paid off (more of which later).

The magic of communication still has the power to wow me and I hope that this book will inspire you to feel the same.

Introduction

Small Talk has two purposes: to help you identify what's going on with your child's communication and to show you how to encourage the natural stages of language development with fun games and activities. I want to teach you how you can make learning fun – both for you and your child.

Whatever questions you may have about your child's language development, I am here to answer them. Maybe you're wondering why your 18-month-old can't say 'Mummy' when all her peers can, or why your toddler constantly shouts? Will a dummy hold back your baby's speech? Does your friend boast that her baby has mastered 100 words, while yours only has 10? Just how can weaning affect language development? Does watching TV help or hinder your child's language ability? Or perhaps you just fancy having a conversation with your ten-week-old? Whatever your query, this book has been written to reassure and inform you.

You may be wondering why you need a book about a process that appears to develop so naturally – when a child suddenly starts talking it can seem like a miraculous event, with very little obvious work on your part. However, as a speech therapist I will show you just how intricate the developmental process is, how early it begins and how instrumental you can be in helping your child. I will explain the various stages of language development and inspire you with games you can play with your baby from birth to help her reach these stages quickly and also to make you aware of what is coming next. After all, intelligence needs language in order to develop and the first few years of your child's life are of critical importance to their development – and how well they do at school later on.

This book begins by guiding you through pre-birth communication. Did you know that during pregnancy, between 24 and 27 weeks, a baby can hear and recognize its mother's voice? I go on to describe the crucial 0–48-month period, which is fundamental to your baby's language development because this is when the brain builds pathways to the jaw, lips and tongue, establishing the foundations of speech.

This early language-development stage is crucial; when I see children aged four or five whose parents have concerns about their communication, the first thing I do is go right back to the start of this speech building process to get to the root of their particular problem. I will ask parents about any feeding or latching problems their child may have experienced as a baby, about when the child made her first cooing sounds and when babble (an early stage of communication, which I will explain fully in chapter three) began. This is surprising to some parents, as many don't realize that all of these things are important for language to develop (why would they?), believing that communication only begins when a child starts talking, which means that they miss critical phases during which their baby's brain power can be boosted. This book is designed to empower you by helping you maximize the guidance you give to your baby during those early stages, and by making you feel confident that you are doing the right thing at each stage to encourage your child's language development while helping to boost her brain power.

I'm going to keep things simple – and super practical. As a busy parent you will be familiar with the sort of day when conversations have been replaced with iPad or TV time as you do the chores or you've had a busy day at work away from your child and find yourself with just five minutes to spend with your little one, but you're not exactly sure what to do, and you want to get it right. To help you make the most of these little windows of time, I've put games, tips and ideas for activities that encourage communication on every page, so you can pick up this book and find something to do with your baby very easily – and have fun with her while she learns. These games are given under the heading 'Small Talk Time'. And if you haven't got time to read the whole book, simply use the contents list (see page v) to flip to the right stage in your baby's development and look out for the 'Small Talk Time' tips for instant inspiration.

THE BENEFITS OF USING MY ADVICE

Make your child smarter

It's a controversial idea but many psychologists believe that a child's grasp of language directly affects their intelligence, arguing that you need language to think and, therefore, the sooner you begin to learn language, the smarter you'll be.

My view on this is that your ability to communicate can never be more advanced than your intelligence level; however, the more you stimulate your child's communication skills, the more likely they are to realize their intellectual potential. All parents naturally want to encourage their children to communicate and I hope that this book will give you the confidence to do this. You are your baby's best resource.

Give your child a head start at school

Researchers at Bristol University have recently released a report[1] confirming that reading and talking to children at home makes starting school easier for them. They found that children with a positive communication environment went on to achieve higher scores on tests of language, reading and maths when they entered school.

The project is the first large-scale study to examine the impact of the child's early environment (before they are two) on their language. The findings emphasize that what parents do with their children, even before they have started to talk, can help prepare them for school and lifelong learning.

Professor Roulstone, Director of the Speech and Language Therapy Research Unit for North Bristol Trust, says, 'The main message is that, as parents, we can have a big impact on how our children learn to talk and the better our children are talking by the age of two years, the better they will do when they start school.'

Small Talk will help you and your child unlock the magic of communication. The way that you communicate with your child will affect not only how she interacts with you, but also how she approaches the world – how she expresses herself, learns, picks up social skills, and achieves and exercises independence. In other words, you are not merely teaching your child how to talk, but how to think, act and be. The skills set out in this book will help you to bring up a child who is, as far as possible, confident, sociable, enquiring and happy.

Stay one step ahead of your child

Small Talk lays out the chronology of language development, allowing you to pinpoint where your child is at and what is coming next. This exciting tool will enable you to stay one step ahead of your child's language development – guiding her on to achieve the next new skill.

Calm tantrums during the 'terrible twos'

If a child struggles to communicate this may be because there is a gap between their current intellectual capacity and their level of speech, and they don't yet have the language capability to express what they want. This can mean they become frustrated and prone to temper tantrums. I believe that this scenario is often the cause of the so-called 'terrible twos' (which, as many parents will know, can start much earlier than two!), when many children are struggling to verbalize their thoughts. So, the earlier your baby can communicate – whether it's to tell you that she wants to play with the red car, would like a drink or is feeling too hot – the less frustrated and the calmer she will be. I hope that this book will help parents to keep tantrums to a minimum; after all, if you can reason with them and they can answer you, you are halfway to diffusing toddler rage.

Of course, a child's inability to communicate what they want or need isn't only frustrating for the child. I know how helpless parents can feel when their child is struggling to tell them something and they simply cannot understand what it is. By creating a great Small Talker, you will help to reduce the frustrations of both you and your child.

Be reassured about what is 'normal'

I know just how much parents love to hear about the process of language development because I'm constantly quizzed by all and sundry – the mothers in my baby group, friends with toddlers, the checkout lady in our local shop who knows what I do for a living and even strangers in the street who have seen me coming out of my clinic. Almost without exception, they want reassurance that what their child is doing is 'normal' for her age, so you will therefore find a 'Milestones' section at the end of each chapter.

As a parent myself, I understand that we all want to know what our child 'should' be doing, no matter how much we tell ourselves that we shouldn't compare or don't need norms. I want to emphasize right from the outset that your child is an individual and will do things at her own pace. I've seen children who can hold conversations at 18 months while others of the same age can barely say a recognizable sound. And both are perfectly acceptable. So take the milestones with a pinch of salt and trust your instincts – all children are slightly different. One might excel physically while another will excel verbally.

If at any stage you are worried about your child's speech, language or communication development, look at the pages 287–92 in the appendix and those 'Milestones' sections at the end of each chapter. If you identify that your child has a difficulty with one particular area, go to the section in the book that provides simple and entertaining games to help your child achieve that skill. Always seek help from your health visitor, GP or a speech and language therapist if you are concerned.

So, this is a book about what happens, when it might happen, why it happens and what you can do to encourage the process of communication. My aim is to motivate you to experiment with words and language, and inspire you to expand your child's vocabulary and language skills, but in a fun, easy-to-do way with no pressure. If you want to turn your little one into a smart, sociable, well-rounded kid and have fun doing it, start Small Talking!

CHAPTER ONE

Nicola's Small Talk Techniques

This book has been written to help you discover more about language development, and it's important to remember that before the words actually come, your baby is already busy learning a range of intricate communication skills, for example, learning to listen, pay attention, be sociable and understand what is being said. These skills are the foundation for being able to talk.

Throughout this book you will find lots of games and activities (under the heading Small Talk Time) to help your baby learn these skills. And as you, the parent, are fundamental to turning your child into a great communicator, we will look at your own parenting style and how to adjust it to benefit your child. Then we will learn six Small Talk techniques – these skills will empower you to get the best out of your child and are relevant to every single interaction you have together. By the end of this chapter you will have all the top tricks up your sleeve and be raring to get going with some Small Talk Times.

WHAT TYPE OF PARENT ARE YOU?

As a speech and language therapist, one of the textbooks that I refer to is *It Takes Two to Talk* by Jan Pepper and Elaine Weitzman. One of the most useful chapters confronts the sensitive issue of the parents' communication style and how it can impact on their child's speech, language and communication development. The authors describe seven types of parent and explain that, throughout the day, mums and dads may dip in and out of all seven 'types', but usually have one dominant parenting style. Read the descriptions below, which have been adapted from Pepper and Weitzman's book*, and see if you can spot yourself:

The Director

This role has the parent leading and controlling a child's daily inter-actions. The parent does most of the talking and tells their child what to do and how to do it. For example, Robert wants to find the page with the monster in his favourite book but his dad is playing the Director role, insisting that they read the book page by page.

The Tester

In this role, the parent asks a lot of questions in order to see what the child has learned. But constant testing doesn't help the child learn – a child learns best when he is having fun and his parents are tuned in to his interests.

The Entertainer

When in this role, the parent tends to take the lead, doing most of the talking and playing, and leaving little opportunity for the child to interact and be part of the fun. However, children need to be actively involved to learn.

---

* The descriptions of parent types have been adapted from the book *It Takes Two to Talk*®: *A Practical Guide for Parents of Children with Language Delays* (Pepper and Weitzman, 2004). A Hanen Centre publication. Reprinted with permission.

The Helper

The Helper does everything for their child, from finishing his sentences to answering questions on his behalf. But when parents are too quick to help, they may not find out how much their child can communicate and what really interests him.

The Mover

This role may be adopted by a busy parent who has 101 things to do that take priority over communicating with their child. These parents often do not notice when their child is trying to show or tell them something.

The Watcher

Sometimes, parents would like to interact with their child but aren't sure how to join in, so they end up watching or commenting from a distance. But to learn language, children need to interact with their parents.

The Tuned-in Parent

This parent is tuned in to their child's interests, needs and abilities. A Tuned-in Parent gives their child opportunities to start an interaction and then responds immediately, with interest.

Out of these seven types, the Tuned-in Parent is the one to aspire to. You can't be a Tuned-in Parent all of the time, but try to play this role more often – be honest and ask yourself if you talk too much, fool around too much, continuously test your child or help your child too often.

You are your child's most valuable resource when it comes to learning to communicate so tune in to being a Tuned-in Parent.

CASE STUDY: JENNY, THE 'DIRECTOR' PARENT

A friend of a friend rang me for some advice when it became clear that her 16-month-old boy, Barney, wasn't vocalizing at all – he was merely gesturing and grunting. First of all I established that he didn't have hearing problems and his other development was normal. The mum, Jenny, felt that Barney understood everything she said and he was able to express his needs and wants non-verbally, but it was becoming frustrating for everybody that she had to continuously interpret his message for people who couldn't understand him. As our phone conversation progressed, it became clear to me that Jenny was very talkative and hardly stopped for breath. I had to think quickly of a way to get her to self-diagnose that she was talking too much and not allowing Barney an opportunity to respond. So I asked her how often she talked to Barney and if she left gaps for him to communicate back. She said, 'Well, I talk to him constantly, because that's what you're meant to do – isn't it?' I explained that while he would absorb a lot from her chatting, it was equally important that she paused regularly to allow him to join in the conversation in his own way. Jenny is definitely a Director Parent! But with my help, some self-awareness and a few simple exercises (such as Attempting Real Words – see page 114) Jenny's now got stiff competition in the chatting stakes.

THE SMALL TALK TECHNIQUES

Now we're going to focus on the most important people – your little ones. So I'm going to set out my six golden rules, referred to as Small Talk techniques, which will equip you with the knowledge necessary for developing your baby's communication skills as a foundation for great language. Don't worry if it takes some time for these to become part of your daily routine – after all, you are learning to become a good 'parent communicator' in the same way that your baby is learning something entirely new, too!

1. Enjoy ten minutes of Small Talk Time every day

The official NHS guidelines are that you should try to spend at least ten minutes every day playing with your child. This sounds shockingly short. But first of all I should emphasize that this is the bare minimum – if you have the luxury of spending three hours of uninterrupted quality time with your baby each day, while managing to maintain his fun and enthusiasm, then do! This is an important point because it is quality, not quantity, that counts when it comes to Small Talk Time.

Aiming for ten minutes of uninterrupted time is, crucially, achievable for most parents, and ten minutes can easily turn into more when you are having fun!

GETTING THE MOST OUT OF STORY TIME

A bedtime story should be additional to your ten minutes of Small Talk Time a day and should be done from a very early age – from birth, in fact. I find that many of the parents I meet at my clinic try to read to their babies every word of a book when, actually, for young babies, it's best to simply point out one or two single words that relate to the pictures on the page. As you 'tune in' to the level of your child's language and thought, you will be able to modify your storytelling accordingly – first reading out one line from each page, then the whole story.

Don't forget to point out parts of the images your child might be interested in that may not always relate to the text – a picture of

---

a dog or tractor, perhaps. Use your baby's finger to point to these things as it encourages the child to look at the same thing you are looking at.

Seek out books with a catchphrase repeated on every page – for example, the *That's Not My . . .* series of books by Fiona Watt and Rachel Wells or, for older children, *We're Going on a Bear Hunt* by Michael Rosen and Helen Oxenbury. Or if you have a favourite book that doesn't have a repetitive line in it, simply add one yourself. I love the book *Where's Spot?* by Eric Hill and tell my parents to say, 'Where's Spot?' each time they turn the page, even though, amazingly, it's not in the text. The goal is that your child should know the catchphrase so well that you can pause as you turn the page, and they will say the punchline for you, learning new words and grammar as they go.

Lastly, photo albums can work just as well as storybooks. Initially, simply name the people in the pictures, then add more detail. For example, first you might say 'Mummy', then this might become 'Mummy swimming' and finally 'Mummy swimming in the sea on holiday last summer' (see page 282 in chapter ten for more hints and tips on reading stories).

2. Set the scene for Small Talk Time

This piece of advice is very important, and more difficult to achieve than you would imagine. It centres on not being distracted for your ten minutes of Small Talk Time. We all know how easy it is to be distracted when we try to sit down and focus on one particular task. You are busy and it's not my aim to make you feel guilty, but try to figure out when in your day the windows of opportunity arise and make the most of them; it could be between supper and the start of the bedtime routine or the ten minutes before you unload the dishwasher.

Try to constantly remind yourself that your Small Talk Time has to be quality time.

You may think you definitely provide this 'quality' time already, but do you really? Research tells us that many of us parents are actually prioritizing chores over uninterrupted one-to-one time with our children. I know that life can be terribly busy, but try not to multi-task or get distracted during your Small Talk Time. Think about a recent time you spent with your little one; did you have your mobile in your hand, the TV on or Facebook at your side while you played or chatted? I often have to remind my husband to put his iPhone down when he plays with our daughter, Jess, as it seems to have been surgically stitched to his hand since the day he bought it! Actually, I mustn't be too unkind to him. Only the other evening, I was reading Jess a bedtime story while watching the television programme *Come Dine With Me* at the same time. It was so natural, sitting in the living room with the TV on, that it was a few minutes before I realized I was short-changing Jess and turned it off.

So ensure the TV is switched off, phones are far away and iPods are silent. When there is background noise, the words you say become indistinct and it's difficult for your child to focus on you – and, don't forget, you are the best role model for language they have. All ears should be on you, so your baby only has one source of information to process.

Sit down with your child, ensuring you are at the same eye level and face to face. If your child is little, sit him in a baby bouncer or prop baby up with pillows on the bed while you sit opposite, otherwise just sit on the floor together. Either way, it is important that young babies are well supported – you'll get more out of your child if he isn't having to focus on balancing in order to achieve head control, or on sitting or standing while trying to concentrate on you.

3. Be simple and clear

Speech therapists agree that understanding is the key to good language development. Before a child can begin to speak, he needs to first understand what is being said. Once your baby can understand that something that is fluffy and says 'woof, woof' is a dog, he can then begin to start to say the word. So, we must use our words clearly as a model for our babies. For example, 'Look, a cat. Meow, meow, cat.' (For more on modelling words, see page 125.)

Parents often fail to appreciate just how *new* everything is to their babies. We as adults have been gabbling for years and years – I, for one, *love* to gabble – but imagine how that must sound to a baby. You are literally bombarding them with strange, unknown sounds that, to them, have absolutely no meaning. This must be even more confusing than if, say, you were abroad listening to people talk in a language you had never heard before, because at least you'd be able to understand the body language, facial expressions and social context.

The best way to help your little one start to make sense of the world is by feeding him bite-sized morsels of language at the right level. So, when your toddler is under the age of one, for example, try to communicate in a very simplistic way using a lot of repetition (see Small Talk technique number 4, below).

Focus on the key words in a sentence and don't worry too much about using correct grammar. A sentence like 'the teddy has fallen out of the push chair' should be simplified to 'teddy fall down', depending on the level of the child's language.

Many parents might worry about adapting the grammar of a sentence, but as your child's language grows, your own language naturally expands and becomes more grammatically advanced alongside your child's. Talking in this simplified way will help your little one to begin to understand what these entirely new words and sounds mean.

CASE STUDY: LINKING WORD AND ACTION

Owen has been taking his son Laurie swimming every week since he was eight weeks old. Right from the start he learnt to say a set phrase to Laurie whenever he dunked him in the water. Several weeks into the course, Owen noticed that Laurie recognized the phrase 'Laurie, ready, go!' and knew it meant he was about to get wet. Even if Owen said these words on dry land, like in the living room, Laurie would blink his eyes and hold his breath in readiness for the water. This proves just how quickly a child can link words and actions together, demonstrating beautifully how a baby of just three months old begins to grasp our language.

4. Repeat, repeat, repeat

Do you remember your school teacher drilling into you rules such as 'I before E except after C' or, later on, French or German phrases like 'J'ai faim' or 'Ich habe hunger'? If you do, this is because repeating words and ideas over and over again helps them to stick in your mind. So, applying this rule to language development, we have to say things, repeat them and stress the words we want the child to learn.

In fact, children love to hear information being repeated (for example, when you tell them the same story for the hundredth time or sing repeatedly about five little ducks who went swimming one day, over the hills and far away . . .). This may be tedious for you but it is a highly effective way for your little one to begin to understand the language that you are teaching him.

However, it is important to try to be consistent with the words or phrases that your child hears. For example, there are hundreds of ways to say that something is 'small' – such as 'little', 'tiny', 'titchy', 'minute', 'wee' and so on – but your child will learn quicker if you drill into him just one such word, so try to pick one and stick to it in the early stages of language development. He will pick up the others later, don't worry.

USING WORDS IN CONTEXT

A study I once read suggested that a child would need to hear a word being spoken in its context at least 500 times before he will understand what the word means, and many more times again before he will begin to attempt to say it. I once told a parent this and she, quite understandably, asked if this meant she could simply say 'cup' 500 times in a row and her baby would suddenly be able to say it. An interesting idea! The answer is no, but do try to repeat certain words often and, importantly, in context. For example, say 'up' each time you pick up your baby, repeat 'down, down, down' when you go down the stairs, 'push the button' when you're in a lift or 'shake, shake, shake' for a rattle. Doing this each time will help your baby learn the word and also reinforce the context in which that word is meaningfully used.

5. Stay one step ahead

As your child gets older and progresses through the phases of language and speech development, as a parent you need to stay one step ahead. So, ideally, you would be able to identify which phase of communication your child is in and know what is coming next – then you can continuously be encouraging him to move forwards to the next phase. This book will help you to do that, and the chapters have been organized to set out, in a chronological manner, the various phases of language development. Many stages do overlap, but being aware of all of them will help you to encourage your baby to progress to the next one.

6. Say What You See

If you only take on board one thing from this whole book, it should be this: Say What You See. This is THE most important technique you can use with your child. I drone on and on about Say What You See because parents need to master this technique in order to promote their child's language development. Simply put, the idea is that language develops through play. So, watch your child play, think about what he might be thinking and provide a comment to put *his thoughts* into words. This might *sound* easy, but it can actually be quite tricky and it takes a lot of practice to get good at it. Using the Say What You See technique helps children feel relaxed and secure, exposes them to language relevant to their play and enables them to receive positive responses as they attempt to communicate.

So all you do is give a gentle running commentary of what your child is doing and what is happening at that moment in time. It involves following your child's lead, observing him closely to see what he is interested in, and commenting and then pausing to give space for the child to respond. We can often talk too much or ask too many questions and not give our children a chance to speak. So, rather than saying, 'What are you doing?', 'Did Dolly fall down?', you should say, 'Dolly's drinking her milk. Whoops! She fell off the chair. Poor Dolly. Ah, May's cuddling the dolly.' (Incidentally, I always use the child's name – in this case, 'May' – or I omit the name, saying, for instance, 'cuddle the dolly', rather than use pronouns such as 'you' or 'I', which, in this case, would be 'You're cuddling the dolly.' To use these latter pronouns can be confusing for the child. For advice on when to use 'I' and 'you', see page 203.)

This powerful technique helps your child to focus on his activity for longer (and the longer he stays with an activity, the more he will learn), become involved in what he's doing and link what he hears to what he is doing or thinking. Crucially, it also helps children feel confident and relaxed because it avoids putting pressure on them to talk or give answers and you will find that they will babble or talk back in response to your comments because they feel under no obligation to speak.

Having said all that, it's not nearly as easy to hold back as it sounds. We naturally want to test, question and direct our children. For example, if a child were to bang bricks together, perhaps not playing with them in the traditional way, instinctively you would want to say, 'Build me a tower,' but what you *should* say is 'Bang, bang, bang go the bricks.' By saying 'bang, bang, bang' you are verbalizing your child's thoughts, showing him your interest and valuing what he's doing rather than directing their play – so you become a great playmate rather than

SAY WHAT YOU SEE WITH OLDER CHILDREN

A work colleague of mine tells a wonderful story about her grandson who is nine. She took him to the park and he said, 'Granny, will you do that thing where you say what I am doing?' And she remembered having continuously used Say What You See when he was a child. She willingly obliged, saying, 'Up, up, up the steps. Sitting down at the top of the slide. Getting ready . . . weeeee, down you go.' He was clearly loving the fact that she was totally involved and enjoying his play, which gave him a sense of confidence and security.

This just proves that Say What You See is for children of all ages and, honestly, all children love it. Sometimes when you carry out this technique with a child for the first time, they look at you in amazement and then do something else to see what you'll say. Obviously, if they were to throw the toy you'd reprimand them as usual, but that's the beauty of this technique: you can dip in and out of it as much as you like throughout your day. Please, please try it today!

a teacher. And next time he repeats the action or play sequence, he will hear your voice in his head, almost like a scratched record, and eventually want to say it for himself.

These Small Talk techniques require you to learn a lot of new information and you are unlikely to take it all in at once. Please don't panic. Learn as your child learns – in 'bite-sized' pieces! Try to incorporate one of these techniques into your daily routine at a time until they become second nature. Practice makes perfect!

CHAPTER TWO

What is Language and How Does it Develop?

A recent survey by the 'Hello' campaign* found that 82 per cent of parents wanted more information on how children develop speech, language and communication skills. So, if you are one of the 82 per cent who want to understand more fully what's going on in your baby's brain during the crucial first four years of life, I will try to explain it to you, while keeping things as simple as I can.

WHAT IS LANGUAGE?

Speech, language and communication involve a variety of skills:

- attention and listening – how we focus and concentrate on the person talking in order to receive a message.
- comprehension – how we understand the language that we hear.

---

* The 'Hello' campaign was aimed at prioritizing children and young people's communication in homes and schools, with special focus on those with speech, language and communication needs. It was run in the UK in 2011 by the Communication Trust in partnership with Jean Gross, Communication Champion for children, was sponsored by BT and Pearson Assessment and was backed by the Department of Health.

- expression – how we form words into sentences and use appropriate grammar to convey a message.
- speech/phonology – how we use sounds to make up a word.
- social skills and pragmatics – how we interact with someone in order to receive a message and use language appropriately to communicate, such as body language, eye contact, tone, volume, etc.
- memory – how we remember and store words and sentences in our brain.

The diagram below demonstrates this beautifully.

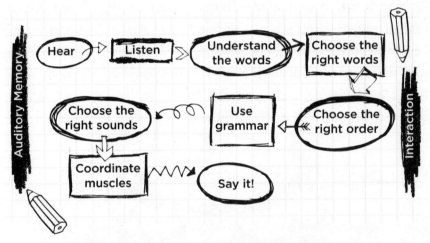

WHAT HAPPENS WHEN WE LISTEN AND SPEAK?

Based on a diagram designed by Anthea Williams and Jacqueline Woodcock

HOW DOES LANGUAGE DEVELOP?

It's pretty amazing that children learn language. It is thought to be the most complex skill human beings develop and we still don't understand it fully. Psychologists and linguists debate endlessly about what exactly enables a child to acquire language – is it nature or nurture? How is the brain wired in order to concentrate and to process language?

Numerous models are drawn to try to represent these processes, but I think the two diagrams below represent language development most clearly. The Language Cake shows the general outline of the components a child needs to acquire in order to speak, and the Language Tree shows this in more detail, along with what the parent can do to influence this process.

The Language Cake

Imagine trying to serve a cake without a plate. It would crumble and disintegrate. So in the illustration below, the plate represents the skills that need to be mastered before language can develop. These skills, the foundation for language, are: showing an awareness of others; having a desire to communicate; listening; waiting; turn-taking; memory; attention; symbolic play (most often called imaginative play); and eye

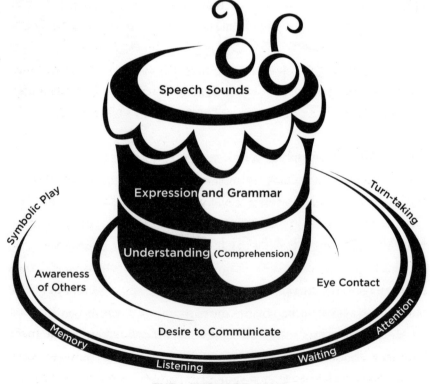

THE LANGUAGE CAKE

contact. These pre-verbal skills are all essential to a greater or lesser degree, depending on the child, in order to acquire spoken language.

Once the skills shown on the plate are in place, a child will start to respond to verbal language because she now has the tools to begin to understand spoken language. For instance, take the word 'bye-bye'. Imagine a set of parents, frantically waving and saying 'bye-bye, bye-bye' to their pre-verbal child. This child needs to have an awareness that someone is communicating with her, a desire to communicate by looking, listening and attending/concentrating, remembering, taking her turn, etc. and then, when these skills are established, the child will begin to understand the word 'bye-bye', attempt to say it, possibly by saying 'ba-ba' or 'dye-dye' in the first instance, and then will adjust it to 'bye-bye' once her speech skills are developed.

I see a lot of children who aren't talking and often their parents are desperate for me to start therapy that targets saying words. I have to explain to them that the pre-verbal skills shown on the Language Cake plate need to be addressed first. So I might focus on playing turn-taking games or listening to environmental noises (e.g. the washing machine, the birds in the garden) to improve a child's attention and verbal under-standing. Only then can we proceed with actually saying words.

The Language Tree

The Language Tree shows how the Small Talk techniques directly influence a child's language development. The roots of the tree are attention/listening, understanding of language and thinking – without these, the tree would fall down. The tree then grows and spoken language/expressive language appears. Words form the bulk of language – the tree trunk – and, from this, sentences emerge. The fruit and leaves on the tree are most noticeable to the eye and are what make it pretty – speech sounds and grammar are what make language sound pretty, but you could understand language with-out good speech sounds or eloquent grammar (in the same way you

THE LANGUAGE TREE

can grasp the meaning intended when a foreigner speaks broken English). Without sunshine, the tree would not grow at all. In this diagram, sunshine represents parental input and praise, and the rain represents the things a parent can do to help the tree to grow. In no particular order, these are: create positive interactions; use single words and short sentences; allow time; give instructions in small steps; avoid lots of questions; offer choices; talk about the 'here and now'; have realistic but high expectations; develop listening skills; repeat, repeat, repeat; follow your child's lead; and use Say What You See (see page 17).

THE FIVE WAYS IN WHICH CHILDREN LEARN LANGUAGE

Research by Coupe, O'Kane and Goldbart in 1998[1] concluded that there are five fundamental principles of how children learn language[2]:

- A child needs a reason to communicate.
- A child begins to use language when she understands it is a better way to get what she wants.
- A child learns language through meaningful interactions with an adult who is providing both appropriate models and appropriate content. This is NOT a passive process.
- A child needs an adult to provide repetition and clarification in order for her to develop the ability to decode what is being said.
- A child needs to develop cognitive and social skills alongside language skills in order to continue developing language.

Now you can see the complexity of learning to speak, let's go right back to the beginning – in the next chapter we'll start with talking to your bump.

CHAPTER THREE

• • • • • • • • • • • • • • • • • • •

The Pre-Babble Phase (0–6 months)

In the previous two chapters, we identified seven types of parent inter-action styles (see page 7) and set out the golden rules – the Small Talk techniques. They emphasized the importance of being a Tuned-in Parent, who is able to identify a baby's attempts to communicate and respond accordingly. We then discussed the intricacies of what language is and how it develops.

In this chapter, we look at the pre-babble phase. Many adults might think that the time before words emerge is irrelevant; that the sounds a baby makes are chaotic, arbitrary and meaningless. This is far from the truth. In this phase, the baby is forming the building blocks he needs to be able to use words and language. In other words, the pre-babble phase of moaning, groaning, screeching and squeal-ing is absolutely essential and, as a Tuned-in Parent, you can identify and reward your baby's attempts to communicate, helping him on his journey towards spoken words.

Interestingly, this journey starts far earlier than you might think – at 24 weeks your baby's ear is now structurally complete, although researchers believe that he might be able to hear sounds from outside the womb as early as 16 weeks. The most prominent sounds are your heartbeat and your tummy gurgles. Encourage your partner to talk to your bump – voices with lower frequencies are believed to penetrate the wall of your abdomen more easily, so he might hear his voice better than others.

Babies are born instinctively sociable and can interact with you from birth by copying you – if you stick out your tongue, so will they, and when they are crying, they are telling you that they are either in pain or discomfort (due to a dirty nappy, feeling too hot or too cold, and so on), or feeling tired or hungry. Crying noises are made of long vowel sounds such as 'argh', 'ur' and 'ugh'. And, before long, your baby will start to use these vowel sounds and experimental noises as a way to 'talk' and here begins pre-babble, a way of communicating that must be responded to in order for the babble phase to start.

In this chapter, I want to share two main points. Firstly, I set out the various phases that you will be able to identify, and then reward, to help your baby along his journey. Remember, though, that these phases can and do overlap, so don't expect them to arrive in a strict chronological order. For this reason, I haven't tried to link the phases and you can read each phase section as stand-alone information. Secondly, I want to discuss issues that may arise during the pre-babble phase, such as using dummies, tongue tie, beginning to sign, excessive dribbling, controlling TV time and autism. So, let's get started . . .

TALKING TO YOUR BUMP

Amazingly, babies in utero can recognize their mother's voice between 24 and 27 weeks, and studies have shown that a baby's racing heartbeat will calm down to the sound of their own mother's voice. With this in mind, I would urge you to try to talk to your bump every day and encourage your partner to talk to it, too. You may feel a bit silly, but it really can make a big difference to their future language development.

You can also try to communicate with your bump in a couple of other ways. If you feel your baby move, push back where you felt the kick, and your baby may then respond with another kick and, hey presto, that's your first mother–baby interaction!

BABIES' LANGUAGE STARTS IN THE WOMB

A study published recently in *Current Biology* suggests that infants begin picking up elements of what will be their first language in the womb.[1]

Kathleen Wermke, of the University of Wurzburg in Germany, who conducted the study, says, 'Not only did we find that babies are capable of producing different cry melodies, but they prefer to produce those melody patterns that are typical for the ambient language they have heard during their foetal life, within the last trimester of gestation.'

This means that human foetuses are able to memorize sounds from the external world by the last trimester of pregnancy, with a particular sensitivity to the melodies in language.

Wermke's team recorded and analyzed the cries of 60 healthy newborns, 30 born into French-speaking families and 30 born into German-speaking families, when they were three to five-days old. That analysis revealed clear differences in the shape of the newborns' cry melodies, based on their mother tongue.

Specifically, French newborns tend to cry with a rising melody pattern, whereas German newborns seem to prefer a falling melody pattern in their crying. Those patterns are consistent with characteristic differences between the two languages, Wermke says.

The study shows the extremely early impact of native language and highlights the importance of talking to and singing to your baby from as early as 24 weeks of gestation. Some mums feel rather odd about doing this and even feel embarrassed talking to a baby once it's born, but it is so, so important. The earlier we talk to babies, the more in tune with our language they'll be and the quicker they'll learn it.

Another idea is to sing a little song to your bump in order to interact with your baby. Try singing the following song to the tune of 'Skip to My Loo'. It goes like this: 'Pat, pat, pat my bump, pat, pat, pat, my bump, pat, pat, pat my bump.' Then you can change the word 'pat' to 'rub' and 'tickle'. Over time, your baby will start to recognize this tune and then, when he or she is born, you can sing the same tune to many different activities, for example, 'wash, wash, wash your toes', etc., and your baby will be familiar with the tune. Singing is wonderfully calming for babies and children, which is why we sing when our children are distressed or want to sleep, etc. When children are calm, they can focus better and learn more.

EYE CONTACT

From the moment your baby is born, he instinctively wants to look at your face. Can you imagine hearing the same voice for nine months and not knowing where the sound is coming from? Sure enough, soon after birth, your baby will begin to actively check out the source of the sound – your face. Amazingly, within 15 hours of birth, a baby can recognize which face their mother's voice is coming from. At birth, a baby is able to focus at a distance of 20–30cm (8–12in), which is the rough distance between a baby's face and his parents' when he is breastfeeding – perfect planning by Mother Nature.

Establishing good eye contact helps you to develop a strong social and emotional bond with your baby, encourages your baby to look at your face to see where the sound comes from and, a few weeks down the line, copy and experiment with his own voice.

HOW EYE CONTACT DEVELOPS

Outlined below is the developmental pattern for eye contact:

- **A newborn** is able to look for short periods at a human face and is attracted by movement.
- **At two months**, a baby will 'lock' on to a human face, especially when the face is accompanied by a voice, and can track his eyes between two people, objects or patterns – even at some distance.
- **At four to six months**, a baby recognizes familiar people and smiles, but is also drawn towards the novelty of a new face or objects.

Why is eye contact so crucial for communication?

I am reminded of the importance of eye contact every time I take case histories from parents who have children with speech and language problems. I notice that when I break eye contact, the person stops speaking. When I maintain eye contact, the person continues talking, knowing that I am interested in what they have to say.

The same idea relates to babies. When a baby gives and receives good eye contact, they begin to gather information about language through watching your facial expression, gestures and signs. This is the beginning of social interaction.

Poor eye contact

Poor eye contact is a characteristic I often see in children who have autism. It is by no means the only characteristic of this condition, so please don't assume that if your child's ability to make and maintain eye contact is poor, he has autism. Conversely, a child who gives appropriate eye contact can still be diagnosed with autism. (For more information about autism and a checklist of signs to watch out for, see pages 53–58.)

Don't panic. In most cases, a baby or child not giving eye contact is simply another phase in the developmental process and no cause for concern. During my years of working with children, I've noticed that while babies tend to gaze adoringly at their parents for the first two months, at about eight to ten weeks a baby's eyesight improves and they start actively looking into the wider environment and become fascinated with what's going on around them – rather than with you! Your baby's interest in faces will return as quickly as it went and, after a few weeks, he'll be desperate to look at people again and start flirting and crowd-pleasing with beautiful wide eyes and beaming smiles all over again.

CASE STUDY: DISTRACTED FROM EYE CONTACT

Recently, one of my mummy friends called me in a panic. She feared that her baby, who had suddenly started to avoid eye contact, had autism. She said, 'After a month or so of baby Ellie and I endlessly gazing into each other's eyes, she is no longer interested in me. She is looking at lights and other objects in the periphery and seems to actively avoid my eyes.' I reassured her that I had gone through a similar thing with my baby Jess and told her to ride it out for two weeks. Sure enough, within ten days she called me to say that Ellie was back to staring at her – as well as taking in her surroundings.

TUNED IN TO HUMAN CONTACT

Babies as young as three months can tell the difference between a happy and a sad voice. At this age they can also tell human voices from other sounds. A research team from the Institute of Psychiatry at King's College, London, studying babies from three to seven months,[2] found that coughing, sneezing, yawning, lapping water (reminiscent of bathtime) and the squeaking of toys all activated part of the brain known to process speech. But human sounds lit it up far more.

Small Talk Time **Boosting eye contact**

One of the most amazing things that a baby can do at birth is to copy some oral movements that their parent makes. For example, if the parent pokes out their tongue or makes an 'ooo' shape with their mouth, the baby will, too. Give it a try! Also try the Small Talk Time games below with babies that are three to four months and older. Actively encourage your baby to look at you when you play these games.

- Wear funny glasses, hats, noses, wigs or bright lipstick (go on, dads – don't be shy!).
- Look in the mirror and make funny faces at each other. Wait for your baby to try to copy you.
- Sing some songs and rhymes in the mirror and point to the appropriate body parts. Here's a rhyme to try:

> *Two little eyes to look around,*
> *Two little ears to hear each sound,*
> *One little nose to smell what's sweet,*
> *One little mouth that tastes what to eat*

Opposite is a song that's great for this activity (see the Small Talk website – www.smalltalktime.com – for a video of this song):

I look in the mirror and who do I see?
Who is that boy, looking at me?
I look in the mirror and who do I see?
That face in the mirror is me

- Pick up a noisy or sparkly toy and move it slowly from left to right in front of your baby's face. Go slowly, so that you can see his eyes tracking the toy. Make it disappear behind your head or back and

PARENT-FACING BUGGIES

The Talk To Your Baby campaign, run by the Literary Trust (www. literacytrust.org.uk), is continuously asking leading pushchair manufacturers to produce parent-facing (known as rear-facing) buggies. They say parents communicate much more with their children if they are facing them and, in my experience, this is true.

I have the use of two pushchairs, one of which is parent-facing, the other rear-facing. When my daughter Jess sits in the parent-facing buggy, I have noticed that I talk to her a lot more (perhaps too much!). I basically think aloud, saying things like 'I wonder if Daddy's home?', 'Mmm, what shall we have for lunch?' or 'Oh, I think there's some yummy cheese in the fridge.' However, when Jess is forward-facing, I have the same thoughts but don't bother to say them out loud.

And I'm not alone in this. Research carried out by Dr Suzanne Zeedyk, developmental psychologist at the University of Dundee,[3] and published by the Talk To Your Baby campaign in November 2008 examined interactions between parents and their infants who were seated in both parent-facing and forward-facing buggies. The report concluded that parents are twice as likely to talk to children in parent-facing buggies, which could impact on language development. I recommend a parent-facing buggy if at all possible.

wait for your baby to make eye contact. Give him a big smile and say, 'Yes, you are looking at Mummy!'

- Peek-a-boo is another great game. Initially, use a gauzy, transparent scarf or piece of fabric (muslins are great for this) and briefly trail it over your face, so your baby can see your face and then you momentarily disappear. As your face is covered, start saying 'Peek-aaaa . . .' then pop out and say, 'boo!' Babies often find this hilarious and will give lots of smiles. You can then try trailing the fabric over baby's face and use the same routine – encourage your baby to pull it off. Once he gets the hang of it you can make the game more interactive by leaving a long pause after saying 'Peek-a- . . . (pause)' for your baby to make an excited movement or a noise (and then you say 'boo') – the baby's noise should eventually become a 'boo'. This type of game is known as an anticipation game – you are anticipating that your baby will say a sound or attempt a word at a particular point.
- Try sticking a sticker next to your eyes or on your nose to encourage better eye contact – a simple, cheap and effective idea.

CRYING

Understanding your baby's cry

You might think newborns do very little other than cry and sleep but, when they cry, they are, in fact, trying to communicate one of four basic needs: pain, discomfort, tiredness and hunger. Each cry sounds slightly different and, before long, the parent begins to recognize these cries and can therefore react accordingly.

That's the theory, anyway, but I must admit that, with my baby Jess, detecting the differences between the cries was quite hard work and, even now, I have to listen carefully to the cry and am still often uncertain about what the actual problem is. Then, even if I think I know it's a discomfort cry, for instance, trying to figure out what the discomfort is often proves quite a mission in itself.

I remember one occasion when Jess woke up from a nap screaming and I knew immediately that she was in pain. It was another matter trying to find out what the source of the pain was. After trying milk and cuddles, I decided to change her nappy and then I discovered the problem – I had put a pair of silly glittery tights on her and, when I took them off, her legs were covered in a bright red rash, poor love.

So, my advice (aside from not buying any sparkly tights) would be not to worry if you never manage to decipher your baby's cries exactly. Just ensure you are listening and, occasionally, resist your instinct to rush to your crying baby's assistance. Instead, pause to listen to the sound of the cry for a few seconds before you respond:

THE LISTEN, WAIT, RESPOND TECHNIQUE

Have you ever really listened to your baby cry? Usually, we're so quick to jump up in a panic and cuddle them that we often forget to actually listen. Next time your baby cries, listen hard for just ten to thirty seconds to the type of cry he is making so that you will gradually feel more confident in interpreting his cries and figuring out what he wants. The only cry that must be addressed immediately is the pain cry, which is very distinct so you can't mistake it for something else – there will be no doubt that your baby is in pain.

Types of cry
The types of cry your baby makes are:

- pain cry – a sharp scream followed by a moment of no breathing, and another sharp scream.

- discomfort cry – a whiny sound, almost like a fake cry, which doesn't stop when the baby is picked up.
- hunger cry – a low-pitched cry that rises and falls with a rhythm. It usually gets progressively louder and the baby can't be calmed down. The baby might root for the breast or suck on his hand at the same time.
- tired cry – a soft, rhythmic, moaning cry as the baby tries to settle to go to sleep.

When crying becomes talking

It may surprise you to learn that newborn babies are virtually silent – unless they are crying – because they haven't yet learnt how to make any other sounds. Crying noises are made of long vowel sounds – 'argh', 'ah', 'hur', 'ur', 'ugh'. And, before long, your baby will start to use these vowel sounds as a way to 'talk', so you will begin to hear little 'aahs' and 'uurs' popping out as he kicks on his playmat. This will probably happen at about 10–12 weeks. I bet you didn't think that crying is, in fact, nature's way of enabling a baby to climb the language development ladder! Crying is the first spoken means of communication and, even though there are no fully formed words within a baby's cries, the seeds of those words are there and are encouraged to grow through the crying process.

But there are also ways that you, as a Small Talker, can help to nurture these seeds. The best way is by playing games, and below are a few suggestions.

Small Talk Time **Encouraging early vowel sounds**

We have already established that crying noises sound like more desperate vowels, so the next step is to play games involving vowel noises anytime from around three months. Try the following games:

- Fall to the floor and say, 'Argh!' Children are highly motivated by sound and movement, so can you imagine how rewarding it would be to a baby to see a grown adult fall to the floor, saying, 'Argh!' right in front of his face?
- Prop your baby up so he can see you clearly, then spin around and say 'eeee'.
- Yawn in a very exaggerated way, saying 'hurrrh' with a big stretch. You could stretch your baby's arms up at the same time.
- Sit your baby on your lap, facing you. Bounce him up and say, 'weeeee' and then lower him down, saying 'oooooooohhhh'.

The key with these games is to play them a few times to establish the routine and to get your baby familiar with the noise that is paired with the action. Then, play the game again and pause before your big finale, enabling your baby to join in and attempt appropriate sounds too – which may take some time. Once your child realizes that his sounds are intentional and meaningful (so that, if he says 'eee', he is rewarded by you spinning around in response to him), he will continue to move forwards with his communication. This is another anticipation game, where you are anticipating your baby's movement or noise as he interacts with you during the game. It can be noisy, but great fun!

VOWEL SOUNDS

There are five vowel letters in the English alphabet (A, E, I, O, U). But in the speech and language therapy world there are many more vowel sounds – depending on the accent, it's more like somewhere between eleven and twenty. Say the following four words and listen to how different the letter 'a' sounds each time: father; cat; about; pay.

So, when you hear your baby begin to 'talk', it is this wide range of vowel sounds that you will hear – 'ah', 'ur', 'ooo', 'ei', 'uh', 'aya' and so on rather than A, E, I, O and U. As I mentioned in the previous section, vowel sounds are derived from crying noises. I suppose the best way to explain it is that they are like spoken crying noises that the baby uses to experiment with his voice.

Once your baby starts to use them, it's really important that you react and reward him by smiling, talking back and making good eye contact. Say things like, 'Are you telling me a story?' and 'And then what happened?'. This way, you are encouraging your baby to say more.

HOW BABIES LEARN WORDS

The other day, a friend of mine said 'Guess what? Milly [six months] has started saying "iya" [as in 'Hi-ya']. Can it really be true?' Well, the answer is yes! Initially, a child says something by accident, which sounds like a real word. At six months, it was probably the case that Milly was saying this word accidentally, as part of her experimental speech, but because her parent was so delighted, Milly was rewarded by having the word said back to her, for example, 'Iya, iya, Milly'. Then, sooner or later, Milly would have begun to understand that she was communicating with her parent and repeated the word – randomly initially, then she began to use it in the correct context. The realization that you and your baby are intentionally communicating with each other is really exciting.

Small Talk Time **More vowels, please!**

Try the following games to encourage your baby to say some vowel sounds.

- Get down on the floor so that you're at your baby's level and play with a toy you know he really likes, preferably something that makes a noise. You could even lie on the floor together and encourage a bit of tummy time. Don't make a sound yourself but create a sound from the toy. Don't give your baby eye contact unless you sense that he is not looking at you or the toy and, if this is the case, move into his line of vision again until he looks at you. The idea is to encourage him to get your attention by using his voice. If he makes a sound, respond immediately by bringing the toy closer to him and showing it to him. Give him a big kiss and the toy to play with and say, 'You're so clever, you were calling Mummy.' If your baby doesn't make a sound, respond to a physical movement in the first instance, for example, a wave of his arms or an excited kick. Keep rewarding his efforts and respond extra specially enthusiastically when he does make a sound.

- Make various vowel sounds to your baby in the mirror and wait to see if he copies you. In the first instance, you could try 'ooo', 'eee' and 'ah'. Say the sounds your baby makes back, too.

- Sing songs that include vowel sounds to your baby – not only will this help to develop the vowel sounds in his vocabulary, it will also boost his listening skills. A favourite with my patients is the classic 'Old MacDonald Had a Farm', simply because of the chorus, 'E I E I O', which is made entirely of vowel sounds. The key is to sing it very slowly so your baby can listen and join in. Another good song is 'Row, Row, Row the Boat', with the version of the ending that goes 'If you see a crocodile, don't forget to scream – argh!'.

HELPING YOUR BABY TO FOCUS

Remember that if your baby is sitting on your lap and working hard to hold his or her head up, you won't hear as many sounds from him because all his energy will be going into head support. Try laying him down on his back so his body is well supported. You are likely to hear many, many more noises and sounds this way.

- It sounds obvious, but you can say 'aah' whenever you cuddle your baby or a teddy, and say 'ooo' whenever you see anything surprising or interesting.
- If you're really keen, you could make simple and bold flashcards for your baby. Try a ghost for 'ooo', a mouse for 'eee' and a crocodile for 'argh'.

DEVELOPING A CONVERSATION

If you've been practising the exercises given in this book so far, your baby will now understand that he is making sounds that people seem interested in because he is being rewarded with smiles and replies from you for these attempts to talk. At this stage, you will notice a boom in the amount of vocalizations your baby makes as he intentionally attempts to 'talk' – this is a very important step.

So how do you create a conversation? It's all about the art of turn-taking, and here's how to do it . . .

Small Talk Time **Turn-taking**

Have a chat with your baby

Wait for your baby to say something. Once he has finished 'talking', leave a slight pause in case there is more. Then make a comment yourself, such as 'Yes, it really is cold today.' Try to keep your utterance at a similar length to the that of your baby's, or slightly shorter, and wait for your tiny talker to say some more. If he cuts you off, let him. Hopefully, you will now be turn-taking in a bit of 'small talk'. Try to keep this 'conversation' going for as long as possible by giving him lots of smiles and eye contact to show that you are finding his story incredibly interesting. You are being a Tuned-in Parent (see page 9). Bravo.

As your little chats develop, you might hear vowel sounds, or screams, or you may even hear some consonant sounds, but the key to having a conversation is gaining eye contact, listening and waiting. If your baby doesn't say anything, say something yourself, then simply wait. So you might start with 'Where's Rhodri gone?' Wait . . . 'Where is he?' Wait . . . Wait again . . . 'We took him to school.' Wait . . . 'Ah,' says the baby and you immediately respond: 'Yes, he's at school.' Then wait some more. If a sound is made, either copy it or use some 'motherese' (see the box on page 42) to try to expand it.

Work on turn-taking when you are alone with your child and when there is no background noise – it's much harder to get your baby to 'share' the conversation when brothers and sisters are running around or colourful, noisy adverts keep popping up on TV. A good time to practise is when you are in close proximity, such as at nappy change time or perhaps after a feed.

Play copycat

A very important part of developing a conversation is encouraging your child to copy the sounds they hear from you, another family member or another child. Copying is an important skill to learn. If we can't copy others, how can we learn to speak? Copying also involves cooperation and interaction between two people – an essential part of communication. We usually teach a child to copy non-verbally before we encourage him to copy verbally.

I am a big believer in the value of play dates, as they give your baby the opportunity to spend time with other children, whether they are younger, older or the same age. You will notice your baby reaching out to touch the other children and then beginning to copy their noises and actions. Whether it's a cough or a scream, or just a gesture, this copycat play is an important part of learning to speak.

MOTHERESE

When we talk to infants, regardless of the language we speak, most adults alter their voices to attract the infant's attention, use short, simple sentences coupled with higher pitch and exaggerated intonation, and talk at a much slower rate to communicate effectively. This is usually known as 'motherese' or baby talk or, in the scientific community, as infant-directed or child-directed speech. Research tells us that babies are pre-programmed to listen to such coochy-coo voices and, as parents, we often naturally and unconsciously talk to our babies like this to help them tune in to our speech. It's Mother Nature's way of encouraging that parent–baby bond.

When we use motherese we speak in short, slow sentences with repetitive words, we stretch out vowel sounds, add vowel sounds (e.g. doggie), and exaggerate intonation patterns, making our sing-song speech more attractive to a baby's ear than a flat voice. (Don't worry if you end up saying 'doggie' or 'horsey' for some time. Some people disapprove of teaching children these 'childish' words, but it does no harm and, before long, your little one will start correcting you, which is when you'll know it's time to use the proper word.)

When you are chatting to your baby using motherese, you shouldn't worry too much about the length of your sentences. However, when you want to help your baby learn something new, stop, say it clearly and simply and repeat it. The following is an example of how to use motherese and teach new words at the same time: 'Let's go into the kitchen and see what's in the fridge for lunch. What about a nice ham sandwich?' Then, when you get out the bread and show it to your baby, instead of saying, 'Here's the bread', stop, say it clearly and simply and repeat it: 'Bread, it's bread. Bread on the plate.' By pausing, simplifying and repeating the single word 'bread' you are adapting your motherese and teaching a new word. You may think your tiny baby is too young to learn new words, but I can guarantee that you are doing this subconsciously already. You may be talking to your baby about Daddy at certain points throughout the day, saying things like 'I wonder what Daddy's doing? He might be getting in the car and driving home' (motherese). When Daddy actually comes in, picks up your baby and you say, 'Daddy. Daddy's home' (adapted motherese). This teaches your baby a potential first word – 'Daddy'.

LANGUAGE BUILDING BLOCKS

I remember once I was in a swimming pool changing room with Jess and another mum who had a six-year-old boy with severe autism. As I tried to wrestle Jess into her swimsuit, as usual, she started to grizzle and moan, and this little lad on the other side of the room began to copy her. This was the first intentional noise his mother had ever heard him make and she was delighted. This was the stage of communication he was at – copying crying noises. I found it fascinating because it reaffirmed to me that children need to go through these crucial building blocks before they use real words.

EXPERIMENTAL NOISES

Once your baby has acquired a range of vowel sounds and is becoming confident and competent at using them, the noises you hear him make will become more adventurous and amusing (this will happen at around three to four months). He is beginning to experiment with his lips, tongue and jaw in order to make many different sounds, such as screams and squeals, blowing raspberries, grunts and growls and you may even hear some consonant sounds appearing (all sounds that are not vowels – more about these in the next chapter). He will also be experimenting with volume and tone – here's where the tuneful nature of your coochy-coo voice begins to pay off, as you'll hear your baby beginning to imitate your intonation patterns.

My daughter growled a lot. Even my friend's two-year-old noticed and one day said, 'She thinks she's a lion!' I had to consider why she was making this noise as, I can assure you, it wasn't a noise she was copying from my husband or me. My explanation was that the growls make a lovely vibration in the throat and therefore gave Jess a lot of tactile feedback – so she wanted to say 'grrr' again and again!

The purpose of these experimental sounds is to prepare the mouth for consonant sounds by building the neurological pathways from the brain to the jaw, lips and tongue (known as the articulators). In other words, the more you say a particular sound, the easier it becomes, because your brain creates pathways from the speech centres to the articulators so that they can move quickly to form a shape in the mouth.

By creating these neurological pathways and using them over and over again, the coordination and strength of the muscles in the jaw, lips and tongue improves, ready for the production of the more difficult stage of producing consonant sounds. Say the vowels out loud and you will notice that your mouth stays open and quite still. Now say 'shhh' out loud and you will notice that you move your lips, tongue and jaw far more, which makes consonants much more complicated to master.

No wonder your baby finds it exciting making these new noises. This experimentation is the workout for the main event! Just as a child can't jump without first practising to stand, walk and run, a baby can't say words without going through the vowel and experimental noise phase.

Small Talk Time **Anticipation games**

Now that your baby is making experimental noises, you are at the point where you can move forward the art of turn-taking, by expecting your baby to fully interact with you. In a way, you are putting a little bit of pressure on him to respond verbally – you are anticipating a response from him and he is anticipating a word or an action from you. The key to this technique is in establishing a routine, so your baby knows exactly when he has to do an action or say a sound to receive his reward. Below are some games to try.

- Peek-a-boo is a great anticipation game (see page 34). Your child will begin by passively watching your actions and then, eventually, will participate more actively by removing the cloth from his own face and attempting to say 'boo'.
- Put your mobile phone to your ear and say 'hello', then put the phone to your baby's ear and wait as you look at him with an expectant face and nod to encourage him to make a noise.

Ready, steady, go games

The following games will encourage your baby to make experimental noises:

- You'll need two rattles, one for you and one for your child. Say, 'Ready, steady . . . go' and make as much noise as you can with your rattle and with your voice. Then shout 'Stop!' and see if you child is quiet. Repeat, repeat, repeat, until a routine is established. When the routine is established, say, 'Ready, steady . . .' and wait. Wait for a sound or a movement from your baby as his way of saying 'go' before you vigorously begin to shake the rattle again. The movement your baby makes might be an expression of excitement, such as a leg stiffening or a reach of the hand. A movement is likely to come before a sound but, as time goes by, wait for your baby to pair a movement and a sound (and, later, make just a sound) before you react.

- Build a tower of bricks. Say, 'up' as you build and encourage your child to say, 'up' – 'uuu . . . '. Then say, 'Ready, steady . . .' and wait in anticipation for him to make a noise or movement, before saying 'go!' and knocking them down.
- Seat your child in a Bumbo seat or lay him on the floor. Take a ball or a car and say, 'Ready, steady . . .' and then, when he makes a sound, roll the ball or wheel the car as fast as you can towards your child. For a car, make a raspberry noise, and for a ball, say 'wee'. Try singing this song – 'Roll the ball, roll the ball, roll the ball to Libby. Libby has got the ball, now roll it back to me.' (See the Small Talk website, www.smalltalktime.com, for a video of this song.)

Songs and rhymes

Try the following simple anticipation songs and rhymes:

- Sing 'I can hear Jamie, running down the street, one two three, can you hear his feet? Ahh . . .', then wait in anticipation for your child to make a sound. Once he does, finish the rhyme off with 'Run, run, run, run, run', moving his feet up and down.
- Old favourite 'Round and Round the Garden Like a Teddy Bear' is a really fun anticipation game. Move your finger in a circular motion around your child's palm when you sing it, then continue with 'one step, two steps . . .' as you move your fingers up his arm, then wait for your child to make a noise and say 'tickly under there' and tickle his chin. He will love it.
- Lay your child on his back and hold his feet down on the ground. Sing the song 'London Bridge' but change the words slightly by singing, 'London bridge goes up, up, up' and lift his bottom up. Once he becomes familiar with the song, wait in anticipation for him to vocalize. Then you say 'up, up, up'.

WHY 'MOTHERESE' BOOSTS SPEECH

Researchers have long known that babies prefer to be spoken to in a sing-song manner associated with motherese (see page 42). But Erik Thiessen of the Carnegie Mellon University has revealed that infant-directed speech also helps infants *learn words more quickly* than normal adult speech.[4]

In a series of experiments, he and his colleagues exposed eight-month-old infants to fluent speech made up of nonsense words. The researchers assessed whether, after listening to the fluent speech for less than two minutes, infants had been able to learn the words. The infants who were exposed to fluent speech with the exaggerated intonation contour characteristic of infant-directed speech, or motherese, learned to identify the words more quickly than infants who heard fluent speech spoken in a more monotone fashion.

SIGN LANGUAGE AND BABY SIGNING

Now that your baby is experimenting with his mouth, encourage him to experiment with his hands as a means to express himself – let's start signing.

All babies learn gestures or signs before they learn to say words, for example, waving for 'bye-bye' or arms up for 'lift me up', so encouraging your baby to use these signs, and furthermore, will give him a head start in learning to intentionally communicate his wants and needs. The success of baby signing is due to the fact that, if you sign, you provide visual information and words simultaneously. Signs are considered to be visual cues, which reinforce spoken language, so your baby will grasp language more quickly. Baby signing can be used with babies who hear and communicate perfectly well for their age.

Speech therapists are passionate about baby signing because it gives a baby a means to communicate before he can actually speak, inspiring him to expand his communication skills more rapidly.

We will go into baby signing in a lot more detail in the next chapter, but there are a few signs that I recommend you try to introduce during the pre-babble phase – these are signs that you will probably be using without even realizing because they are almost an extension of natural gestures. These are 'bye-bye', 'up', 'finished' and 'more'.

Bye-bye

Up

Finished

More

The four signs shown here can be incorporated easily into your every-day routine – 'up' each time you lift up your baby, 'finished' at bath time or when his milk has finished and 'more' each time he is having fun playing a game with you.

Having set out the various stages that you would expect to see in the pre-babble phase, and having shared my tips and techniques to help you to encourage your little one to develop through these stages as smoothly as possible, I will finish this chapter by giving you my insights and advice on other issues that might crop up during this period. The first centres on the controversial issue of the dummy.

Using a dummy

Dummy or not? There is no universal rule, but everyone seems to have a very strong opinion about it. So what do the professionals say?

You may be surprised to hear that there are some situations in which a speech and language therapist would recommend a dummy to strengthen the mouth and help a child establish a good suck for feeding in the very early stages. At other times, a child with significant speech sound difficulties might come to a speech therapist for an assessment and an experienced practitioner would know immediately that the child sucks a dummy, on account of the shape of his lips, teeth and tongue or the child's excessive dribbling. It would not be unusual for the speech therapist to refuse to see that child again until he no longer used a dummy. Sucking on a dummy can restrict the movements of the lips and tongue, causing major difficulty in articulating sounds.

We all know that babies like to suck, and dummies can help them to self-soothe at nap times or when a baby is tired or grumpy. But regular or constant use of a dummy can hamper your child's speech, simply because a child is likely to start talking with a dummy in his mouth restricting the movement of his tongue, lips and jaw and encouraging bad habits to develop even when the dummy is not in his mouth. (This is different to thumb-sucking as a child who sucks his thumb will usually take his thumb out of his mouth to speak.) Take the 't' sound for instance. It is articulated by moving your tongue upwards in the mouth to touch the ridge behind your top teeth. This sound is pretty impossible to make when a massive obstacle is in the way, so the child might say 'k' instead and, therefore, 'toe' becomes 'koe'.

The advice is to wean your baby off a dummy by eight months before he becomes heavily dependent upon it and will therefore have the dummy for longer, and definitely before 12 months – the phase when many children start to utter their first words (see page 260 in chapter ten for more tips on how to ditch the dummy).

Tongue tie

Everybody seems to be talking about tongue tie at the moment, and it's often blamed for feeding problems at birth – as it can prevent the baby from latching on properly – and speech delay in older children. So, what is it?

Look in the mirror and stick your tongue up towards the roof of your mouth. You will notice a flap of skin that joins the underside of your tongue to the floor of your mouth. In babies with a true tongue tie, this flap of skin (called a frenulum) extends right to the tongue tip, which restricts the tongue so that it cannot protrude beyond the front teeth or reach back to the far molars to clean them after a meal. In extreme cases, this 'pulling' at the tongue tip forms a heart or bulb shape.

While true tongue tie affects a very small percentage of babies, a large majority of children will have an element of tongue tie. And this is where the problem lies. Some people immediately blame the tongue tie for latching difficulties, whereas a poor latch can be caused by a whole range of factors, including reduced muscle strength or coordination in the mouth, positioning, and difficulty turning the head to one side to name a few. They also tell concerned parents that tongue tie can hamper or delay speech. And both of these reasons are used to explain why the baby needs 'the snip'.

Health professionals might suggest a minor operation in which a pair of blunt-ended sterilized scissors are used to snip into the frenulum to free the tongue (it should not be too painful because it has few nerve endings and blood vessels). The baby is put to the breast instantly so that the milk can work its antibacterial and anti-inflammatory magic and the practitioner can see the baby's new feeding action and help mum to position correctly for the 'perfect' latch.

In my view, thousands of unnecessary tongue tie operations are being carried out all over the country and I honestly think this is the latest 'fad' to sweep the nation. While researching this chapter I came across a website that focuses on breastfeeding information, support and education. It cited a study revealing that 10 per cent of all babies born in Southampton had tongue tie. It went on to list 28 different symptoms that may indicate tongue tie – I had to laugh when I realized it included everything from colic to snoring and excessive flatulence. No wonder parents are confused! How can they possibly be confident about a diagnosis when the alleged list of symptoms is as long as your arm and also includes so many common or 'normal' complaints?

I didn't realize that tongue tie diagnosis was so rife until I had problems with feeding myself (and, let's be frank, who doesn't?). When Jess was about a week old and breastfeeding was a painful nightmare, I was told that Jess had a tongue tie, creating a click when she was feeding, which led to air entering her mouth, causing a latching problem. I was amazed. I could see instantly that Jess was not tongue tied. In fairness, she did have a very slight bulb shape at the end of her tongue, but it clearly wasn't restricting her movement as she could move her tongue into a flat shape and even beyond her lips at times. In fact, it turned out that poor Jess had oral thrush and, because of the furry coat it gave her tongue, she could not feel when the nipple was inside her mouth and couldn't get a good latch, especially as her mouth was feeling uncomfortable and possibly painful.

51

Luckily, I was confident in my convictions – but only because it's my profession – or I would have been press-ganged into getting Jess's tongue snipped and putting her through an unnecessary and costly operation (which sometimes costs as much as £300).

In another case, a friend of mine who's a nurse was also told her baby was tongue tied, causing feeding problems. She went to her GP who told her that there was a six-week waiting list to have the frenulum snipped on the NHS. She was so desperate to get feeding back on track that she went private and to this day she is convinced that this minor operation did make all the difference. I am not so sure – I think it was probably the two hours of breastfeeding coaching after the op that did the trick.

Lots of professionals are advocating the snip zealously, as if it is always necessary and as if tongue tie is the obvious cause of speech and feeding problems. Firstly, let me deal with the speech difficulties issue directly. Even if the tongue is tied all the way to the tip, this does not have any bearing on articulating speech sounds – it can still move around the mouth into all of the positions necessary to articulate all of the sounds in the English language. Therefore, tongue tie is NOT a cause of speech sound difficulties, so the snip is not a solution for speech sound problems.

Some professionals might argue that a snipped tongue has greater freedom of movement. This is true, but largely irrelevant. A tied tongue will achieve the same clear sounds with the same ease, even if its positioning is slightly different to an untied tongue. The fact that so many health professionals are advocating the snip stems from a lack of knowledge about particular fields of specialism, such as speech therapy. The result is an off-the-cuff and misguided recommendation, which hormonal and sleep-deprived new parents are prone to believe is the right thing to do.

With regards to feeding problems, I would be overstepping my field of expertise (and, therefore, as guilty as the professionals who advocate the snip as a solution for alleged speech sound difficulties) if I were to take a bold stance. However, my view is that most babies have feeding difficulties in the first two or three weeks and there are many different causes. To believe that the snip is the panacea for every kind of problem is very simplistic. The snip is a modern-day fad – at least half of my antenatal group of eight were told to get their babies' tongues snipped even though, when I examined them, there was absolutely no sign of a tie.

So, even if you are desperate for an answer to feeding difficulties in those early few weeks, I'd advise you to think carefully about a tongue-tie snip. There may not be any lasting damage as a result of having this minor operation (although the snip could cut through a blood vessel, leading to bleeding and pain, and the tongue may feel loose for the baby afterwards, which can cause the little one to gag and cough), but why pay a great deal of money for a procedure that isn't always necessary? I believe that a lot more research needs to be carried out into this matter because the current default advice to get the snip is unconvincing and worrying.

Autism

I've decided to tackle autism head on in this book as it's something I know lots about because it's one of my speech and language therapy specialisms, and I want to share my knowledge with you.

I am quite certain that many parents, somewhere throughout this early nought to six-month period have wondered, 'Is my child autistic?' All it takes is for your baby to seemingly avoid eye contact for a few days and paranoia sweeps in. And, unlike many childhood disabilities, syndromes or structural abnormalities, there is no neonatal test to diagnose autism. Cue more worry. After all, isn't that a parent's job?

More than likely there won't be any cause for concern and those babies who had seemed disengaged, difficult or 'quirky' at times quickly become the most sociable children you know. But with the incidence rates forever increasing and early diagnosis and intervention thought to be paramount, parents need to be aware of the symptoms. So, don't be alarmed by seeing the 'A word' in this section. Just read through and be informed.

What causes autism?

According to the National Autistic Society, the exact cause or causes of autism have not yet been fully established. Research suggests that autism can be caused by a variety of conditions that affect brain development and that occur before, during or after birth. They include, for example, maternal rubella, tuberous sclerosis, lack of oxygen at birth and complications from childhood illnesses, such as whooping cough or measles. Twin and family studies suggest a genetic link in autism, but the sites of relevant genes have yet to be identified.

What is it?

A child with autism has difficulties in three specific areas (often referred to as the 'triad' of impairments). These areas are:

1. The ability to understand and use verbal and non-verbal communication.
2. The ability to understand social behaviour and to interact with other people.
3. The ability to think and behave flexibly.

These impairments go hand in hand with resistance to change and the need for repetitive routines. Children with autism also have unusual sensitivity (either heightened or lowered) to sight, sound, smell, touch and taste.

Detecting early signs of autism

The average age for an autism diagnosis is between three and four years old. Yet many parents first become concerned around eighteen months

THE AUTISM SPECTRUM DISORDER

Due to its broad range of symptoms and levels of ability, autism has been called a spectrum disorder – a person who is suffering with mild autism or high functioning autism (Asperger's Syndrome) is at one end of the spectrum, while a person with severe autistic symptoms is at the other end. Autism is now often referred to as the Autism Spectrum Disorder (ASD) and, more recently, an Autistic Spectrum Condition (ASC).

– it's usually around this time that problems with the triad of impairments emerges. However, the latest research indicates that many autistic children show signs of autism in their first year, when developmental delays – particularly with regard to language and communication, the areas most associated with autism – become evident.

Below are the phases of development that a 'normal' nought to six-month-old should be displaying:

- **By 4 months**, your baby should react to movement and bright colours and track a moving object with his eyes. He should turn towards sounds and seem interested in faces. He should also be interested in his hands, reach for an object, be able to hold an object and support his head.
- **By 6 months**, your baby should show joy by laughing or squealing, smile often when playing with you and smile back at you. He should be able to move one or both eyes in all directions and will only occasionally cross his eyes. He will babble and coo when happy and cry when unhappy. He will try to copy sounds and 'partake' in a little conversation.

If your baby does not display these phases of development, bear in mind that not all delays are indicative of a developmental delay. But if you have concerns, *don't* suffer in silence. Contact your GP or health visitor if your child exhibits any of the following behaviours at around six months of age:

- seems either very stiff or very floppy
- refuses to cuddle
- shows no affection and doesn't engage with those who care for him, seeming disinterested or isolated
- seems sullen and avoids eye contact
- does not respond to sounds
- seems inconsolable at night after the age of five months
- cannot roll over, either front-to-back or back-to-front by five months

Making an autistic child feel content and secure

If you suspect that your child might be autistic, make your day as predictable as possible. Use 'objects of reference' to help signify what is about to happen. Bring a familiar bib to your child when it's time for eating, or cut off a piece of your tablecloth to show him that you are about to go to the table to eat. Show your child a rubber duck when it's bath time and use the duck in the bath. Use photos of the swimming pool, nursery or childminder to help your child to understand what is about to happen. Sing the same songs when you are about to do a particular activity so that your child knows what's going to happen and he won't feel alarmed. For example, 'We're going in the car, we're going in the car, hey-ho the merry-ow, we're going in the car (to the tune of 'The Farmer's in the Dell').

Children with autism may have a heightened or lowered reaction to sensory stimuli or difficulty integrating their senses (known as 'sensory integration difficulties') so you should be aware of noises, tastes, textures, touch, smells, and sights in the environment that could be triggers for distress for your child. These might include the smell of your washing powder or coffee machine, clothes labels, scratchy or rough fabrics or even heavy seams and pockets, multiple textures on one plate of food (let your child feel what he is eating so that he can get as much sensory information from it as possible), high-pitched buzzes from the TV, noises from the central heating pipes or the sun shining in his face.

Small Talk Time

Games to try if you suspect your child is autistic

- Try to play as many of the pre-babble Small Talk Time games featured earlier in this chapter as possible.
- Encourage as much face-to-face interaction as possible to promote eye contact – play copycat faces in the mirror (make a funny face and wait for your child to respond) or look at a book together so that he can see your face and the book at the same time (you kneel on the floor with the book in front of you, facing the child, at his level). Be very animated, making your voice rise and fall, use different voices and lots of facial expressions, and be very repetitive and predictable.
- Play 'ask an adult games' that involve people rather than objects, because children with autism struggle most with social interaction. For example, Peek-a-boo, singing action rhymes such as 'Row, Row, Row the Boat', tickling, chase, jumping and other rough-and-tumble games.
- Try to encourage interaction through anticipation games and routine. So, if your baby loves rough and tumble, practise a game where you say, 'Ready, steady, go!' and throw your little one up in the air. Then, when the routine is established, wait after 'Ready, steady . . .' for your child to interact with you, either kicking his legs, looking at you or saying a sound, before you throw them up and say, 'Go!'

- Encourage your baby to make as much noise as possible and copy any vocalizations in order to try and develop a turn-taking 'conversation'.

SPEECH AND LANGUAGE DEVELOPMENT MILESTONES: 0–6 MONTHS

The UK government has released a set of milestones for speech and language development as a guide for parents. As I keep saying, all children develop skills at different rates, but by six months, the government says that usually your baby will:

- turn towards a sound when he hears it.
- be startled by loud noises.
- watch your face when you talk to him.
- recognize your voice.
- smile and laugh when other people smile and laugh.
- make sounds to himself, such as coos, gurgles and babbling sounds.
- make noises, like coos or squeals, to get your attention.
- use different cries to express different needs (for example, one cry to signify hunger, another to indicate tiredness, and so on).*

---

* These milestones have been provided by the website www.talkingpoint.org.uk and are reproduced with kind permission.

CHAPTER FOUR

Weaning
(From 4 months)

THE IMPACT OF WEANING ON SPEECH AND LANGUAGE DEVELOPMENT

You might be wondering why on earth I am telling you about weaning in a book that focuses on encouraging communication in babies. You might think that introducing solids to your baby's diet is only important for nutritional reasons but, in fact, a growing number of speech therapists believe the weaning stage is crucial in speech and language development, which is why I have devoted a chapter to it.

As a speech therapist, I am trained to the same level as a doctor in the anatomy and physiology of the head and neck. I also have specialist training for problems related to eating and drinking. So, not only do I understand what happens when we speak, but also when we eat and drink. This means that I see a lot of children who have speech and feeding problems as a result of weak or uncoordinated muscles in the mouth. And my expertise in this area has driven home to me the importance of the weaning process and what type of eater a child is (e.g. fussy, slow or erratic) and the impact these things can have on a child's mouth.

Eating boosts the strength, speed and control of the muscles in the mouth – in particular the jaw, lips, tongue, palate and cheeks (the articulators), which assist in sucking, licking, biting and chewing.

It's important that the articulators work efficiently to help your baby make the sounds she needs for speech development.

This theory is quite controversial in the world of speech therapy and, while most therapists believe that the development of feeding impacts on speech and language development to the same extent, not everyone agrees. Some argue that developing good oral muscles for feeding has nothing to do with the movements needed for speech – in other words, keeping your lips together as you chew *won't* help you make the lip sounds 'p', 'b' and 'm'. But to me, the connection is glaringly obvious.

Let's think about this. Saying the phonetic sound 'b' out loud involves raising up your jaw so that your lips meet each other and tightening your lips together. When do we get the most practise in opening and closing the mouth, exercising the jaw muscle? When we are sucking and chewing. And when do we get the most practise in tightening our lips together? When we close our lips around a spoon to take food from it. So, it might sound unlikely, but while your baby is smearing apple purée all over her face, her highchair and you, she's actually at the verbal gym, giving her articulators a really good workout.

This section focuses on when to start weaning and the different stages involved. I'll also tell you about the traditional weaning method, in which you offer your baby purées from a spoon, and we'll also learn about an alternative known as baby-led weaning. We will look at how the mouth moves when we eat and drink, what happens if it doesn't move in the right way, the impact this has on speech and how we can help. We'll also focus on moving from a bottle to a beaker or a cup.

This chapter isn't a definitive guide to weaning, but rather an overview of how your weaning decisions could affect your baby's speech. And, as well as giving you the best advice I can so you can confidently make these choices, I've included lots of fun foodie games for you and your baby to try. Remember the saying often used by health visitors – 'Before one, food is for fun'!

WHEN TO START WEANING

Weaning is *the* biggest challenge most parents face at the six-month stage – or maybe a bit before – and comes just when you are in a nice routine with milk feeds, so you might feel a bit anxious about rocking the boat. Rather than worrying, try to think of how exciting it'll be to give your baby her first taste of all those lovely flavours. I still clearly recall the time when my co-author Tracey's baby, Minnie, tried chocolate ice cream for the first time. She licked a bit off the spoon and her face immediately lit up. She was literally chomping at the bit for more!

Is your baby ready?

Parents often ask me when they should wean their children but there is no set answer: each baby is different. However, as a rough guide, you'll probably start to see signs that your baby is ready for weaning any time from four to six months. The official World Health Organization and government guidelines recommend that introducing solid food should be delayed until the baby is six months (26 weeks) old because breast milk or formula provides all the nutrients a baby needs for the first six months of life.

It's worth noting, though, that until 2003 the British government advised that weaning was safe from four months. Confusingly, this has made weaning one of those parenting hot-potato issues on which everyone has their own opinion – ask your sister, best friend, mum or grandma and they've probably all got different advice on the matter.

I tell parents that they need to trust their instincts, ignore any peer-group pressure (there was a mum in my baby group who weaned early and couldn't help but boast about her baby's new love of roast dinners, which made us mums who hadn't yet moved on from milk feel rather inadequate) and tune in to the signals from their babies. When babies are ready to eat, they usually make it pretty clear.

SIGNS YOUR BABY IS READY FOR WEANING

The following signs are all good indicators that your baby is ready for weaning:

- She is still hungry after finishing a milk feed.
- She demands milk feeds more often.
- Having previously been sleeping through the night, she begins to wake regularly.
- Her weight gain may slow down.
- She can't be settled by the normal means, i.e. changing a nappy, or having a cuddle.
- She can sit up unaided.
- She has lost her tongue-thrust reflex (small babies instinctively use their tongues to push foreign objects out of their mouths – until this reflex fades, they are likely to do the same thing to a spoon of purée or a piece of banana).
- She starts to reach for food at mealtimes.

There are two common tendencies in babies of this age that parents often misinterpret as weaning signals. The first is if your baby is constantly putting her fingers in her mouth. This is usually her exploring or teething. The other thing babies do that often has parents reaching for the blender is that they will watch you intently while you eat. In reality, this is probably because they find it fascinating. But, if they start trying to grab your food and eat it, well, that's a different matter!

THE TWO METHODS OF WEANING

Once you have decided that your baby is ready to be weaned, your next decision is *how* to wean. Generally speaking, there are two schools of thought – the traditional purée method (in which you blend up everything for your baby and feed it to her on a spoon) or going straight to solid finger foods, known as baby-led weaning (BLW).

Traditional weaning: the basics

In traditional weaning, a baby moves systematically through different stages in order to learn how to chew. Starting with smooth purées, she will, over the course of a few months, progress to lumpy, then chewy foods. You can use shop-bought puréed baby food or make your own by blending up steamed vegetables, fruits and rice, gradually moving on to fish and meat. Good first foods include puréed vegetables such as carrot or butternut squash, and puréed fruit like apple or pear.

As a guideline, if you start weaning at around six months, by the end of this 6–12-month phase, your baby should at least be able to manage a lumpy and textured meal (see stage 2, on page 67). She will also be taking in a lot less in terms of milk feeds during the six-to-twelve-month period, but breast milk or formula will still form an important part of her diet.

If you are using jars or sachets to wean your baby, you will notice that the stages and approximate ages are marked on them. Some brands are much easier for babies to eat than others so, if in doubt, spoon it onto a plate before feeding it to your baby and have a good poke through with a spoon to ensure there are no lumpy surprises. For example, in one jar you might find a smooth, thin sauce and a rather large cube of carrot (I explain why this is difficult for a baby to deal with below under the heading 'Help! my baby won't eat lumps!' on page 75) and, in another jar, you might find no lumps at all. Meanwhile, homemade food tends to be blended together and, therefore, the texture is more consistent and easier for babies to eat.

Baby-led weaning: the basics

BLW is a method of weaning a baby straight from milk onto solids. It bypasses the purée stage and encourages the baby to self-feed on a range of soft solid foods (see page 69). Self-feeding allows the baby to decide what, how much and how fast food passes through her lips. It generally starts with a range of soft foods such as:

- fruits – banana, mango, plum, soft pear
- cooked vegetables – sweet potato, carrot batons, broccoli, roasted peppers, parsnip
- strips of omelette (after six months)

The idea is that your baby takes as much or as little of each food as she wishes. Initially, she explores the textures and tastes, actually swallowing very little. But, over time, as she becomes more comfortable with the textures, tastes, colours and smells, the strength of the muscles in her mouth will increase and she'll begin to eat. As with all weaning, milk is continued in conjunction with the solid food, but reduces in quantity as the amount of solids increases.

Devotees of BLW say that this method fits perfectly with a baby's general development. At six months babies are grasping and mouthing toys, so this is the ideal time to begin introducing finger food. Babies at six months are generally able to sit upright unsupported (if not, they could sit on a lap or in a highchair with support) and should be eager to participate in mealtimes – in other words, they'll probably be trying to grab food and put it into their mouths.

BLW allows a child to explore food by picking it up, playing with it or licking it before moving on to chewing and swallowing it. This allows her to receive a lot of information about the food – such as its size, weight, shape, consistency, etc. – that will help her to know how to chew it.

And, according to the BLW gurus, babies weaned using the baby-led method are actually less likely to choke on their food, as they are not capable of moving food from the front of their mouths to the back until they have learned to chew by moving their tongue appropriately.

ARE YOU THINKING ABOUT BLW?

Before you embark on the BLW method, ask yourself the following questions:

- Has my baby got reasonable strength in her mouth? You should have a gut instinct about this, but watch to see how her mouth moves when she mouths toys.
- Was my baby premature? If so, she may not be developmentally ready to accept finger foods at six months.
- Did my baby have feeding or swallowing difficulties with milk in the first six months of her life? Was she a poor milk feeder?
- Is my baby developmentally ready for solids (i.e. sitting upright with good head control)? If your baby was premature, it may take her longer to achieve a good sitting posture and head control.
- When do I return to work? Children often take less food over a longer period of time with BLW, and nurseries tend to have fixed snack and meal times, which could be harder for a BLW baby to adapt to.
- Has my child had difficulty putting on weight? If so, it's harder to fortify finger food with richer foods such as cream or cheese, to provide additional calories for underweight babies.
- Am I informed about BLW? I recommend the book *Baby-led Weaning* by Gill Rapley, and that you talk to your health visitor, breastfeeding councillor or others who have used this method.

My verdict

A lot of experts and parents think of weaning as a black or white issue – you either choose traditional weaning or BLW. But my opinion is that you should do both together – it's more realistic and you get the best of both worlds.

With my baby Jess I started with a couple of days of puréed food and, each time I gave her the purée, I gave her her own spoon so that she felt part of the meal (at six and a half months, Jess was able to put the spoon into her mouth successfully – although the carpet wasn't too happy about this!). After a couple of days of purée, we went straight to easy-to-bite-and-chew foods (see page 69) – I gave her a soft carrot stick from my plate and, afterwards, a chunk of banana for her to manage herself. I also remember having a salad in a restaurant (salad in a restaurant is not a common experience for me!) with a chunk of pineapple that Jess reached for at about six months and I willingly gave it to her to suck and practise biting on. She then wanted the lemon from my drink and, much to the horror of my in-laws, I gave it to her, peel and all. Yep – sure enough, she loved it! Mum: 1, in-laws: 0!

You could try giving your baby purée if she is eating on her own (which can help because babies often have meals at strange times – lunch at 11.30 a.m. or supper at 4.30 p.m., for example), but give her easy-bite foods to play with when she sits with you during family meals. I wouldn't advise giving purée and finger food during the same meal for the first few weeks because it may be confusing, but, after that, the world's your oyster and you can have as much fun as possible with food.

There is little chance of your baby choking on easy-to-bite-and-chew foods if you ensure she is well supported (sitting slightly forwards rather than leaning backwards, for example, in a recliner seat) and has good head control. Mother Nature has designed a perfect safety mechanism by placing a gag reflex much further forwards in babies' mouths than in adults' mouths, so if their food slips towards the back of their mouths, they will gag it up.

To keep a meal sociable, try to eat something alongside your baby so she is exposed to the range of foods you eat. Be confident and enjoy watching her as she devours your culinary delights!

THE STAGES OF WEANING: HOW THE MOUTH DEVELOPS

By moving the jaw, lips and tongue during eating, your baby strengthens and learns to coordinate all the muscles, ready for speech sound production. This development occurs in four stages and below is a rough guide to each, outlining what your baby should be able to manage if you are following my advice and combining the two methods.

Stage 1

Sucking milk, whether it be from a bottle or a breast, involves a simple up-down movement of the jaw, and the tongue extends forward in the mouth (protrudes). When solids are introduced, babies replicate this up-down movement as an early form of chewing – we refer to this as munching. During stage 1, babies are learning to bite and munch food – they are practising the early movements for more advanced chewing. (When you chew, your tongue goes from side to side and moves diagonally, and your jaw moves up and down and round and round.) Babies at this stage may also experience tongue protrusion during swallowing or at rest (it should disappear by six months), replicating the tongue movement used for sucking milk, when they are trying to eat – food enters their mouth and their tongue pushes it straight back out. Therefore, they must learn to keep the tongue inside the mouth and how to move it from side to side to control food in the mouth.

Stage 2

During this stage of weaning, babies are biting off small pieces, munching and moving the tongue from side to side.

Stage 3

In stage 3, babies are chewing using side-to-side, round-and-round and diagonal movements of the tongue and jaw.

Stage 4

During stage 4, babies are chewing all kinds of consistencies and textures of food.

TOLERATING TEXTURES

As well as considering what movements your baby's mouth can manage at a particular stage of weaning, you need to think carefully about the types of textures and consistencies she is able to tolerate.

We've just learnt that babies go through stages of weaning as they develop the mouth control necessary to manage different consistencies and textures of food. Unfortunately it's not always as straightforward as this – it's very common for children to have problems with weaning, such as food refusal, eating incredibly slowly, choking, gagging, and so on.

Remember, until weaning begins, your baby's mouth has only ever been exposed to the thin, smooth texture of milk, so you have to gradually allow her to experience new textures in her mouth. Whether your baby has taken to solids like a duck to water or is struggling, I hope that the list below can guide you through the natural progression of food textures. Once your baby is managing one consistency efficiently, you can move on to the next.

All children have fussy food days and research suggests that we need to offer food 12 to 14 times before they will accept it, but most parents give up after three or four times. If your baby is struggling with weaning, you will need to pinpoint the textures she *can* and *can't* manage successfully. To help her move forwards, you may need to go back a level and repeat some stages along the way.

Nicola's work-through weaning list

As you wean your baby onto solid foods, introduce textures in the following stages:

Purée

Begin with smooth textures, moving on slowly to grainy purée.

Mashed

Start with food that is whisked or blended for less time than your usual purée, leaving a texture and a roughness to it. When your baby tolerates this, move towards fork-mashed food.

Bite-and-dissolve foods

These foods melt in the mouth and do not require chewing. They are a good 'next step' for children who will not tolerate lumps in puréed food. However, if your child is managing to nibble on banana or parsnips, you may want to go straight to 'easy-to-bite-and-chew' foods (see below).

As you will notice, the list of bite-and-dissolve foods here is not particularly wholesome! You can try sponge fingers, sponge cakes (such as Madeira cake), cheese straws, rusks, meringue, Cheerios and homemade yogurt ice lollies. The brands Organix and Goodies produce a range of healthy snacks, some of which literally melt in the mouth, such as Organix carrot sticks.

Easy-to-bite-and-chew foods

These foods require some preparation in the mouth before being swallowed, so watch as your baby munches and moves her tongue to practise grinding down the foods (babies tend to suck food initially or squash it with their fingers!). You can introduce the range of food shown below immediately if you are doing the BLW method or a combined approach (see page 63). There are many of these foods:

Fruit and vegetables
- soft pieces of potato, sweet potato, plantain, parsnip, carrot, beetroot, cauliflower, swede

- banana (whole or small pieces) and other very ripe peeled fruit, such as pear, peach, mango, nectarine and avocado
- seedless grapes, either peeled or squashed and cut in half lengthways
- squashed blueberries, raspberries or strawberries

Breads
- white bread and butter
- lightly toasted white and wholemeal bread (not granary) with melted butter
- sandwiches made with white bread (crusts are probably better removed in the initial stages), filled with smooth fillings, such as tuna mayonnaise, Marmite, cheese spread, jam, hummus, lemon curd and so on
- chapatti/parathas
- garlic bread (without the crust)
- pancakes, croissants, cheese straws, waffles

Note: some breads can be sticky and can cause chewing or swallowing difficulties; also the doughier or crustier it is, the more difficult it is to chew and swallow.

Pasta
Ensure pasta is cooked until it is soft. Some shapes are easier than others for infants to hold – penne is a good one to try.

Dairy
- pieces of soft cheese such as Wensleydale, Cheshire, Lancashire or Laughing Cow triangles

Meat, fish and poultry
- small pieces of corned beef
- small pieces of sausage with skin removed

- small pieces of well-cooked fish (fresh, tinned or frozen, with bones and skin removed)
- fish fingers and fish cakes (you may need to remove the crispy coating)

Harder-to-chew foods

When your baby has mastered easy-to-bite-and-chew foods, move on to including the following foods in her diet:

- raisins
- pineapple
- flapjacks
- pizza
- hard cheese
- firmer vegetables such as peppers or celery
- rice cakes
- Shreddies
- lettuce
- dried apricots
- meat
- doughnuts
- scones

Other categories

There are also other categories of texture that you should be aware of. This is because some children don't like the feel of these textures in their mouth or because they are tricky to make into a ball (bolus) in order to swallow.

- **Bite-and-crumble/splinter foods** – This category includes most biscuits (other than soft ones), oat cakes, cream crackers, Ryvita, rice crackers, poppadoms, bread sticks.

- **Sticky or tacky foods** – This category includes cream cheese, tahini, peanut butter, honey (only allowed if your baby is over twelve months) and some white breads (such as bagels and naan bread).
- **Bite-and-stay-firm foods** – These include: dried banana, some biscuits, fruit sticks and nuts.
- **Mixed textures** – Examples include apple or banana added to yogurt, custard with fruit in it, pasta with a thin sauce, soup/casseroles/sauces with vegetable pieces and hard pieces of cereal floating in milk.

`Small Talk Time`
Making the link between eating and speaking
Do as much as possible to connect the neural pathways for eating and speaking, by keeping your child stimulated while he eats. You can do this by encouraging babbling during mealtimes. For example, say, 'Mmm' when your child is eating to encourage lip closure (you can't make this sound without closing your lips), and say 'b-b-b-biscuit', 'yum yum' or 'd-d-delicious'.

`Small Talk Time` **Don't forget food play!**
This is when things start getting really messy! But when your baby first starts to wean – and even well beyond this stage – you must allow her to play with food. It's crucial that she is given opportunities to feel and lick food in order to gather sensory information about it, particularly if it is new to her. The more information your child receives about the food she eats, the more she will want to eat it and the stronger her oral muscles will become. Remember – 'Before one, food is for fun.'

If your child is not tolerating lumps in her mouth, note that this often goes hand in hand with being tactile defensive (a negative reaction to your hands being dirty or messy). If this is the case, it is crucial that you do lots of food play.

Food play games to try

Warning! If you've got a fussy eater, you might have to accept that not all the games revolve around organic 'healthy' food but, trust me, a bit of chocolate mousse won't hurt them and, if it gets them interested in eating, who cares? These games are aimed at babies aged around eight months who are not tolerating lumps.

- Put an apron on and practise painting with chocolate mousse or Marmite – encourage your baby to lick her fingers, but do not force her.
- Try drawing with a tube of icing.
- Help your baby to make a mask out of a paper plate by sticking on dried pasta shapes for the eyes, nose and mouth. The tricolore pasta (that is, orange, green and white pasta) works well for this game.
- Try vegetable stamping by cutting interesting shapes in potatoes, carrots or other hard vegetables, dipping them in paint and printing them on paper.
- Try painting with broccoli sticks or carrots.
- Sprinkle hundreds and thousands on buttered bread to make a pretty pattern.
- My personal favourite game is hiding toy animals or cars in jelly or cereal. Children are always delighted to find their dinosaurs or doggies buried in squidgy jelly.

DRINKING

Just as the foods that your child eats will have an impact on her speech, the way she drinks is also very important. The reason for this is that when you suck from a bottle, your tongue comes forwards and rests just above the lower lip, encouraging tongue protrusion. If this mouth shape is reinforced over time (through sucking on a teat or on a dummy), your child could end up with a lisp – the most common type of lisp is when your child's tongue pops through her teeth when she says 's'.

When you suck from most beakers or a straw, your tongue retracts in the mouth, creating a cavity in the base of the mouth to receive the fluid so you can then swallow it. This is the position of the tongue in the mouth that we need to encourage.

In order to encourage the optimum tongue position, as soon as your baby starts on solid foods, introduce a beaker of water with every meal. It's important to do this when your baby is as young as six months because, by one year of age, she should have been weaned off a bottle completely.

Choosing a beaker

When you buy your baby's first beaker you'll be totally baffled by the range available in the shops – they come in all sizes, shapes, colours and designs. Below is my advice:

- Choose a beaker with just *one* small hole – this will stop too much water from coming out as your baby sucks. Later, once your child has mastered the technique, move on to two or three holes.
- Choose a beaker that has a spout that can be raised or lowered so that it is portable.
- Speech therapists disapprove of non-spill valves (these are little contraptions located in the spouts of beakers that stop the fluid from pouring out if the beaker is overturned). Why? Because they are clearly devised for the adults who don't like spillages, with no thought for how this will impact on a child's articulators. Drinking from a beaker fitted with a non-spill valve is similar to sucking on a teat and, therefore, encourages tongue protrusion. So choose a spout that is free-flow rather than non-spill. If you want to keep spills to a minimum when you travel, buy a beaker with a non-spill valve and simply remove it before your child drinks from it.

- Beakers with a straw attachment are also good, but might be a bit tricky for a six-month-old. Introduce these at about nine to ten months onwards. You can also use a regular straw but it'll be easier if you cut it so that it is shorter in length – your baby won't have such a long way to suck and it will therefore make it easier and quicker to get the drink. (One day I simply placed a straw in my daughter's mouth and, as if by magic, she sucked and drank. The second time I tried it, which was sometime later, she looked at me as if I was mad and didn't even attempt to suck!).

OTHER WEANING ISSUES THAT MAY ARISE AT THIS TIME . . .

Are you sitting comfortably?

Setting the scene for mealtimes is important, so try to have a routine in place for meals, just as you have an established bedtime routine. First off, be sure to sit your baby in a highchair in which she is well supported – she shouldn't be wobbling about. If she is, stuff a towel down the side for a snugger fit. Your baby's feet should also be flat on a surface; if her legs are dangling, then it'll feel to her as if she is sitting on a gym ball as she eats (i.e. very, very unsteady). Don't feed your child in a recliner seat – it's tricky for babies to control their head movements and, depending on the level of the recline, the food can rush to the back of their mouth too quickly to swallow it and can result in coughing and spluttering.

Help! My baby won't eat lumps!

A bumpy transition between smooth purée and lumpy or mashed food is very, very common in young children. In my experience, the food that is the most problematic for babies is the kind that has two consistencies in one spoonful – you'll often find this in stage two baby jars. In some jars you will find a smooth purée and then a small chunk of onion or cube of carrot, which can come as quite a shock. Can you imagine how difficult this is to eat if you're not used to having food in your mouth? While your gums are dealing with the fairly hard carrot cube, the thinner purée, the sauce, has slipped to the back of your mouth and you're choking! Not choking badly – perhaps just a cough or two – but if you repeatedly have this experience over a period of time, you could imagine why a baby might refuse the next mouthful or meal. It is at this stage that panicking parents will complain to their health visitors that their child isn't weaning properly and babies are then referred to the feeding team at my clinic.

My advice to the parents I see – and to you – would be to keep the consistency of the food the same and mash down the lumps into one consistency. (With my baby Jess, I sometimes blended the contents of a jar or added mashed potato, baby cereal or sponge cake for a sweet dish, so that the consistency was more even.) You can still gradually serve your baby thicker purées with slightly more texture, but every spoonful should be the same texture. It'll be some time, perhaps as much as another six months or more, before your baby can manage two consistencies of food in one spoonful (such as yogurt with big fruit lumps).

If your child is refusing your culinary delights, consider how each piece of food she rejects might feel in her mouth. Is the food crunchy, spicy, bitter, sour, cold? Is there a pattern to the food she refuses? What size and shape is it? How wide is it? How thick is it? Can it be easily moved around the mouth? Does it scatter when it gets inside the mouth, therefore making it difficult to create a ball (or bolus) ready to swallow? (See page 71 for more on bite-and-crumble/splinter foods.) How hard does your child need to chew and how much pressure does she have to exert? Is one mouthful all of one texture and the next mouthful, another texture?

Did you ever think eating could be this complicated? Imagine all the information your baby's brain has to consider when a mouthful comes her way! You've been doing it for years so it's second nature to you, and you don't even have to think about it, just as you don't have to think about driving a car.

CASE STUDY: MEALTIMES HAVE BECOME A BATTLEGROUND!

Kal was ten months old when he was referred to me. He'd started eating solids at six months and was having lumpy solid food at about seven months old. Right from the offset of the introduction of lumps, Kal would gag and was occasionally sick. He always had to be in the right mood for food. Tears were common and often he point-blank refused to eat – and would not even open his mouth to try.

On my home visit I watched a mealtime unfold. Sure enough, Kal started crying as soon as his mum took him towards the high chair. She then put on the TV and started singing along. While Kal was distracted she slipped a spoonful of spaghetti bolognaise into his mouth. He looked totally shocked and spat it out and started to cry, reaching to be lifted out. Mum looked at me in a panic – no wonder they both hated mealtimes. So together we formed a plan.

- It was paramount to take the stress out of mealtimes and to try not to approach them with a sense of dread. We decided to go back to the food we knew Kal liked – smooth purées, especially yogurt – so we would offer a savoury purée followed by a smooth yogurt and, over time, we'd make the savoury purée more textured by adding mashed vegetables, and the yoghurts would stay as they were.
- We would offer milk and finger foods for snacks as usual in between meals, but not give extra milk to compensate if Kal hadn't eaten his solid meal. His weight would be closely monitored by the health visitor.

- His mum would present the savoury purée in a small bowl, so Kal didn't think he had a lot to eat – and she would allow him to feel and play with it.
- During a meal she would try to encourage him to take control over whether he was going to eat or not. She would only offer the food three times. If he took it, great, but if not, that would be that – she'd accept it and not force-feed him.
- Kal's mum would also offer finger-food snacks away from mealtimes.
- It was important not to let Kal get upset at mealtimes and to keep everything as positive and upbeat as possible. Kal's mum would praise him if he ate – not going too OTT – and praise him if he put his messy hands to his mouth.
- It was important for mum to keep her language consistent, so we decided she'd say, 'Finished?' with a head shake if Kal clearly didn't want any more, and teach him to use the 'finished' sign (see page 48) so that Kal could understand what she was saying more clearly and he'd have a means to communicate when he didn't want any more.
- I spoke to Mum about altering the whole tone of mealtimes, with less emphasis on analysing what Kai had eaten and how much of it he'd swallowed, and more attention given to making mealtimes something he would look forward to. Reading a book at mealtimes was ok and much better than the TV.
- If Kal continued to get upset when he was put into his high chair, his mum would have to feed him on her lap so that he could enjoy feeling close to her and secure whilst he ate. His mum would then insist that Kal sat in his high chair for family mealtimes, initially offering no food unless he reached for it, then, over time, offering finger food from her plate and working towards him having a little plate of his own.

- Away from mealtimes, all sorts of games around food were to be encouraged, starting with dry food play, then wet and then sticky – and lots of exercises for the lips, tongue and jaw were encouraged.

The result: I visited three times over the space of a month and Kal greatly improved. We slowly introduced more and more lumps, bite-and-dissolve foods and easy-chew finger foods (see page 69). He loved the mouth games and his weight nearly returned to its original trajectory.

A problem at stage 1

If you find that your baby is not taking to her purées well during stage 1 (see page 67), encourage her to have lots of sensory experiences in her mouth. This is called mouthing, and it allows her to become accustomed to having a variety of textures in her mouth. If she's seeking the sensory experience of mouthing toys, you must encourage it and not stop it (within reason) because this is an important stage in tolerating food. In fact, get together all of your child's favourite teething toys and allow her to have a good chew and explore these toys with her mouth as often as possible.

Other ideas
- Use a food pouch – this is a little net in which you can put soft food, such as, say, mango, in for your baby to suck and chew. These can be bought in most supermarkets for a few pounds.
- Make purées thicker and rougher over time. This can be done by adding smooth mashed potato, parsnip or sweet potato.
- Under supervision, allow your child to experiment with some bite-and-dissolve and easy-to-bite-and-chew foods (see page 69). The

reason for introducing bite-and-dissolve and easy-to-bite-and-chew foods is to help strengthen her mouth by encouraging her to chew. Place the food in the side of her mouth, between the top and the bottom teeth, so that she will have to move her tongue to the side of her mouth to munch it, and prepare it for swallowing by moving it to the centre and towards the back of tongue. (You try eating a biscuit without using your tongue – it's virtually impossible.)

A problem at stage 2

If your baby is having difficulty biting, munching and moving her tongue from side to side to tolerate slightly more textured food, try placing bite-and-dissolve foods down the side of her mouth between the top and bottom teeth to develop the side-to-side movements of the tongue which are vital for chewing.

Also, sweeter foods that are long and thin, such as fruit bars or licorice, will increase saliva production, which can promote chewing. Encourage your child to feed herself so that she can control the rate, size and speed at which she eats. You could also try using food pouches (see page 79).

A problem at stage 3

If your child is finding it difficult to make the side-to-side movements of the tongue and round-and-round movements of the jaw associated with stage 3 (see page 67), and is not comfortable with purée of a rough consistency or finger foods, try to reduce the amount of puréed foods she is offered in the hope that she will take more finger foods. Also, offer soft-chew foods (such as cheese, pear, pasta, avocado, banana, soft-boiled vegetables, etc.) and, again, place food in the sides of her mouth.

If you meet your mum-and-baby group regularly, ask each of the mums to bring a snack that their child eats but yours won't. Seeing other children eat food that your child won't works wonders!

Perfect your spooning technique

We parents often want to keep mealtimes as mess-free as possible – understandably, because it makes our lives easier. I was guilty of this as my kitchen wasn't big enough to have a table in it; therefore all mealtimes took place in our carpeted sitting room. After realizing that mealtimes were never going to be spill-free, I put a plastic tablecloth under Jess's highchair – not ideal but very necessary. Be prepared for a bit of mess – that's half the fun!

Some of the tricks we use to avoid spills – such as using your baby's lips or teeth to scrape the food off the spoon when you are spooning food into her mouth, can be counter-intuitive. Instead, if you rest the spoon on your baby's bottom lip, she has to work harder, using her lips, jaw and tongue to remove the food. This will, in turn, encourage closure of the lips and, consequently, the lip sounds ('p', 'b' and 'm') will soon be heard in babble. Also, try using a fairly flat spoon, moving towards a deeper spoon, so that over time your child has to close her lips further to receive the food.

As well as placing the spoon on the bottom lip to encourage lip closure, perhaps with every third mouthful, try putting the spoon down the side of your baby's mouth to increase the sideways move-ment of the tongue as mentioned above.

Messy eaters and dribblers

If your child is a messy eater and finds it hard to keep the food in her mouth when she chews, it might be due to a muscle weakness in her mouth. If this is the case, you may also see her coughing or overfilling her mouth. (Imagine one baked bean in your mouth – in order to chew it you'd have to have very precise movements of your tongue. So sometimes it's easier to overfill your mouth in order to manage food and this is a very common tactic used by babies.)

Another symptom of weak oral muscles is having indistinct and imprecise speech – she'll be making babbling noises but they will be muffled and unclear. This means that you need to do some exercises (see below) to improve the muscles and the speech sounds.

Watch out for excessive dribbling, too. My daughter dribbled a lot. We initially thought she was an early teether but she didn't have any of the other obvious symptoms, apart from chewing her whole fist (some of the other symptoms are a slightly raised temperature, crying and dribbling). So on second thoughts, I decided that the muscles in her bottom lip must be a bit weak and that was why the saliva was simply gushing out of her mouth. I tried some of the exercises below and, within weeks, she wasn't dribbling any more.

Small Talk Time

Exercises to strengthen the muscles for feeding

Although it may be controversial to think that building the muscle strength around the jaw, lips and tongue will affect speech and eating skills, I stand firm in my belief that these exercises are worth pursuing.

Jaw

First encourage your baby to practise chewing the following foods:

- cubes of hard cheese, such as Cheddar cheese
- strips of white meat, such as chicken or turkey
- processed meat, such as ham, chicken or turkey
- cheese on toast, cut into strips
- eggy bread (French toast) (after six months)
- omelettes, cut into strips (after six months)
- crunchy cereals
- fresh soft fruits, such as banana, mango and pear
- tinned fruits.

Then move on to:

- sausages
- meatballs
- chips
- chicken nuggets
- ravioli
- toast
- hard fresh fruits, such as apple or melon
- firmly cooked vegetables (e.g. al dente carrots)

You could also try a Chewy Tube, designed to help strengthen your baby's jaw muscles. This tool is an essential part of a speech therapist's toy bag, but foolproof for parents to try. It looks like a rubber dog chew in the shape of a hammer and is designed to fit between your child's top and bottom gums. Don't be alarmed if she has a good old chomp – she can't choke on it and it's a medical tool designed for this exact purpose. (I once visited a family who had been giving their child an actual dog chew, not realizing that Chewy Tubes exist!)

Lips

Introduce your child to blowing, which will strengthen the muscles of her mouth and face. You can buy penny whistles, which are incredibly sensitive and by simply breathing on them a sound will be produced. If your child can achieve this, over time she will begin to close her lips around the whistle and this will really get the muscles of the bottom lip moving in order to reduce the dribbling.

Once the ability to blow has been established, you can then move to more advanced blowing toys such as referees' whistles, party horns, hot food, candles, talcum powder, recorders, feathers, ping-pong balls (make a blow-football game), dandelions, blowing bubbles for a shorter, then longer distance – the world is your oyster! (Perhaps a set of adult-sized ear plugs would be advised, too!)

Another thing to try is sucking games, which are great for strengthening the mouth ready for talking. You may have a baby who knows how to suck through a straw straight away, so try it! If not, you'll need to break this skill down into achievable steps.

The easiest way to start this is to use a carton of juice or a pouch of puréed food, such as those made by Ella's Kitchen. (If you are using a drink carton, I would recommend you replace the very thin straw with a regular thicker straw. To accommodate it, you will have to make the hole in the carton slightly larger – ensure the seal is airtight around it and cut the straw to a shorter length so that it is quicker and easier to suck the fluid.) Place the end of the straw or the food pouch in your child's mouth and, when you see her move either her tongue or lips towards the end, squeeze the carton/pouch until a tiny bit goes into her mouth. Keep the tip fully filled with fluid so that all you have to do is give the tiniest squeeze and the fluid will appear. (If you don't fancy messing around with cartons, you can buy a rather expensive receptacle called a Honey Bear that'll do this exact thing for you. Hopefully, your child will love the taste and be encouraged to do it again until eventually (and this may take some time), she is able to suck.

There is a muscle that completely encircles lips, known as the obicularis oris. This is the muscle that allows you to purse your lips into a circle to say 'ooo' and 'sh' among other sounds, and also to make raspberry noises and kiss! If this muscle is strengthened using the exercises given above, your baby's sounds will be easier to achieve and more clearly articulated. You could try painting lipstick or lipsalve on your child's lips and getting her to kiss a mirror, or simply practise kissing each other. My friend's baby, Cecilie, was sucking up spaghetti at the age of nine months – a fantastic exercise for the lips, and great fun!

Small Talk Time Tongue

Having a strong tongue will help your baby move the food around her mouth to chew it and to articulate clear and crisp speech sounds. Have a go at the following licking games and tongue exercises:

- Plant a bit of yogurt on each corner and on the top and the bottom of your baby's lips. Encourage her to lick it off – this is probably best done in a mirror so that she can see what she's doing.
- Put some chocolate flakes at the bottom of an egg cup and encourage your baby to lick down to taste them.
- Encourage your child to lick her lips before you wipe her messy mouth.
- Make funny faces in the mirror using your tongue.
- Make up a story about Mr Tongue! It goes something like this: 'Mr Tongue wakes up one morning and comes out of his house [your mouth]. He decides to have a good stretch right up to the sky [move your tongue upwards]. And then down to the ground [move your tongue downwards]. And then he sees a dog wagging his tail and he tries to copy [move tongue from side to side]' and so on.
- I also love a song about a little green frog (see the Small Talk website – www.smalltalktime.com – for a video of the song). The key feature is that you must poke out your tongue as you sing and it's great fun for you and baby!

Still worried about feeding problems?

If you are still concerned about a feeding problem, speak to your health visitor; if he or she thinks there is a serious problem, they might consider referring your child to your local speech and language therapist. Below are questions a speech therapist is likely to ask you, so have a think about them before your appointment:

- Can you make a judgement on the general muscle tone in your child's mouth?
- Can your child poke out her tongue and lick her lips?
- Does she gag? If so, on what food consistencies or textures? What does she manage well?

- Is she gagging when food is presented or when she tries to swallow?
- Have there been any signs of reflux in the past? (The main signs are vomiting more than five times a day on a regular basis, crying excessively after feeds and coughing a lot after feeds.)
- How do you present her food to her? Does she eat purées or finger foods?
- Is food being scraped off the teeth or gum with the spoon?
- Can the child self-feed or finger feed?

CHAPTER FIVE

● ● ● ● ● ● ● ● ● ● ● ● ● ● ●

The Babble Phase
(6–12 months)

In the last chapter we learned that the seemingly meaningless squeals, screeches and cooing noises (called pre-babble) your baby makes in his first six months are actually the crucial building blocks from which he'll begin to form words and language. I also revealed how, as parents, you can tune in to these sounds and begin to identify and reward your baby's attempts to communicate.

And, thanks to all the fun you've been having Small Talking (playing Peek-a-boo, Ready, Steady, Go and my other Small Talk Time games) hopefully, by the beginning of this new 6–12-month phase, your baby should be starting to understand that communication is a two-way process.

Now the fun really begins as nodding, waving, babbling, clapping, signing, pointing and book-sharing become huge fun (you'll be amazed at how infectious a baby's giggle is), while singing and playing games like 'Round and Round the Garden' are endlessly entertaining – for you and baby. And he'll want the fun to go on and on – Peek-a-boo can last an eternity and simply *never* seems to get boring.

This is when you really see the well-worn speech therapy phrase 'language develops through play' coming alive. Your baby will become super interactive during this phase and you'll notice that his personality and sense of humour will start to shine through. Your babbling baby is well on his way to becoming a cheeky, charming, chatty child.

Another key feature of this stage that always delights and amazes me is the change you'll notice in your baby's social skills – he will become really sociable, craving human contact and attention. You'll spot your baby having great fun engaging strangers by making eye contact in a supermarket aisle, or at the till – all with the aim of getting a rewarding response such as a smile or a comment.

He'll want to 'play' with and take notice of his baby friends, too, and will crawl after them, pull their hair, reach for them and, towards the end of this phase, have a 'conversation' with them, rather than studiously ignoring them and acting as if he's in his own little bubble.

Of course, I can't help but get carried away with the communication side of things, but I should probably mention that this six-month period is also exciting because an awful lot is happening physically, too – your child will learn to roll proficiently, sit up unaided, crawl, walk and begin trying solid food.

You may find that during this phase there is less of a noticeable change in communication skills, as the most obvious changes are happening physically. But I can assure you that lots of things are happening under the surface that are crucial to speech and communication. This chapter looks at what's happening in your baby's brain at this time.

Let's start, though, by looking at how your baby's babble will develop.

YOUR BABBLING BABY

What is babble?

Babbling usually starts between five and seven months. During the pre-babble phase your baby will have mastered the vowel sounds and now, during the babble phase, you will start hearing the first consonant sounds – 'p', 'b', 'm' and 'w', and then, later, 'd' and 'g' – speech sounds appear in a pre-determined developmental order.

Babble is the sound made when the same consonant sound is added to a familiar vowel noise, for example, 'ba ba' or 'goo goo'. This is known as reduplicated babble. It then moves to adding two consonant sounds together, such as 'mu bu' or 'du wu' – known as variegated babble, which should appear by about eight to nine months. By ten months the babble becomes more elaborate, reaching four or five syllables, and varied tones. This is known as conversational babble or gibberish – 'goo-eee-yah', 'bay-me-ooo-du', 'ka-da-bu-ba'.

Obviously, as most real words are made up of consonants and vowels, being able to make babble sounds is a crucial step on the journey towards using real words.

We had real problems with our daughter Jess during the babble phase. She got into a habit of saying 'buh guh', which, unfortunately, sounded very much like b**ger – obviously, not a great first word. She'd say it at the most inappropriate times – when my husband's great-aunt came to stay, when visiting the dentist and continuously down the phone to all and sundry. The trouble was, it got a lot of attention and Jess knew it. My dad and father-in-law would continuously repeat it and even initiate a conversation with, 'Buh guh, buh guh'. We had to draw a line when things got worse and she started saying, 'Hiya, buh guh' – no word of a lie! So I began not reacting at all and insisting that no one else did either.

This is how babbling and, later, real words begin – they all happen accidentally. A baby might say 'mu mu' in play, but is rewarded with a response along the lines of, 'Oh, yes – mu mu, mu mu,' and then he wants to say it again because he enjoyed the reaction he got. If an experimental noise or babble sound is not rewarded, after some time it'll fade away. So, bye-bye beastly 'buh guh'!

What's happening in your baby's brain?

While your baby is busy babbling, a vast network of neurological pathways are being created in his brain and the reason babies babble

in such a repetitive way is that it helps the brain to generate and practise using these neural pathways. (Just to remind you, these are the
connections that run from brain to mouth to enable speaking.) So,
the more a baby says 'ba ba ba', the more deep-routed and robust the
neural pathways for making that sound will be.

Newborns arrive with a limited amount of neurological wiring.
There are some very basic connections in terms of vision, hearing and
the other senses. But in the cerebellum (the 'little brain' tucked under
the main hemispheres), nothing is wired at all; the hardware is in place
and ready to 'wire up', but requires real-life experiences and human
interactions so that the cells can join together, creating a network of
neurological pathways that will become the foundation for thinking
and reasoning, language, and social and emotional behaviours.

Let's think about this in terms of understanding. Each time you
say the word 'Nana' when your baby is looking at Nana, those links
in his brain are getting stronger and stronger and will become so well
established that, when you say 'Nana' and she's not visibly there, he
will still know who you are talking about. Eventually, the pathways
will run from the brain down to the articulators (the jaw, lips and
tongue that help us to form sounds that become words) so that, in
time, your baby will try and say the word 'Nana'. So, whenever you
communicate with your baby you are helping to develop his thinking
and concentration skills. (These skills fall under the heading of cognitive skills, which are perception, thinking and learning skills.)

Early experiences and interaction with a responsive and attentive
caregiver are the most critical factors in a child's brain development –
from birth, the brain rapidly creates these connections that form our
habits, thoughts, consciousness, memories and reasoning. If you want
to learn more about this, look at the attachment theory section in Sue
Gerhardt's bestselling book *Why Love Matters*.

This is why the brain of a three-year-old is supposedly two and a
half times more active than an adult's as, during the first three years of

life, a child's brain builds an estimated 1,000 trillion links through the experiences he encounters. Babies are continually looking, listening and moving, so just imagine all the experiences they are having and all the connections their brains are making.

It's so clever, isn't it? So when I see a child who has a speech or language delay in my clinic, one of the first questions I ask the parent is, 'Did your child go through a babble phase?' as it is integral to later speech and language development.

Small Talk Time **Encouraging babble**

Just as babble is made up of a chain of repetitive noises, it is really important to repeat the same games over and over again so your baby will continuously hear the same words and sounds. Even though it might seem boring to you, babies enjoy endlessly hearing the same fun, lyrical words being used repetitively as it helps them to build neural pathways. Below are some games to try:

- The first thing to do is copy the noises your child makes. Try to develop a turn-taking conversation – baby says 'du' and you say 'du'. Wait and see if he says anything else. If so, repeat it. Then you say a simple babble sound and wait for your baby to say something. He won't be able to say your sound straight away but if you repeat this activity over and over again, hopefully a little copycat will be brought to life.
- Copy each other's noises in the mirror. Make sure you can both see each other's face and your child will have a better chance of modelling your mouth shapes.
- Use puppets to generate noises by making the puppet say a stream of babble sounds in a conversational way, such as 'ah babababababa'. Stop and wait for your baby to join in. Then try again with 'ah baba' – be as animated as possible. If you haven't got a puppet, make one from a sock.

- Make a babble bag (available from our website) – a set of toys that encourage your child to babble, for example, a pretend mobile phone, a talking toucan (a bird that repeats the noises you say), a microphone, a mirror, a noisy book, a kitchen-roll tube that makes an echo when you speak down it, a couple of animals that make distinct noises, such as 'moo moo' or 'woof woof', a car (so you can say 'brum brum') and two puppets to experiment with.
- Try singing interactive songs or clapping games, such as 'Pat-a-Cake'. The crucial thing about these games is that you are communicating with your child at his language level and expecting him to join in with you (see page 100 for more information on singing).

A CLASSIC CLAPPING GAME

Say the following nursery rhyme to your baby, adding some clapping where indicated:

- Pat a cake, pat a cake [clap hands], baker's man
- Make me a cake as fast as you can
- Pat it [pat your knees] and prick it [point to the air] and mark it with 'b'
- And put it in the oven for baby and me [point to baby and point to yourself]
- For baby and me, for baby and me [continue pointing]
- Yes, there will be plenty for baby and me [continue pointing]

REASONS TO COMMUNICATE

Babies need a desire and then a reason to communicate. I've always found the following list of reasons why a baby might try to communicate very helpful for making parents aware of all the instances when their 0–4-year-old might be communicating, particularly when he might only be using his voice rather than real words to do so. Once you know what motivates your baby to want to communicate, whether it be as a request or a protest, you can provide many opportunities during your day to encourage him to tell you his wishes. Take your lead from the situations below*, then watch and wait to see how your baby responds.

- Responding – 'Yes'/'Bye-bye'. Does he use his voice to respond to other people?
- Requesting – 'Biscuit'/'More.' Does he use his voice when he wants something?
- Protesting/refusing – 'No!'/'Go away.' Or when he doesn't want something?
- For getting attention – 'Muuuummy!'
- For making comments – 'Look!'/'Big bus.'
- To give information – 'Me fall down.'
- For seeking information – 'What's that?'/'Where's Daddy gone?'
- Thinking and planning – 'After tea'/'Bath time.'
- And sharing ideas – 'Let's go park!'/'I like sweeties.'

LISTENING FOR LANGUAGE

Developing the skill of listening

In order for a child to acquire the words he eventually wants to say, he first has to learn to listen to language, so he can recognize, remember and repeat words. Listening is fundamental to this phase as your baby transitions from babble to attempting first words.

---

* Adapted from the Natural Autistic Society's *Early Bird Programme Parent Book*.

You might think that listening is a skill that just comes naturally, but listening is different to hearing. A child may have normal hearing but might find it difficult to listen, so we have to teach them to listen.

The ability to listen is greatly affected by your child's ability to concentrate and, during the 6–12-month period, your baby should be able to focus for a little longer than he has done before – perhaps for as long as two to three minutes by the end of this phase.

If your baby has good listening skills, he'll have good concentration, which means that he will stay with a game for longer, allowing him more time to think about it and learn the words that are associated with the game. Thinking and concentration come under the category of cognitive skills and, therefore, the better you are at these skills, the higher the chance of realizing your intellectual potential.

CASE STUDY: FINN LEARNS TO LISTEN

One of the tricky things about my job is when I see something in a friend's child that I think could be helped with a couple of simple tricks. This happened with Finn, who was nine months. He rarely said anything and nobody seemed at all concerned. He had three older siblings, all under the age of five, and lived in a busy, noisy house. He was a sociable boy who smiled a lot and gave great eye contact, but rarely spoke. One day I plucked up the courage and said, 'Finn is quite quiet when we meet up. Is it because he's mesmerized by all the others running around?' The answer was, 'Umm, I hadn't really noticed. I suppose it must be.' Me: 'Does he say a lot at home?' Answer: 'Yes, I think so.' Me? 'Oh, that's good.' End of conversation.

Two nights later, the phone rang. 'Hi Nic, it's Gaynor. I was thinking about what you said the other day about Finn being quiet and I've noticed that he hardly says a word at home.' 'Well, what does he say?' I asked. Answer: 'He copies the dog barking and makes a loud "ahh" sound when the others are making a lot of noise'. Hmm, I was right: there was a problem. So here's what we did.

- Firstly, I referred Finn for a hearing test. His hearing was slightly down on both sides and he had a history of ear infections in both ears, suggesting that at one point, maybe a critical point in his development, he would have found it difficult to hear and perhaps that, even now, his hearing was fluctuating.
- Every day we gave Finn ten minutes Small Talk Time when he had a bit of one-to-one with mum, dad or me, with as little background noise as possible. We had to train his ears to listen – this may have been because his hearing was low at one point and he got into a habit of not listening because there was nothing to listen to. You have to hear sounds in order to try to copy them!
- Each Small Talk Time started with the adult saying, 'Shhh', and then waiting for a sound to listen to. (One day, I set my mobile phone alarm off and hid it under the cot just so that he would hear a different sound to that of children making noise!)
- We made a babble bag (see page 92).
- We also had a sound sack for Finn to play with. This consisted of a bag of objects that made specific speech sound noises that are used in the English language, and are easy for baby to say, for example, a monkey ('ooo ooo ooo'), a mouse ('eee eee eee'), a teddy ('ahhh'), a train ('ch ch') and a rabbit ('ff ff'). It was much easier to collect the objects together so whenever we had five minutes we could literally pull something out of the box and get stuck in straight away.

Within a month, Finn was making a much wider range of noises and everyone was a lot less worried. He continued to make good progress and didn't need any official speech therapy support.

THE BENEFIT OF CAUSE-AND-EFFECT GAMES

I encourage all my patients to play with cause-and-effect toys – these are games with which an action from the baby results in an exciting reward for him. So you might push a button and an animal pops up, squeeze teddy's tummy and he starts to sing, clap your hands and Iggle Piggle starts dancing, pull a string and the duck quacks, and so on.

Why am I such a fan? Think about communication. If a child understands the concept that his actions will make something happen, then he will be likely to attempt a word to get what he wants. In other words, he realizes that if he says 'more', Daddy will tickle him again, or if he says, 'drink', he'll get a drink, and if he says 'duck', Mummy starts singing 'Five Little Ducks'. This is a learnt behaviour from playing with cause-and-effect toys.

Try not to predict your child's needs and wants all the time. For instance, if at 10.30 a.m. your child usually gets a drink and a biscuit, wait until 10.45 a.m. and see if he communicates what he wants by pulling you, pointing, signing or trying to attempt the word. Remember – communication can be verbal and non-verbal during this phase.

Small Talk Time **Learning to listen and concentrate**

Listening for language can be very difficult when there is a constant background noise such as the TV or the radio – you might want to look back at the Small Talk technique in chapter one (see page 12) about setting the scene, as all the same rules still apply. The games below start with the most basic listening skills and get more complex, so try to run through them in order.

Make lots of noise as you play

Shake keys and rattles, bang drums and saucepans or biscuit tins. Play together and copy each other.

Noise, then no noise

- I love rainmakers or rain sticks, those toys full of tiny beads that you tip up to hear the sound of rain. You need to say, 'Listen to the rain, raining, raining, raining. Stop.'
- Is the washing machine on? Listen out to hear it spinning and then stopping.
- Try presenting your child with an array of containers, some that have things in and some that are empty. Try using dry rice or pasta, a toy car and frozen peas to put into the containers. I sometimes walk around the garden with a plastic take-away container and, when my daughter looks at something, I will put it into the box and shake it to see what sound it makes.

There's a great song for which you will need something very noisy such as bells or metal tins full of metal spoons. It goes like this:

Shake and shake and shake and stop [make the silence last a while, then repeat three times]
And then we're going to shake some more – shake, shake, shake, shake, shake, shake stop.

Listen to noises in your environment

- Go outside and say, 'Shhhhhhh' and wait . . . what do you hear? Cars, birds, roadworks, dogs, trains, leaves blowing in the trees, a helicopter, or perhaps silence? Try to verbalize what you hear to your baby.
- If there is a sound in your house, for example, the vacuum cleaner, the washing machine, dishwasher, doorbell, phone or

kettle boiling, draw your child's attention to it. Say, 'Shhhhhhh,' again before you draw his attention to the noise, so that he knows that he has to listen.

Where is the noise coming from?

First of all, turn off other noises like the TV or radio. Now, find a noisy toy or an alarm clock and play with the noise so your child becomes accustomed to the sound it makes. Then, when he is not looking, put the toy behind him and say, 'Where's Tigger/the clock gone?' Encourage your child to look for it. Once you have done this a few times, hide the toy somewhere further afield (under a table, in a cardboard box or behind the sofa, for example) so that your child can crawl and find it.

Symbolic noises

- Listen together to things that make a distinctive noise, for example, vehicles (cars, trains, emergency service vehicles and airplanes) or different kinds of animals.
- Toy animals are also great for this game – hold two up and say one animal's noise, watching to see if your baby looks to or reaches for the correct one. If the animal doesn't have a specific noise, like a rabbit, I usually give the animal a speech sound noise such as 'ff, ff, ff' (biting your lip with your front teeth). For giraffe I always say, 'j, j, j' (bear in mind that giraffe starts with a 'j' sound rather than a 'g' sound).
- Favourite toys can also be given their own noise – with dolls I usually say, 'Ahh,' when they get a cuddle, and for ball it's 'b, b, b, b' – intentionally the first 'sound' of the word.
- Make a babble bag (see page 92). Put the noisy objects your child likes the most into a bag. Besides the suggestions on page 92, you could add a cuddly toy with a large nose to press and say 'beep, beep', a Teletubbie that says 'eee ow', a cat that says 'meow' or a

fire engine that goes 'nee nor'. Pull them out one at a time and when you look at these objects, say their sounds over and over again. Help your child to listen to and learn the noises. Say the sound 'brum, brum' whilst the car is moving and go silent when it stops. You could also try putting a mirror in the bag to encourage your child to say the sounds and to look at the way his mouth moves as he says them.

- Make a sound sack (see page 95).

Listening to voices

- Hide behind the curtains, behind the sofa, under a blanket, under the table or behind the door, then call your child's name. Can he find where you are hidden? Say 'peek-a-boo' when he finds you. (Health warning: this game can go on for hours!)
- Ready, steady, go games – get your baby to knock down a tower of blocks or roll a ball in response to you saying, 'Go.' Try tickling him after you say, 'Go,' and so on.
- Sing a familiar song and then wait for your child to react when you pause by the key word, for example, 'If you see a crocodile, don't forget to . . . scream . . . argh!' (For more on why children love songs so much, see pages 100–104.)

Babies can lip-read

Babies don't learn to talk just from hearing sounds. New research suggests they're lip-readers, too. Scientists in Florida have discovered that, starting around the age of six months, babies begin shifting from the intent eye gaze of early infancy to studying mouths when people talk to them. 'The baby, in order to imitate you, has to figure out how to shape their lips to make that particular sound they're hearing,' explains developmental psychologist David Lewkowicz of Florida Atlantic University, who led the study.[1]

Apparently, it doesn't take babies too long to absorb the movements that match basic sounds. By their first birthdays, babies start shifting back to look you in the eye again – unless they hear the unfamiliar sounds of a foreign language. Then, they stick with lip-reading for a bit longer.

This research confirms just how important it is to get down to your baby's level and have quality face-to-face time with him (as opposed to sitting him in front of the latest baby DVD) when it comes to speech development.

SINGING

Parents have been singing songs and lullabies to their children for thousands of years, passing down the rhymes through many generations. Children love songs and rhymes – have you ever noticed that when a song from an advert comes on the TV or when you put a CD on in the car, your child stops and calms down? And for good reason – babies love the familiarity of songs and, because of the continuous repetition of the same words, they find learning words through songs easier than learning words through spoken words. And, recently, I heard on the radio that brain scans have shown that when you hear music, the language centre in the brain lights up. Even more reason to start singing.

The same applies to adults – a tune might come on the radio that you haven't heard for years but you'll find yourself singing along because the words come back to you as soon as you hear the music. Having a tune and a rhythm helps you to remember the words.

So, this is why we have a section on singing here when, perhaps you might have thought that, by the age of six months plus, you'd have stopped singing lullabies to your baby and be moving on to speaking. In fact, the opposite is true – I encourage the parents who visit my clinic to keep singing to their children for years!

MY FAVOURITE SONGS FOR EVERYDAY ROUTINES

Choose short and simple songs that are easy for your baby to learn and remember. Below are some of my favourites:

- Whenever you see your child go from sitting to standing, sing the following words to the tune of 'Knees Up, Mother Brown':

  Jess is standing tall
  Jess is standing tall
  One, two, three, four, five
  Jess is standing tall!

- Try tidying up singing the following words to the tune of 'The Grand Old Duke of York':

  Oh, it's time to tidy up, it's time to tidy up
  Tidy up, tidy up, tidy up, tidy up
  It's time to tidy up.

- Carry out your morning routine while singing 'This Is The Way We Wash Our Hands' (wash our face/brush our teeth).
- For teaching body parts, try the old classic, 'Heads, Shoulders, Knees and Toes' or another song I like is 'Put Your Finger on Your Nose', which you sing to the tune of 'If You're Happy and You Know It'. Below are the lyrics:

  Put your finger on your nose, on your nose
  Put your finger on your nose, on your nose
  Put your finger on your nose
  That's where the cold wind blows
  Put your finger on your nose, on your nose

Put your finger on your ear, on your ear
Put your finger on your ear, on your ear
Put your finger on your ear
And leave it there all year
Put your finger on your ear, on your ear

Put your finger on your knee, on your knee
Put your finger on your knee, on your knee
Put your finger on your knee
We're as happy as can be
Put your finger on your knee, on your knee

Put your fingers all together, all together
Put your fingers all together, all together
Put your fingers all together
And pray for better weather
Put your fingers all together, all together

Small Talk Time **Learning through singing**

You are probably going to have to sing 'Twinkle, Twinkle, Little Star' and other nursery rhymes hundreds of times with your baby, so I figure you may as well learn how to get the most out of it! Below, I give you some pointers. If you think your child really enjoys the song and wants more, encourage him to say or sign 'more' (see page 48) before you sing again.

Go slow and praise

Look expectantly at your child to encourage him to join in when singing. This will help him to make sense of the words and enable him to participate in his own way. So you might hear him trying to join in the 'quack, quack, quack' part of 'Five Little Ducks', scream when he 'sees' the crocodile in 'Row, Row, Row the Boat' or indicate that he wants more in the rhyme 'Round and Round the Garden' by pulling your hand or lying his hand flat.

Just don't go so slowly that the rhythm is lost, or that your child's attention is compromised. Try to focus on one song for five minutes a day.

Stress and repeat words

Choose songs in which the same words appear time and time again (for example, 'Five Little Ducks' offers plenty of repetition). This enables you to stress that word time and time again. There is a reason why children love the dreaded rhyme 'The Wheels on the Bus' – the lyrics are simple and repetitive and the word 'bus' gets repeated time and time again.

Sing songs with actions and signs for the words

This helps the child to understand the meaning. Two of my favourite action songs are 'Incy Wincy Spider' (where you use your hands to show a spider climbing up the water spout, and then being washed down and fan your hands to show the sun coming out), and 'Twinkle, Twinkle, Little Star' (where you wiggle your fingers to show a sparkling star above your child's head and form a triangle shape to show a diamond in the sky).

Encourage participation

Decide what your child should do to take part, for example, clap, sign (see page 104 for information on signing) or sing a word, and begin to teach him the song with the aim that he will start filling in the gaps. Just as with anticipation games, when you pause during the song (ideally, before the key word or action), stop, look at your child expectantly (sometimes for a time that feels far too long for an adult, say, five to eight seconds) and wait for your child to respond in some way. This won't be the real word initially, but, instead, a look, body movement or sound suggesting that he knows he has to say or do something at this time. Remember to give lots of praise.

If your goal is to get your baby participating with a clap or a sign (for example, in 'If You're Happy And You Know It'), take his hands in your own and help him to move them appropriately, then move your hands further down his arms so that he moves his hands alone, then simply push his elbows to show that you are expecting him to clap.

If you want your baby to contribute a particular word, then choose the word carefully – the word at the end of the phrase often stands out, or the word that is frequently repeated. Slow down before the word appears and look expectantly at your child, in anticipation, then say the word yourself if he doesn't say it, so that you don't lose the thread of the song. Initially, you'll encourage him to say one word, then increase it to two, three, then more words.

ACTIVITIES FOR LANGUAGE DEVELOPMENT

Research by Dundee University found that activities including singing nursery rhymes, sharing books and reminiscing, such as looking at photo albums, all promote language development.[2] Researchers found that repetition is also important – if children are learning new words, they remember them better if they look at them again and again in the same book.

USING GESTURE AND SIGNING

From as young as seven months, but usually around eight to eleven months, a baby starts to use natural gestures such as waving, reaching and pointing to communicate. This suggests that coordinating the movements of our hands is far easier than coordinating the lungs and articulators in order to speak. So try to make the most of your child's ability to use his hands functionally and teach him to communicate with them!

Pointing

Did you know that we are the only animals that point? Well, I suppose most animals have paws, which makes it a bit tricky, but even chimps raised with humans rarely point and never point to other chimps.

That must mean that it's a very intelligent thing to do – it draws someone else's attention to what *you* want them to focus on, even when that object is some distance away. It might be as a request for something, or to demonstrate your interest in something to another person. When two people are focusing on the same thing, it's known as joint attention and, for good communication, it's a very important skill to acquire. Amazingly, babies who can't talk will even point to each other as a form of communication! Babies will understand a point long before they start to point themselves, and will turn their heads or look to respond.

Most children should be pointing by 12 months and start pointing at around 10 to 11 months. You might see your baby point to food he wants in the fridge, to people he wants to be picked up by, to pictures in a book that he wants you to name for him or to the door if he wants to leave.

Sometimes, the point may be accompanied by a sound but, often, it is not. And a baby usually looks at you before and after the point, to check that his message has been received. (This is different to a child on the autistic spectrum, who may point when nobody is around to receive their attempts to communicate, therefore not understanding the concept of joint attention.)

With just a tiny flick of an index finger, a whole new world opens up for your baby. He'll point and, instinctively, you'll look at the object and name it. This could happen time and time again as he learns the words and stores them in his word bank, ready to use in a few months' time.

POINTING AND THE ACQUISITION OF SPEECH

This simple gesture is so important that the rate of speech acquisition is correlated with the onset of pointing. Luigia Camaioni, of the University of Rome, found that the earlier babies begin to point, the more words they know at 20 months of age.[3]

Small Talk Time Pointing

- Firstly, establish whether or not your child understands the purpose of pointing. To find this out, direct his attention with your finger to an object within close range. Don't point to an object that is making noise (a radio, television, telephone, and so on) because he may follow the noise rather than your finger's aim. Does he look at the object to which you are pointing? Or is he looking at your finger? How does he respond? Then establish whether he understands the function of his own point. Take your child's finger and use it to point to something – does he look at where his finger points to? If not, use lots of tactile books, such as the *That's Not My . . .* series and encourage him to point to pictures that will provide sensory feedback and to look where his finger is placed.

  It's important that your child understands your point because he may not attempt to point himself until he understands this. So, if you feel he doesn't understand the function of pointing, start pointing all the time at things in your environment. Point to things that are in close range, like facial features, then toys that are just beyond your finger, then things that are slightly further away, like a bus or a police car.

- Once you think your child understands what's going on when you point, try singing the following finger-based songs – 'Round and Round the Garden', 'Peter Pointer', 'Two Little Dicky Birds' and 'Heads, Shoulders, Knees and Toes'. This will encourage him to isolate one finger.

- Play with toys that encourage fine motor development (intricate movements with the fingers), such as an old-fashioned phone, a pop-up game or even, dare I say it, an iPad or an iPhone, for which isolating one finger is integral. Scatter cereal such as Cheerios on the table and encourage your child to eat them by picking them up using a pincer grip (finger and thumb together). Once he can isolate one finger to form a pincer grip, mould his hand into a pointing shape – you may have to put your own finger in his palm so that he can grip something in order to hold his other three fingers down.

- Put something you know your child loves just out of his reach and, when he reaches for it, give it. Then try it again. Adjust your child's hand into the pointing position for the required object. Repeat this again and again using a range of very motivating objects.

Signing

So, seeing as your baby is naturally beginning to use gestures, why don't we teach him more gestures and start basic signing? You could enrol onto a baby signing course with your little one or buy a simple baby signing book, such as *My First Signs* by Annie Kubler.

Signing does not hold back speech development

Often, when parents come into my clinic with their children and I encourage them to start signing as part of the therapy process, they object, saying that they want their child to talk, not sign. There is a myth that learning to sign hinders talking but, in actual fact, this couldn't be further from the truth and is a common misconception I am very happy to bust, right here, right now.

If you think about a child's developmental stages, children naturally use gesture before they speak. For example, they wave, clap and reach their arms up to show they want to be picked up. Making these gestures doesn't stop them from eventually saying those words, it merely helps them to communicate their needs and wants when they haven't yet got the words to express themselves. Once the word is learned, the gesture or sign should fade away.

Another way to think about the relationship between signing and speech is in terms of crawling and walking. We all accept it's good for children to go through a phase of crawling because it helps them to develop the motor skills they need to master in order to begin walking. But when they start to walk, they stop crawling fairly quickly. So, crawling is a natural step towards walking, just as using gesture and sign is a natural phase to pass through before talking begins. I assure you, signing will actively encourage your child's first words, not hold them back.

The benefits of signing

- **It's easier to sign than it is to speak** – Research into language development has shown that signs and gestures are easier to learn than spoken words – for more on this, visit the Makaton website (see Resources on page 299). After all, as I showed you in chapter two, speech is a very complex process – it involves the coordination of breath, vocal folds, the jaw, the lips and the tongue and an explosion of brain cell activation. For your baby to utter just one word, he may have to coordinate five or more mouth shapes. By contrast, a gesture requires far simpler brain and body processes because, at this stage of development, babies have better visual and physical than verbal skills.

- **Babies can see the signs they are making** – To make things even harder, when a baby attempts a word, he cannot see if he is getting it right because he can't see his own mouth. This, in my opinion, is where signing comes into its own. A child can watch his arms, hands and fingers moving when he waves or points 'up', which makes the motion easier to control. You can also physically assist a child to sign, further reinforcing the sign and its meaning, but you can't do this with speech.

- **Signing helps parents simplify their language** – Given that most parents master signs at the same time as their baby, signing also helps the talker to simplify and slow down their language, enabling the child to hear a clear model for language. For example, an adult might say, 'Do you want another apple?' but if you only know the signs for 'more' and 'apple', you are more likely to say, 'More apple?'

  Signing also helps the talker to use consistent language. The signer will only know a certain number of signs so they will tend to use consistent signs for the same word. So, without a sign an adult might say, 'Do you want din dins?', 'Are you hungry?' or, 'It's tea time!', but if they only know the sign for 'eat', the parent will usually say, 'Let's eat.'

  And, as you hopefully have already learned, repeating the same word or sign constantly is the best way for your baby to learn what this word means, and the context in which to use it. Once he understands, he will try to say it.

- **Signing reduces frustration** – In all children their level of understanding and thinking is greater than their ability to express themselves verbally. In other words, by ten months of age, your baby should be able to understand some single words like 'Daddy', 'bath', 'drink', or 'milk', but won't be able to say them. Imagine how frustrating this must be – just think about being in a foreign country where you don't speak the language, but you know exactly what you want to say and you just can't get your message across.

Children often become frustrated when they can't express themselves. Young children may communicate this through behaviours such as tantrums, screaming and kicking. By using signs, we are helping them to communicate in a more acceptable way.

- **Signing boosts understanding** – Signs also add extra information to the child's attempts to speak, helping parents to understand what their baby is trying to say. When a child first starts talking he may use the same utterance for many different words. For example, 'bu' may mean 'bus', 'book', 'boo', etc., but if the word attempt is made alongside the sign then the listener will always know what the word is.

- **Signing helps concentration and listening** – Children find it easier to focus on things that are moving, so when your hands are moving to create signs your baby is more likely to look and listen. If two people stand next to each other and say the same sentence, but one is moving their hands as they talk and the other just talks, a child will most definitely be looking at the person moving their hands. Think about how your eyes are drawn to a flickering fire or a moving TV screen, even though you are not particularly concentrating on it.

- **Don't be intimidated by the thought of learning sign language** – Some parents panic at the thought of learning to sign as they think they have to master a full signing vocabulary, but I want to reassure you that you only need to master the basics. And the good news is that signs are usually pretty logical and often look like the words they mean. For example, the sign for 'car' is like driving a car where you pretend you are turning a steering wheel.

In fact, many are so obvious, you actually already do them without even realizing – how often have you signalled to someone that they should ring you by simply pretending that you are holding a phone to your ear – this is the sign for 'phone'! And guess what – the sign for 'goodbye' is waving.

Nicola's signing rules

- Gain the child's attention and make eye contact before you sign.
- Always accompany signs with clear speech and facial expressions.
- Only sign key words – words that are important for the meaning. Keep your sentences, and therefore your signs, simple and short. So, rather than saying, 'It's ten o'clock. Let's get your coat on and go swimming,' it's far better to say and sign 'swimming time!'
- Reward and praise any attempt to communicate.
- Signs need to be used by everyone in the child's environment, so encourage your partner, older siblings, Granny and Grandpa and the childminder to get involved! Ask your local speech therapist about free signing courses and encourage as many people as possible to attend. If you can get a group of willing candidates together, I'm sure the speech therapist will train your self-assembled group if you ask kindly!
- Keep signing even if, at first, the child doesn't attempt to sign back.
- Many children need hand-over-hand help to start signing, in which you assist your child by taking his hands to mould them into the right position for the sign, just as you take your child's hands when you encourage him to wave.
- Remember that signing skills are developed over time through practice and repetition. The time it takes depends on the age of the child and the frequency at which he is being signed to.
- Remember to have fun. Signing shouldn't feel like a chore or something extra to add to your to-do list. The more you do it, the more it'll feel like second nature, part of the way you communicate.

CASE STUDY: EVIE GETS SIGNING

Beckie is a speech therapist friend of mine who has two daughters, Evie and Leila. She is a great advocate for baby-led weaning and she also taught her daughters to sign.

Beckie starting signing with Evie when she was six and a half months old. In hindsight, she thinks this is too young for most non-speech therapy folk as Evie didn't sign back until about ten months and, because it took so long, most non-speech therapy people would have given up long before as there was no immediate gratification.

Beckie started with only a handful of signs that were meaningful for Evie – 'more', 'finished', 'eat' and 'drink' – and she bombarded her with them during as many everyday activities as possible. Once Evie started signing back, Beckie really stepped up the pace and often used the hand-over-hand method (see above) to encourage Evie with new signs and, by 14 months, Evie had a spoken vocabulary of 20 words, a signed vocabulary of 20 words, and interestingly, there were only two words that Evie could both sign and say. That's forty words by 14 months – amazing!

It seems that the area in which Evie really gained the most benefit from Beckie's signing was in her understanding. She had fantastic understanding and that makes perfect sense – the spoken words were backed up visually by signs to support learning. And, because she had such good understanding at an earlier age, she had a wider vocabulary at an earlier age.

UNDERSTANDING

Between nine and eleven months your baby's memory builds dramatically and he will begin to understand more of what you say. Remember – children usually understand words long before they actually use them.

You'll know your baby understands you when you say, 'Daddy's home!' and your little one looks at the door, or when you say, 'Ball,' and he crawls right to it. Or when you say, 'Kiss,' and he brings his head towards yours. By this stage, your baby should respond well to his own name and should look up (or at least pause) when you say a firm 'stop'. He may even respond to little phrases like 'come here', 'bye-bye', 'give me', 'blow kiss', and so on.

You will notice that your baby's understanding is improving every day and, by the end of this six-month period, he may understand as many as 50 words!

Small Talk Time Boosting understanding

Keep what you say short and simple

Talk about toys and read stories using single words or very short phrases. If your child can only understand single words or very short phrases, such as 'Finished' or 'What's that?' then you must speak to him at this level so that he remembers the words, understands them and then starts to copy them.

Use repetitive language and keep your routine language consistent

If you tend to say, 'Wash your face,' repeat this phrase rather than changing it to 'Clean your mouth' after the next meal. When you go into your baby's room in the morning, try to run through routine language, saying, 'Hello, gorgeous boy. Did you have a lovely sleep? Coming up? Ah, up to Mummy for a cuddle. Open the curtains. Good morning, trees, good morning, garden, good morning, swing'. Similarly, at bedtime, use consistent language as sleep time cues, such as 'Night-night, James. Night-night, Teddy. Sleep tight. Say "Night-night, Mummy". See you in the morning.'

Talk about the here and now

This allows your baby to get immediate feedback about what is happening in his life (refer back to my Small Talk Time tip Say What You See on page 17).

Remember the importance of eye contact
When you say something, ensure you gain eye contact with your baby and get his attention.

Use gestures and signs
Use natural gestures, signs and body language to support your spoken language (see pages 104–112).

ATTEMPTING REAL WORDS

Hallelujah! Just when you thought you were going to hear nothing but crying and experimental noises for ever more, all your hard work finally pays off and you begin to see and hear your baby making an attempt at real words.

In the speech therapy world we spout the statistic that a child needs to hear a word at least 500 times, in its context, before he or she will start to say it. So over the past few months you've been saying 'up' every time you pick up your baby, 'car' every time a car passes and 'hello' every time he sees you, and your child has now understood what that word means and is mustering up the ability to remember it and articulate it.

The key thing during this stage is praise. Your child will talk more if you reward his attempts, so you have to think very laterally about what he might be saying as the words won't be completely clear yet. This is because he is still fine-tuning the neural pathways, practising using his facial and mouth muscles to form the intricate movements needed to make specific sounds.

For example, it takes some parents a while to realize that when their child attempts a word like 'bye-bye', his initial attempt might sound more like 'dye-dye' but if you watch and think laterally you can notice his attempt and reward his effort. And this attempt at the word needs to be rewarded or he won't know to try to say it again.

'Hiya' is another example. A lot of children might start saying, 'Hiya!' and you think to yourself, 'I never say "hiya", I always say "hello".' Well, 'Hiya' is a very immature way of saying 'hello' and as the parent recognizes 'hiya' and models 'hiya' rather than 'hello', the child enjoys saying and repeating the word over and over again.

A word is defined as a consistent utterance in response to a particular stimulus, so listen out for consistent sounds or responses each time your baby sees the same object or action.

Having watched children make their first words for fourteen years now, I've noticed that most babies attempt the same words in the same way – you might hear 'bo bo' for 'bottle', 'ga ga' for 'daddy', 'bibib' for 'biscuit' or 'dar' for 'car'. But to an untrained ear these are not obvious words. I've had some parents come to see me to say that their child isn't talking and I've immediately been able to 'translate' their experimental words for the parents, who were delighted to realize that speech was, in fact, well on its way but not clearly articulated yet.

So, just to reiterate, don't be disappointed if you can't recognize the actual word your child is trying to say; just listen for any consistent sounds or noises for a particular object or action and establish what he is using the word to refer to. Once you have cracked this you can keep repeating the word back to him ('Yes, that's right, it's a CAR!') and he will soon perfect the word.

The more you use Say What You See (see page 17), repeat words, simplify your language, keep your language consistent and stick to what your child is familiar with (always using the same phrase for a specific activity or item, so concentrate on saying, 'Let's eat!' at each meal time rather than 'It's din dins', 'Tea time!' or countless other variables, for example), your child will start to attempt to copy things you do and say. And you will be rewarded with lots of lovely words!

Often, there can be a lot of frustration during this phase and sometimes screams can be heard rather than first word attempts (see the case study on page 119). You might encounter this scenario if your child is given one grape instead of the whole bunch, if another child comes near his toy or if something falls on the floor. Try to stay calm and say the words that describe what has happened or what the child wants – 'More grapes, Mummy,' 'Lou Lou's turn,' 'Book gone,' and so on.

While being calm and patient will help, in my view the very best way to minimize your baby's frustration is to give him another form of communication – signing (see pages 47–9).

Small Talk Time **Attempting first words**

Help your child to make that first leap from experimental noises into words by trying the Small Talk games below. In these games, you repeat the same words over and over again during everyday routines so you create a habit of saying a particular word in a particular instance. For example:

- Line up some toys by the bath and say, 'Ready, steady, splash!' as they fall into the water. Then, once your child is familiar with this habit, say, 'Ready, steady . . .' and wait to see if he attempts the word. Whatever he says, give him lots of praise, because this might be an attempt at the real word and, over time, it'll begin to sound more and more like it.
- Use the same technique for, 'Wash, wash, wash. Wash wash . . .' as you wash your baby's body, and 'Rub, rub, rub. Rub, rub . . .' as you dry him with a towel.
- Your baby will love climbing up the stairs, so climb with him and say, 'Up, up, up.' He may first say 'bu' or 'u' so reward his attempts.
- 'Diddle diddle' can be an early attempt at 'tickle tickle', so say, 'One, two, three, tickle. One, two, three . . .' whenever you tickle your baby.
- Say, 'Ready, steady . . . go!', then chase your baby around the room.
- Say, 'Clothes off!' when you are getting ready for bed, and get specific . . . 'Sock off, sock off, trousers off, nappy off, top off,' and so on.

- If your child is really enjoying something, encourage him to say, 'More,' and do the sign for 'more' too – this works especially well at mealtimes when he'll be rewarded with another spoonful.
- Laugh when other people are laughing around you and encourage your baby to join in. Look at him and say, 'Ha ha ha.'
- Say, 'Bye-bye,' during container play each time you put a brick into the box.
- Say, 'Weee,' when a dolly or your baby goes down the slide.
- Try reading the *That's Not My* . . . series of books with your baby. Read 'That's not my . . .' and wait for your child to have an attempt at the word – 'bear', 'car' and so on.

OTHER ISSUES THAT MAY ARISE AT THIS AGE

Discipline

You really don't want your baby's first word to be 'no', although I must stress that this is very common and it doesn't mean that your baby's experience of his or her first eight months has been negative; it's just such an easy word for a baby to say and, despite your best intentions, you may have said 'no' rather a lot!

But wouldn't you rather your child's first utterance was 'Bye-bye,' or 'Mummy'? If so, at around ten to twelve months, when your baby starts throwing food on the floor, pulling his friend's hair, biting, chasing the dog, crawling away when you're trying to change his nappy or rearranging his grandmother's favourite fine bone china, you have to think hard about how to manage the situation.

At ten months, your baby's memory starts to improve dramatically, and he begins to retain the new words you say to him. So, instead of saying, 'No,' you have to think of something different to say. Below is my advice.

Firstly, choose your battles. In other words, if your baby wants another biscuit when you're visiting relatives and you want to avoid a meltdown, then offer one! It's just not worth battling over every issue – and getting stressed and upset yourself. If you are going to refuse, you must stick to your guns or your baby will quickly realize that his tears and tantrums get him his own way and, next time, will immediately launch into the tantrum, knowing that it worked last time.

Remember that when you scream 'No! No!' in a high-pitched, loud and energetic way it can be mistaken for a great game and actually reward the very thing you've said 'no' to, encouraging your baby to do it again to get the same fun response.

So, decide what you DO want to be strict about – whether it's not throwing food on the floor at mealtimes (so that you can confidently take your baby to the pub for lunch, knowing he won't leave a trail of devastation behind him!), not pulling hair (be it other babies' or pets'), or not pulling Grandad's glasses off his face.

Also, I encourage my mums and dads to try 'positive parenting' and tell their child what they *want* them to do, not what they *don't* want them to do. Here are some examples:

- 'Quiet voice now, please,' instead of 'No screaming!'
- 'Not for Ben' or simply 'Stop!', rather than 'No Ben' when he tries to put a stone in his mouth, as you quickly replace the stone with a ball or a shaker (also known as the distraction technique).
- Say, 'Gently,' instead of 'No!' when your little one tugs at the dog's tail or pulls out your dad's last remaining lock of hair.
- If getting dressed always causes tantrums, turn it into a game by saying, 'I'm going to catch your hand!', 'I'm going to catch your leg!' or 'Hello, hand,' (as it emerges from a sleeve) or 'Hello, foot,' (as it pops out of a trouser leg) instead of simply saying 'No, William, will you lie still!'

Stranger anxiety

At around six to eight months your baby will go through a very sociable phase but, confusingly, this will almost definitely be followed by a phase of clinginess and stranger anxiety. Babies start to only have eyes for the people they know well, usually their mother, and experts suggest that this is a basic survival instinct that maintains the powerful bond between the child and the person who feeds, clothes and comforts him and keeps him safe. All babies will experience this, whether it's for one day, one week or several months. Thankfully, there are a few things you can do to help your baby through this tricky time.

Small Talk Time **Stranger anxiety**

During this period, try to expose your baby to as many people as possible, in as many different places as possible. Go to groups and activity centres, family gatherings and friends' houses. Encourage your little one to be held by others – only if he wants to – and interact with them. Your hard work will pay off when you don't have a child stuck to your hip for months on end!

CASE STUDY: SCREAMING TO COMMUNICATE

I had a mother walk into my drop-in clinic with her nine-month-old daughter, called Ami, who was constantly screaming in a blood-curdling, extremely high-pitched tone. Her mother had initially thought that she was trying to communicate, but the screaming had become so persistent, upsetting and difficult – especially when in public places or with friends or family – that she felt she couldn't cope anymore and had become worried that there was something wrong with her daughter. She was desperate to see a therapist for some specialist advice – firstly to know if there was something wrong and, secondly, to know how to deal with the screaming.

I understood immediately what she was going through because my daughter Jess went through exactly the same phase. It seems to happen from around seven to twelve months, just when your child is starting to babble and communicate intentionally, when he has a greater understanding of what's happening in his world, but lacks the ability to make his wants or needs understood. While there isn't an official term for it, I've seen (and heard) it so many times that I simply call it the screaming phase.

For example, if Jess saw me getting a yogurt out of the fridge in the morning for her packed lunch to take to the childminder, she'd scream like a banshee, which meant she wanted one now. The way I dealt with it was not to react to the scream by raising my voice, but to respond in a quieter voice than normal so she had to shush to hear me. I would then say, 'Yes, Jess – a yoggie' – whilst doing the sign for yogurt, then add, 'eat at Lyn's house', therefore, acknowledging and affirming her communication but not giving it to her. Giving her the yogurt would have reinforced the scream as a reasonable and effective way to communicate.

I won't lie – it took a lot of patience and repetition (and ear plugs!) but, in a month or two, she was using the sign for yogurt rather than screaming for it. At this age, babies can get frustrated if they don't get what they want, so signing really is a god-send.

Also I tried not to ignore the screaming. Jess's screaming was a direct attempt at communication and, if I did ignore it, it would get even louder, which is not helpful.

Ami's mother was delighted to hear that a speech therapist had also had similar issues with screaming, and was reassured that it was perfectly normal and natural – and, in fact, a sign that Ami was potentially a very good communicator! She took away a sheet of basic signs and I never heard from her again, which I took to be a good sign.

SPEECH AND LANGUAGE DEVELOPMENT MILESTONES: 6–12 MONTHS

Children develop skills at different rates but, by one year, usually a child will:

- listen carefully and turn to someone talking on the other side of the room.
- look at you when you speak and when his name is called.
- babble strings of sounds, such as 'no-no' and 'go-go'.
- make noises, point and look at you to get your attention.
- smile at people who are smiling at him.
- start to understand words like 'bye-bye' and 'up', especially when a gesture is used at the same time.
- recognize the names of familiar objects or people such as 'car' and 'Daddy'.
- enjoy action songs and rhymes and get excited when sung to.
- take turns in conversations, babbling back to an adult.*

---

* These milestones have been provided by the website www.talkingpoint.org.uk and are reproduced with kind permission.

CHAPTER SIX

• • • • • • • • • • • • • • •

Single-word Phase (12–18 months)

Whether your baby's first word is cake or cat (or 'buh gah', in the case of my daughter Jess), chances are that it will all kick off at around 12 to 18 months. And once words start coming, things begin to get really exciting as your baby says more and more words and her personality shines through.

Typically, children have around four to six words at 15 months and about 20 words at 18 months. When your child hits the magic 50-word mark, she'll begin to copy everything, instigating a language explosion, and you'll be astounded by the ease with which she learns new words. Until this point, though, she will have picked up a word here and there, with no real speed or urgency, which will leave you chomping at the bit for more. This is totally normal, so just enjoy the words she does have and trust that more are on the way.

And if you arrive at 12 months only to find that your baby isn't yet talking, fear not. Many children will be 15 months old before they utter their first real word. It's well worth the wait!

You'll recognize some of the skills I cover in this chapter from previous sections – expanding your child's language, understanding, listening and social skills. But now I'll show you how to take them up a notch, making the games and interactive play slightly more complex so that you stay that one crucial developmental step ahead of your baby, effortlessly encouraging her on to the next stage – which is gibberish (yes, really).

You can expect a few hurdles, too – persuading your baby to give up a bottle is one of the biggest issues most parents face at this age. I advise all parents that babies should be taking their morning and bedtime milk in a beaker or cup at 12 months, as drinking from a beaker or cup puts your toddler's tongue in a better position for producing clear and precise speech sounds (see page 74).

First, though, let's look at how babbling develops into gibberish.

My baby's talking gibberish

Of course, babies don't just stop babbling and start talking. At around 12 months or slightly earlier, you will notice that the babble begins to change and your baby starts talking double Dutch, otherwise known as gibberish, conversational babble or, in the speech therapy world, jargon.

Your baby will start to talk to you as if she is telling you the most elaborate story you have ever heard, with varied tones and many different consonants. It sounds as if she is talking in a foreign language, and she looks at you as if you should understand every word, whereas in actual fact you haven't got the foggiest idea what she is going on about.

If you haven't already seen it, I recommend you watch the YouTube clip of the toddler twins talking to each other (search for Talking Twin Babies) – it really is the perfect example of gibberish in action. They haven't yet got any real words and aren't even using that many consonants, but they're having an intricate chat using intonation, gesture, turn-taking, body language and appropriate sentence length (see the skills on the plate of the language cake on page 22). It's as hilarious as it is fascinating and you get the impression they know exactly what they are talking about.

Enjoy this slightly comical gibberish while it lasts because, sadly, by about 20 months, the gibberish goes almost completely as your baby prefers to use proper words to communicate.

Before she reaches this stage, you need to encourage your toddler to copy us as much as possible in order to get her gibbering.

It may sound silly, but it's a key step along the way to proper words because it enables her to practise putting a variety of consonants and vowels together in single 'words' or 'sentences', and experiment with elaborate intonation patterns, continuously creating those crucial neural pathways.

Alongside the gibberish, you will hear more of those long strings of babble sounds (reduplicated babble – see page 89) that we encouraged in the previous phase – 'gugugug' or 'tatatata' – especially incorporating the consonant sounds that your toddler hasn't mastered yet and which you should try to encourage if you can. There will also be some shortened utterances – listen out for 'uh', 'ah', 'ba', 'ga', and so on, perhaps accompanied with a point at a particular object or person. You will probably also hear 'ah' quite often, as in 'give me that', or to seek attention, for example, when your child wants to do something, like hold on to your toothbrush or climb the stairs, and knows she shouldn't.

The consonant sounds you should be hearing by now are 'm', 'n', 'p', 'b', 'd', 'w', 'h', but again, each baby is different and will do things at her own pace. Right up until 14 months, my daughter Jess couldn't say 'd' or 'w' and I was very aware of this. She said 'g' instead – a sound that, developmentally, usually comes a little later. This meant 'dada' was 'gaga' which rather amused me, and water was also 'gaga'.

So don't worry about the sounds you are hearing at this age. Just be aware that your child should be making consonant sounds as well as vowel sounds in a meaningful way, trying to get her message across.

Want to boost your baby's gibberish? Below are some Small Talk Time copying games to encourage just that. It is important to adjust the way you communicate to make it easy for your toddler to understand you, so she will try to copy your words. Reduce the number of words you say to single words when drawing her attention to something, sharing a book or playing together.

Small Talk Time **Copycat**

Because language development is all about being a copycat, it's very important to teach your child how to copy so she can begin to 'model' (or copy) your language. Remember – everything that you do with her will be lapped up eagerly as her brain is like a sponge.

The easiest way to develop your child's ability to copy is through play. In fact, you will have already been doing this with games such as Peek-a-boo and the action songs you have been singing. Copying non-verbally in play is a prerequisite to copying verbally.

I remember running a playgroup for eight-month-olds and we were amazed once when I was playing Peek-a-boo with Mattie and Rory and, suddenly, Amelie, who wasn't even part of the game, picked up a piece of paper and started playing, too. She was copying! And this is such an important skill to learn for later language development.

There are many things you can do to encourage your toddler to copy you. My husband and I play Paper, Scissors, Stone to determine who will change Jess's latest dirty nappy and now Jess joins in too, because she has learnt to copy us. (Unfortunately, if she loses, she doesn't follow through with the punishment and change her own dirty nappy!) Below are some other games to try:

- Fill two boxes with identical items, such as musical instruments and sensory objects (for example, a scourer, washing-up brush, flannel, spoons and a foil food wrapper like an empty rice-cake wrapper). These are known as copy boxes. Give your baby one box and you keep the other. Whatever your baby does, simply copy her every move. Then try role reversal.
- The *Tweenies* on CBeebies sing a great song that goes like this (see www.smalltalktime.com for a video of the song):

    Everybody do this, do this, do this. Everybody do this just like me!

As you sing, you make an action for your child to copy – patting your knees or your lap, touching your nose or shaking your hands. Once you've sung it through once, say, 'Your turn,' then copy literally anything your child is doing with her hands, and then sing again. It's great fun and very catchy!

- Encourage your child to copy you as you play. Try hugging a baby doll, banging two bricks together, bouncing a tiny ball, putting a hoop on a stick, and so on.
- Play copycat games in the mirror using noises and sounds. The key lies in waiting. You say something and wait for your child to respond before making more sounds.
- Sing familiar nursery rhymes and change the lyrics to babble noises. For example, to the tune of 'Twinkle, Twinkle, Little Star', sing 'da da da da da da da', and to the tune of 'Wind the Bobbin Up', sing 'wa wa wa wa wa' – you get the gist!

LANGUAGE DEVELOPMENT IN TWINS

You may or may not know that twins are at higher risk of speech and language delay than singletons. There are a number of reasons for this but the main ones stem from being premature or having a low birth weight, or possibly because parents don't have as many opportunities to spend one-to-one time with each twin. So, what can you do to help? Try the ideas below.

- Find as much time as possible for each twin to have your undivided attention. For example, during nappy changing or, consider bathing them separately from time to time, occasionally have separate bedtime stories, allow one parent and one twin a head start in a walk, and so on.
- Be aware that you are your children's best resource when it comes to learning language and the more time they have with

you, the better. Remember to spend ten minutes of Small Talk Time every day with each child independently, or at least as often as you can. This will provide an opportunity for each child to practise and improve her communication skills.

- You will have to be even more committed to using the Say What You See technique (see page 17), ensuring that each twin knows that you are commenting on her play and not her sibling's. Remember to back up what you say with signs (see page 47).
- Read to each twin separately. Reading is a fantastic way to encourage language development in all children.
- When you are chatting to your twins, make sure there is an equal balance in the conversation – be aware of turn-taking, ensuring that one twin is not dominating the conversation or your time! Allow each twin time to speak, saying, 'Gabriel's turn, Alice's turn.'
- Be aware of your twins talking in their own language – twin language, otherwise known as idioglossia. This is very common: one study suggested that twin language occurs in 40 per cent of twin pairs.[1]

Twin language usually develops as a result of twins being so in tune with each other that they copy each other's words, even when these attempts at words are incorrect. For example, one twin attempts to say 'thank you' by saying 'agoo' and, before long, they are both using 'agoo', giving the impression that they have created their own unique language. Remember to always model back the correct version of the word for the child, for example, 'Thank you. Well done, you said "thank you".' If you are worried, act quickly and get in contact with your local SLT.

FIRST WORDS EMERGE

Alongside the gibberish, you will hear your child say the occasional real word – remember that the speech and language therapy definition of a word is a consistently spoken utterance that represents a particular object or person. These attempts need to be repeated and praised in order for them to be heard again.

I often hear a parent say, 'I think she said "ball"!' and I say, 'Yes, great! She definitely did say "ball" and the more you repeat and praise her attempts, the more that word will appear.' This is how language develops – a baby accidentally says something and then gets lots of praise or attention so says it again and again.

This happened once when I was bathing Jess. I had forgotten a towel, so I called to my mother-in-law, saying, 'Pat! Pat!', and no sooner had I stopped then my little parrot, thirteen-month-old Jess, started shouting, 'Pa! Pa!' She received a big laugh and another rendition from me, 'Pat! Pat!' so she said it again and again. Great fun – although possibly not so much fun for Pat who is now at Jess's beck and call!

And this is why I love this phase of a child's language development – things start to get really interesting as your toddler's personality begins to shine through.

Small Talk Time **Games for emerging words**

Say What You See

I mentioned this strategy on page 17. Whether your baby is just a few months or a chatty three-year-old, I still look upon Say What You See as *the* most important – and simple – thing you can do as a parent to boost her speech and communication skills.

It is *so* crucial to give your child a running commentary of what she is doing when she plays. In other words, you must put her thought to word, as she explores and plays, so that she can hear that word time and time again in its context, remember the word and begin to try to say it herself. For example, if your child:

- has a favourite game, say, putting hoops on a stick, add a repetitive commentary. In this case, you could say, 'On. On. On' each time a hoop goes on.
- loves being chased around the sitting room, say, 'Fast. Fast. Fast' or 'Run. Run. Run.'
- bangs her spoon on her high chair while eating, say, 'Bang. Bang. Bang.'
- loves watching the cars go by, say 'car' every time one passes.

Remember to keep your language simple – so you would say 'car' rather than 'another car'. You may think you sound foolish but, I assure you, you are doing the best thing for your child's language development.

Don't get into the habit of asking, 'What's that? What's that?' or you might end up with a child who says 'da' – 'that' – for everything. Instead of asking 'What's that?', use the Say What You See technique and name objects – 'tree', 'dog', 'bus' or 'bird'. This way, your child will be learning the words she needs, at a level that suits her.

If you feel the need to test your child to see if she knows the name of an object, say, 'It's a . . . ', look at her encouragingly and pause to see if she wants to fill the gap. If she doesn't, say the word for her.

Name family members

Make a scrapbook or buy a small album to stick photos of your toddler's nearest and dearest in. At this stage only say their names, for example Mummy, Daddy, Grandad, Baby Wilf and Aunty Char Char (we tend to repeat the syllables, as this is closer to the kinds of utterances we are hearing from the baby).

You could even try making a PowerPoint presentation or online album of family members so that your baby can flick through the pictures on an iPad.

ONE WORD FITS ALL: OVEREXTENSION

Toddlers tend to use the same word to refer to a number of different objects. This is known as overextension. So, for example, 'wawa' may refer to any liquid, even if it's not actually water, and 'car' might refer to literally anything that moves! You will also soon discover that toddlers usually repeat the first syllable in a word, so two-syllable words will most probably be spoken as a repetition of the same syllable (for instance, mama, dada and baba). For example, my nephew said 'more more car car' when referring to watching a train clip on YouTube until he was about two years old. This means that you'll find yourself translating your child's language for those who don't know it very well and aren't used to her quirky speech. Don't worry about this. It's a perfectly normal phase and will soon pass once your child realizes there is a clearer way to get her message across. Just continue to praise her attempts at language and model the correct word – 'Yes, train. You want more train.' (For more on modelling words, see page 125). It's also possible for toddlers to underuse words, calling only specific objects the right word, rather than all items which are the same. This is known as underextension (see page 207).

Have a word theme for the day

Collect objects that relate to a specific word and play with them for the day. (You should also learn the sign for the word so that your child is bombarded with it through her eyes and ears.) These objects could include a book, an item of clothing, a flannel, a toy, and you could even sing a familiar song. 'Bear' is a great example of a theme. You could:

- read a book about a bear
- have a teddy bears' picnic and encourage your child to give some food and drink to the bears.

- sing 'If You Go Down to the Woods Today'.
- bring a bear to lunch with you or take him for a walk with you – put him on the swings, too.
- throw bears in a box and say, 'Bye-bye, bear,' then bring them out one by one and say, 'Hello, bear.'
- look up bears on Google Images and say 'bear' every time you see one.
- wear your bear pyjamas.

You can use this format for any object you think your baby is interested in and, if you can't think of a song that fits with your theme, simply change the words to a familiar song.

Going UP!!!

Another good word to focus on at this stage is 'up' because it's an easy word to say and it's a high-frequency word. Think how many times you can say 'up' in a day – lift up, climb up, wash up, pick up, blow up, build up, tidy up, clean up, mop up, up in the sky, upside down, up to Mummy . . . the list is endless.

You could cut out pictures from a catalogue with things that depict up and down – e.g. fire engines with ladders on top, dolls houses with stairs, garages with steps, slides, toy umbrellas and sandcastles and stick them into a scrapbook. Other ideas include singing 'Incy Wincy Spider' (climbing 'up' the spout), 'The Grand Old Duke of York' (and when they were 'up', they were 'up') and 'Jack and Jill' (went 'up' the hill). Also, repeat saying 'up' while sucking through a straw or blowing up a balloon.

What's in the bag?

Put objects within a category into a bag and play What's In the Bag? Give the bag a shake to generate a bit of enthusiasm in the game, then say, 'What's in the bag?' and encourage your child to pull something out of it. I usually sing a song to the tune of 'The Farmer's in His Dell' that goes like this:

What's in the bag?
What's in the bag?
E I E I O
What's in the bag?

Then either you or your baby should pull out an object and you say, 'It's a . . . [wait to give your child a chance to say a sound but, if she doesn't, complete the sentence] . . . car'.

Make different sets of similar types of object, such as some balls, a set of hats or a handful of spoons. This way, your baby can copy you and, hopefully, as the bag empties out and you repeat 'ball' each time you bring one out, she will attempt to say the word when you say, 'It's a . . .?', looking at her encouragingly.

Alternatively, try a small range of objects that fit within a certain category or set, for example, vehicles, clothes, snacks, toys or animals. Interestingly, when words are learnt within their particular set, they are stored better in the language centre in the brain (a bit like a filing cabinet in your brain). This then makes it easier for a toddler to retrieve them in order to say the words when they are needed.

Name each item as you pull it out and then throw it into a large container – children at this age love 'container play' and it's a technique I use all the time at my clinic. Continue until the bag is empty and then enthusiastically start all over again.

Small Talk Time

Giving your child reasons to communicate

Let's face it, we all need a little encouragement at times – and I am a firm believer in the power of dangling that metaphorical carrot. Your baby won't necessarily talk unless she is motivated to do so and you'd be amazed at how easy it is to entice her into communicating with you when she wants to get her little hands on something. Lots of opportunities to do this will naturally crop up during the day. Below are some examples:

Offer choices

When your child is reaching or pointing, even when you know what she wants, offer a choice. So if she reaches for a banana, you pick up a banana and a plate and say, 'Banana or plate?' This gives her the model of the words you want her to say and, if you hold the objects either side of your face, she can look at your mouth to see how it moves to form the word.

Ask an adult games

These are toys or games that require an adult to activate them and they can be used in conjunction with the infinitely useful word 'more'. (Once your toddler has mastered it, she can use 'more' to communicate her desire for anything from water, to cheese, to tickling.) So, if your child wants more toy action, she will have a reason to communicate with you.

Objects that require adult input include balloons, bubbles, trip trap tracks (a zig-zag car race track that you race toy cars down), taps, spinning tops and wind-up musical toys. Show your child how the game works. For example, run the car down the track or blow up a balloon and let it go, then encourage your child to ask for 'more'.

I always use the sign, too. If you are just beginning to use signs, try hand-over-hand signing (see page 111 for a full explanation), which means you mould your toddler's hand into the shape of the sign. I started this when Jess was 12 months old and it took just ten minutes for her to pick up that she had to move her hands together to get some 'more' bubbles – I was amazed.

Try playing with a toy that requires your child to ask for pieces so it will work, for example, a Connect 4 game, a train track or a puzzle. Hold the pieces back and encourage her to ask for 'more'. You can also do this with food – give your child a very small piece of biscuit instead of the whole thing and encourage her to ask for 'more'.

Asking for help

You can try putting your child's favourite toy or food in a see-through container or bag so that she has to ask you to get it out for her. This works for puzzles, too, where an adult is needed to help put the piece in. Encourage your child to sign or say 'help me' or 'open'.

Sharing books

The new, politically correct way of saying 'read a book' is 'share a book' – posters seem to be up in libraries all over the country reiterating this message. This then suggests that your baby is taking an active part in the process, so encourage her to do this right from infancy by offering her a choice, such as 'Do you want bear book or tickle book?' and wait for her to point or attempt to say 'bear' or 'tickle'.

When sharing the book, keep your language simple – you don't have to follow the text, just say single words or short phrases of a level that is right for your child. At my clinic I usually simplify and personalize the book (by using the child's finger to point to the things I know she is interested in) and then, every so often, I read the book as it is written – especially when it has a rhyme or a rhythm – which will help with later speech sound development and will extend concentration span.

When reading, say the word, for example, 'cow', and encourage your child to copy you by looking at her expectantly or saying, 'It's a . . .' and pausing to allow her to try to finish the sentence (only finishing it if she doesn't). You can try a role reversal, where you point to a picture and look at her expectantly to see if she says something.

Use books that have the same pictures on every page or in a repetitive line so that your child can join in (for example, *Dear Zoo* by Rod Campbell).

KEEPING ONE STEP AHEAD OF YOUR TODDLER'S UNDERSTANDING

Don't forget how important your child's level of understanding is in this phase. You have to keep *your* language level one step ahead of your toddler's so that you can help her soak up all the words you say. A toddler needs to understand words before she attempts to say them and, for a speech therapist, a child's understanding is far more important than her ability to express herself at this age, as it is a better indication of her intelligence.

In order to understand something, you have to listen to, process and remember words and, as you can imagine, every day this sequence is happening over and over again. By 12 months, a child should understand between 3 and 50 words. By 18 months she should be capable of understanding at least 50 words.

But how do you know what your child understands? I remember going to see a speech therapy friend of mine some years ago whose daughter was about 12 months old. She said 'I know I shouldn't really do this, but watch this . . .' Speech therapists frown upon parents who continuously quiz and question their children but she sat her daughter down with a range of objects spread out in front of her and said, 'Where's the owl/squirrel/frog?' Her daughter knew all of these and more – an extensive range of fairly abstract animals – and I was amazed. So, from time to time, try something like this – 'Where's the . . .?', 'What does a . . . say?' or 'Where's your . . .?' (see Small Talk Time games, below).

Just remember to be careful with questions (see page 00). You don't want your toddler to feel that she is continuously being tested. If you overdo it, your little one won't want to play or talk with you so much. Pick your moment carefully. Remember that, ultimately, you need to be there for your toddler as her language model and not her examiner!

Small Talk Time

Promoting good understanding of language

Keep it consistent

I want to reiterate the importance of sticking to the same standard words and phrases. In English, there are so many ways to say the same thing – 'bedtime', 'time for a little sleep', 'let's go bye-byes', 'off to bed', and so on. If you can, use just one of these phrases consistently so your toddler can understand and anticipate what you are going to say, and try to copy you.

Once you feel you are regularly using the same words and phrases during your daily routine, trigger your child into talking by starting a well-used phrase (a carrier phrase), thereby encouraging the missing to word just pop out. When you start the phrase, look at her questioningly and leave a gap for her to fill in the last word. If she doesn't, do it for her (for example, 'It's time for . . . tea', 'open the . . . door', 'ready, steady . . . go' and 'drink your . . . milk').

Where's the . . . ?/Where's your . . . ? games

Be selective about the objects you ask your child to point to and think of the key words in her environment. Say, 'Where's the light/door/window/nose/hair/eyes/monkey/dog/biscuit?' and encourage her to point. If she doesn't respond, you point at the objects for her and say the word at the same time. Remember to give lots of praise if she gets it right and, if she gets it wrong, praise her effort.

Home in on one word and repeat it over and over again. It is also fun to encourage your child to wash different parts of her body in the bath.

Matching object to object

Assemble pairs of balls, shoes, socks, spoons, cars, teddies, nappies, bananas, and so on. Mix them up and see if your toddler can find the 'same'. If she can manage this, try object-to-picture matching, which is slightly harder. Lay two pictures on the floor, one matching the object you have chosen and one of a different object. Say, 'Find the same,' and encourage your toddler to put the object on its correlating picture.

Say What You See

Remember to use the Say What You See technique (see page 17) when you are playing or are out and about. Look at what your toddler

HOW THE BRAIN STORES WORDS

In the language centre in your brain there's an area called the semantic centre, which is where all your words are processed and stored. In 1997, professors Joy Stackhouse and Bill Wells of Sheffield University came up with a Speech Processing Model that explains this process.[2] They mapped the chain of events that occurs when a new word is heard, recognized as being English, decoded into the sounds that it's made up of and understood. Their findings suggest a very organized way in which a word is stored, so it can be retrieved as easily as possible when the person wants to say that word. This means that the brain cleverly splits words up and stores them in categories. Below is a list of the categories in which words are stored in the brain according to Stackhouse and Wells:

- by their meaning – all farm animals, all clothes, all body parts, and so on
- words with the same sounds at the beginning or end, like 'pan', 'peg', 'poor', 'pig' or 'map', 'up', 'cup', 'shop'
- words with the same syllable structure, for example, 'elephant', 'strawberry', 'telephone' or 'television', 'avocado', 'caterpillar'
- words that rhyme, for instance, 'cat' and 'mat'
- words with the same vowel, for example, 'kite', 'my' and 'night'.

If only my paper-filing system was this robust. How simple life would be!

is looking at and model the words she needs, so she can try to say them for herself next time she sees the same objects.

SOCIABLE TODDLERS

Being sociable with you

During this six-month phase, your little one will become more and more sociable. She will start to take notice of more things going on around her, pointing to things that interest her, like photos on the wall. She is finding innovative ways to get your attention, like yanking your hair, throwing food on the floor or clinging to your leg. And she will pass objects to you or strangers to see what responses she gets.

You may also notice that your toddler starts to imitate the things you do, like pretending to brush her hair or drinking from a mug that you've just put down. She is noticing what is happening, retaining the information and copying it. This then helps her to learn that there is a sequence to events which, later, develops into forming a sequence of words into a sentence or a sequence of events into a story. As she uses these objects in play and practises turn-taking with them, the skills she picks up will transfer to turn-taking in a conversation.

Toddlers enjoy being centre stage and think the world revolves around them. They are entirely egocentric. They will join in when people around them are laughing – having no idea what the joke is – and enjoy trying to make you laugh, too. You'll see them peeping through their legs when they're standing up, clapping when you clap, hand jiving to music, making a funny noise or bopping up and down – all to get a giggle from their adoring audience. They simply love attention and applause. All this encourages them to get more input from their closest adults in order to learn more from them.

Being sociable with their peers

During this phase, your child may take notice of others by pulling their hair, chasing after them, handing them things or snatching things. She is curious about other children, but at this stage they don't really play together.

Towards the 18-month mark, toddlers will start playing in parallel with other children, which means they'll play the same game next to each other rather than actively seeking each other's input to make the game more fun, or turn-taking.

Pretend play . . .

Your toddler will also be embarking on the early stages of pretend play – putting a mobile phone to her ear, pretending to brush her teeth, eating a toy banana or even pretending to go to sleep (especially when singing the 'Sleeping Bunnies' song in my experience!).

Researchers suggest that there are clear links between pretend play and social and linguistic competence. This is because pretence encourages the young child to use her imagination and memory for situations and experiences, and use language for thinking things through. She is thinking of a familiar scenario in her head, then acting it out. This process can also help concentration, problem solving and reasoning. See how the process evolves using a spoon. At first, a baby might bang a spoon. The next time, she might pretend she's eating. Then she might try to feed a toy Peppa Pig. She could then go on to pretend to use the spoon to cook, or use it as a see-saw!

Small Talk Time **The power of play**

Making friends

Firstly, arrange to meet up on a regular basis with parents of two or three other children who are about the same age as your child. Fun outings at this age include trips to hands-on children's museums, playgrounds, petting farms or anywhere your toddlers can run around freely. (Just remember that, during this phase, your child is more likely to engage in parallel play than to play cooperatively with her friends.)

Point out other children in your toddler's environment and talk to her about what they are doing. Support her to watch in the first instance and then go up to the children she is interested in and encourage her to copy the other child's play, play a simple turn-taking game or just play alongside.

TESTING YOUR TOLERANCE – THE TERRIBLE TWOS

During this phase it's common for a child to start to test her parents' boundaries. This may include deliberately throwing or dropping toys or food on the floor and continuously trying to alter her parents' plans through persuasion or protest – such as refusing to put on her coat or climb into the car seat, or ignoring her parents' reprimands.

Why is this? Toddlers during this phase are trying to become independent; they want to accomplish tasks and to communicate on their own, but they don't have the necessary skills. Therefore, it's a very frustrating time for them and having a tantrum is their way of expressing their frustration.

Distract your child in such situations. Try to pre-empt a tantrum by keeping a close eye on her – if she has trouble posting a shape into a shape sorter, give her a helping hand. Tantrums are more likely to occur when a child is tired or hungry so, if you're going somewhere important, give your child an early sleep and an early lunch.

I remember driving Jess around the ring road before her first birthday party so she'd have a quick sleep and, being more rested, hopefully wouldn't have an outburst at her party. I think we had a minor tantrum over some Hula Hoops but she was certainly easier to manage than she would have been without that snooze in the car!

Remember – at this age you should ideally encourage your child to interact with a wide range of people of all ages, in a range of different environments.

Pretend play

First, encourage your baby to feed you or help you to drink at meal-times. Then take a cup, bowl and a spoon and take it in turns to give each other a drink. Make a big slurping noise so it's very dramatic and entertaining for your toddler. Now take turns to feed each other.

Your child may look completely bewildered – this is normal, just carry on. Once she starts enjoying it, the more inclined she will be to join in.

Next, take a doll and a teddy and encourage your toddler to become part of the game. You could go through the three-b routine (bath, beaker and bed) with the dolly. Take teddy with you on outings and include him as part of the family. Your aim is to encourage two-step sequences and then more, for example, bath teddy, dry him, then put his pyjamas on.

OTHER ISSUES THAT MAY ARISE AT THIS AGE

Using TV constructively

There is a lot of evidence that if the TV is on all the time in a home as background noise, it will reduce the number of conversations held and that, in turn, can hinder language development during this crucial 0–48 month period. For this reason, many experts recommend that children under the age of two don't watch any TV at all.

But I am a realist and I know that TV is part of modern life and that, sometimes, it's a lifesaver to be able pop your little one in front of the telly for five minutes while you get on with unloading the dishwasher or hanging out the laundry. The good news is that you *can* use TV constructively. Here's how.

If your child is watching TV, ensure it is a programme for children. It may seem as if I am stating the obvious, but you'd be surprised. A lot of research goes into children's shows these days, with psychologists and language experts all consulted to create a programme that is eye-catching and informative. My favourites are *Something Special* (a signing programme) and *Show Me Show Me* (lots of great repetition and singing), which are both on CBeebies.

To get the most out of a programme, your child needs to engage with it – so the TV isn't just a background noise, it is the activity. This means that, ideally, you should be sitting right beside her, pointing things out, making comments, repeating catchphrases and making links with your own life. So, if on the programme they are having a teddy bear's picnic, encourage your child to gather her teddies, too. Once the programme is over, act out what you have just seen. For example, if it was *Postman Pat*, get out a toy car and pretend you are delivering the mail.

If you are doing chores while your child is watching TV, you can still follow this advice, just to a lesser extent. So, if you are tidying up and see that it's raining in *Thomas the Tank Engine* world, you can say, 'Oh, look, it's raining in our garden too.'

Personally, I also find that TV can be useful as part of a routine. For example, Jess always has a bath at 6 p.m. and then we sit on the sofa together and watch *In the Night Garden*, followed by a couple of books before her bedtime. This is now such a well-established routine that I worry when we go away!

I am not going to give you a guideline of how many minutes of TV a day are acceptable – I realize that every day is different. The crucial thing to remember is that you shouldn't use the TV as company for your child and that even while children's programmes are well made these days, you can't kid yourself that they are educational – you are always the best resource for educational achievement and good language development. Don't have the TV on constantly and be strict about switching it off once you move on to a new activity.

Having said all that, there is one thing I am militant about when it comes to TV, and that is to never have the TV on during mealtimes. Many of my patients and friends have fallen into a pattern of doing this, arguing that a programme will distract their child so that they will mindlessly spoon food into their mouths and end up eating more – without turning the dinner table into a battleground. I am very against this.

Eating should be the most sociable time of the day; you are facing each other so your baby can watch your mouth as you talk, and it's the perfect opportunity for the whole family to chat to each other and be sociable. Even if you have the TV on in the morning while you go about your routine, you should *always* turn it off before breakfast. The same goes for lunch and dinner, too. I know that weaning can be tricky and that most children are fussy when it comes to food but TV is *not* the answer, so please turn it off at mealtimes.

Overly enthusiastic head nodding and shaking

Some babies seem to start nodding and/or shaking their heads at around six to eight months, but others, much later. Once they've picked it up, some seem to do it to excess, becoming little head bangers who wouldn't look out of place in the front row of a heavy metal concert. They nod or shake for 'yes' or 'no', when they are excited, when they are tired, and at almost any opportunity they get.

Parents can see this as a cause for concern (there are forums full of worried posts from parents on this matter on the internet) but it's all perfectly normal and a natural stage (I've even heard one doctor saying that it may be because they enjoy the sensation of feeling slightly dizzy!). Remember when your baby first learned to clap and how she did it all the time? As with nodding and head shaking, once young children discover a new trick they like to repeat it – a lot – especially when you are probably encouraging them by laughing or nodding and shaking back.

THE EVOLUTION OF THE HEAD SHAKE

Research indicates that the head shake, usually meaning 'no', may be an in-born action and evolutionary biologists believe that it's the first gesture humans learn. This theory maintains that when the newborn baby has had enough milk, she shakes her head from side to side to reject her mother's breast. Similarly, a child who has had enough to eat uses the head shake to reject attempts to spoon feed her.

Being careful with questions

Some parents are so desperate to know what their child knows that they get into a habit of asking too many questions. Can you hear yourself saying, 'What's that?', 'Where's it going?', 'What colour is it?', 'How many teddies?'. DON'T. When you ask an adult a question, they answer. When you ask a child a question, they often feel under pressure, which feels unpleasant, so they back off. If someone you met continuously asked you questions, you'd soon find someone else who is easier to communicate with.

So, take all pressure to communicate off your child and you will find that she talks more. Instead of constantly asking questions, keep on using the Say What You See technique (see page 17).

Giving up the bottle

Health professionals recommend that a baby should begin to give up the bottle at 12 months. This is the start of a process that parents manage in different ways. Some bin the bottle immediately and give a beaker or a cup straight away, while others reduce over time the number of bottle feeds a toddler has over the course of a day.

Why drop it?

There are many reasons why we are told that a 12-month-old should start to be weaned from the bottle. Below are listed the main ones.

- **Prolonged use of the bottle causes tooth decay** – If a baby's teeth are in frequent contact with sugars from liquid carbohydrates, such as milk, formula, fruit juices, fruit juice diluted with water, sugar water or any other sweet drink – they are more at risk of tooth decay. Human breast milk can cause tooth decay as well. These liquids break down in the mouth into simple sugars that sit in the mouth, inviting bacteria start to feeding on the sugars, causing tooth decay.
- **Prolonged use of the bottle can cause ear infections** – There is a tube that connects your middle ear to the back of your throat (called the Eustachian tube). Milk can get sucked into this tube and cause a blockage or an infection. Repeated ear infections can cause speech delays because, if you can't hear properly, you don't have a good model for speech and language development. This is why a baby should never be given a bottle when lying flat.
- **Lack of interest in eating** – Why would you bother going through all the hard work of learning to eat new textures and foods if your tummy is full of milk?
- **Excessive weight-gain** – Drinking too many bottles over a twenty-four-hour period can cause your toddler to take in extra unneeded calories.

Aside from these factors, prolonged use of the bottle or dummy cause irreparable damage to the shape of mouth (which affects speech development), in the following ways:

- Just behind your top teeth, there is a hard ridge called the alveolar ridge, which is very important for clear and precise speech, in particular the t, d, s, n and l sounds. If you suck on a bottle over time, the shape of the ridge is affected and there is less room for the tongue to articulate against it to form clear speech sounds.
- When you suck from a bottle your lips and tongue curl around the teat, forming a round shape to the lips, which can become habitual even when the bottle is no longer in the mouth. This shape is detrimental to good clear speech – for instance, try saying 'f' when your mouth is curled into this shape.
- When you suck on a bottle or dummy, the middle section of your tongue becomes strong and, therefore, more dominant when articulating speech sounds. However, it is the tongue tip that needs to be the most agile when it comes to articulating sounds. When the middle part of the tongue takes over, the tongue tip pokes through the front teeth, forming a lisp. The words sound slushy and imprecise (as in the case of Will Young, Jamie Oliver or Chris Eubank, who have a dental lisp). Or if your tongue curls in your mouth, you might end up talking with a lisp, sounding like dance expert and TV personality Louie Spence, who has a lateral lisp.

When I tell parents at my clinic about the harmful effect prolonged use of the bottle may have on their child, they commonly say, 'Well, she only has it once every day before bed.' My response is, 'If I were to do a set of sit-ups every day, I'd have a wonderfully flat stomach'. Even one daily repetition can make a big difference to muscle and structural development of the mouth. So . . . banish the bottle now!

Nicola's tips and tricks: from bottle to beaker

I advise parents to move to an open cup as soon as possible after the age of 12 months, or earlier, if you have the inclination. A receptacle which pours is always best. (Avoid those that demand a suck – this swirls the fluid around the teeth. Also, the mouth position for sucking is not one to encourage – try sucking as you read this and you will notice that the bottom section of your cheeks get pulled in, causing your lower jaw to become misaligned with your top teeth, making it very hard to speak clearly. This is known as an over-bite.)

- **If you're giving an open cup** (one without a lid), help your child to tilt the cup up for drinking and down for pauses, and try to maintain contact between the rim of the cup and your child's bottom lip at all times. Using a constant, predictable rhythm will also help. Another tip for when you first move to an open cup is to use thicker fluids that are less runny, such as a fruit smoothie, so it's easier for your baby to keep them in the cup. Developmentally, a toddler should be able to hold an open cup from 12 months with only a little spillage.

  If going straight to an open cup fills you with fear (I totally understand that no one likes the idea of milk being spilt all over their carpet or pyjamas), take the natural first step and try a beaker, which is much better than a bottle.

- **When choosing a beaker**, the spout should be short to ensure that the fluid is tipped just inside the lips, which will, in turn, encourage the tongue to dip down to the base of the mouth to make a cavity to receive the fluid. This is a better position for tongue movement and, therefore, speech development. Watch to see if your toddler's tongue is sticking out under the beaker spout. If so, find a fatter, shorter-spouted beaker.

  Straws are always great for creating a good tongue position in the mouth. You can buy beakers that have straws already attached but the straws tend to be quite long, which makes it harder for little ones to actually suck up the fluid. Otherwise, try a carton with a straw or simply a cup with a straw.

  Avoid non-spill valves which encourage tongue thrust (see page 62). These types of beaker are almost as bad as a bottle.

CASE STUDY: A BOY ADDICTED TO HIS BOTTLE

Recently, I worked with a boy called Saif, aged 18 months, who only drank from a bottle – not just his bedtime milk, but all his drinks during the day, too. He had a significant lisp. Not only was the 's' sound spoken with his tongue between his teeth, but many other sounds were, too – the 't', 'd', 'n', 'sh', 'j' and 'ch' were all spoken with his tongue sticking out. I gave his key worker at nursery, Jude, some tips. (It was decided the activities should be carried out in nursery as Saif was there full-time and his mum had three other children, making it difficult for her to fit them in at home). Jude worked really hard to wean Saif straight on to an open cup. Below are the techniques she used:

- Helping him learn to hold the open cup.
- Encouraging him to watch the other children drinking.
- Giving lots of praise when he held the cup to his lips.
- Playing with open cups in the home corner of the nursery, and helping the teddies to drink from them.
- Telling the Mr Tongue story (see page 85).
- Doing the Bigmouth tongue exercise programme (the Bigmouth Sound Pack is available from Stass Publications – see Resources), which consists of a set of pictures showing a tongue pointing up and down, moving from side to side and poking in and out. These were conducted when he looked in the mirror by the children's toilets every time he washed his hands. Also, Saif's mother was given the same pictures.
- Sticking pictures of the tricky sounds around the mirror (for example, a snake for 's') and encouraging him to say these sounds with his teeth metaphorically stuck together so his tongue didn't pop forwards.

There was a big improvement in Saif's speech, but then the summer holidays arrived. Saif's mum hadn't yet managed the switch from bottle to beaker at home (even though he'd managed this at nursery) and gave it to him whenever he made a fuss.

When Saif returned to pre-school in September, his lisp was back with a vengeance. It really stood out to Jude and me, and we honestly couldn't believe how much worse his speech was. It completely reinforced the message of the importance of bottle versus cup-drinking and how we needed better persuasive techniques for mum! I also wished we'd done a pre- and post-summer holiday video as this would have shown mum just how badly his speech had regressed.

So, the lesson to be learned here is that parents are not doing their babies *any* favours by giving in to their demands for a bottle – stay firm! Just like my advice on dropping the dummy (see page 49), you can expect a day or two of tears but you'll be amazed how quickly children adapt to change if you make it clear that the bottle has gone for good and that they will only be using a beaker from now on.

When children make mistakes with their attempts at words

When a child points to something and makes a sound, she is trying to say the word. Praise her attempt and model the correct word back, for example, 'Uh – Yes, a bird'.

Leaving off the final consonant from a word (for example, 'bu' for 'bus') is perfectly normal at this age so praise your child's attempt and model the correct word back – 'Yes, it's a 'busssss' (you can emphasize the sound she missed off).

Using an incorrect consonant at the start of a word is also very common (for instance, 'du' for 'stuck'). You guessed it – praise your child's attempt and model the correct word back.

In a nutshell, you should be praising any attempt to communicate, whether it's a sign, a gesture or a word, and modelling the correct version back in a positive way. This will help your child to want to say the word again.

> ## EMOTIONAL DEVELOPMENT
>
> When your child cries and gets cross and frustrated, help her to understand her emotions by voicing them out loud. For example, you could say, 'You're sad because Daddy's gone to work', or 'You're cross because there are no more biscuits.'
>
> Children usually love it when a parent does this; they feel better understood with regard to their feelings and will hopefully be happier and more content accordingly.

Again, again!

A word you'll hear rather a lot during this six-month phase is 'again'. There'll be times you wished the word never existed, like when you've read the same book a hundred times, and other times when you sparkle with delight – when your toddler shouts 'again' as loudly as she can after singing her favourite song in the local song group.

Within reason, try to honour your child's request and do the same task again and again. It really will help to create those pathways that link the ear to the brain's language centre, and the brain's language centre to the mouth. The more your child hears the same words and phrases, the more she will understand and the more she will speak. So, say it again, Sam!

CASE STUDY: WHEN THERE ARE NO WORD ATTEMPTS AT 18 MONTHS

This story is from a mother who came to my drop-in clinic:

'I'm worried about my 18-month-old son who isn't talking at all. He was an early walker and is constantly on the move, running about everywhere. He loves to read books together but mainly just turns the pages and lifts the flaps. He has great fun lining up cars and building towers but doesn't talk when he plays. My husband and I talk to our son constantly about what we're doing, pointing things out in the hope of encouraging him to say words, but he hardly even attempts to speak, apart from a bit of "dadadada" now and then. He definitely understands what things mean, though. If I say, "Where's Dadda?", he instantly runs to the door when my husband comes home from work. If I say "fish", he goes to the fish tank, but apart from saying "boosh" once or twice when asked to say "fish", he just isn't interested. My heart sank yesterday when I saw a little girl who couldn't have been any older than him, talking to her mum in three-to-four-word sentences! He is otherwise a very happy, gorgeous little boy. Should I be worried?'

My response to this mother, which also applies to any parent who has concerns about their toddler's language at this age, is that all children develop at different rates so try not to panic prematurely. More than likely your child will be a little chatterbox before you know it. At this age, it is far more important that your child *understands* language rather than being able to *say* the average of 20 words. It would be more worrying if you felt he didn't understand you.

However, there are things you can do to improve the situation:

- First of all, check your child's hearing. Go to your health visitor or GP and ask for a referral to the audiology department.

- Use the Say What You See technique (see page 17). Put your child's thoughts into words as she plays at a single-word level, for example, 'Ball – it's a ball. Ball.' Lower your language level to single words or short phrases, repeat the key words over and over again and start signing (see page 47).
- Follow his interests in play and talk about the things that he is interested in. Find his motivators – be it cars, cats or cranes!
- Have Small Talk Time every day, when you play together and you model the language that he is motivated to say.
- Makes lots of symbolic noises as you play (for example, vehicle noises) and add random noises like 'wee' as a car goes down a ramp or 'ah' when teddy is touched. Copy your child's noises and sounds, too, particularly babble sounds (for example, for dog – 'wuwuwuw'; for cow – 'moomoommoo'; and for sheep – 'bababa'), creating good pathways between the brain and the articulators. There's a great song to sing to the first line of the tune of 'She'll Be Coming Round the Mountain' (you'll need a car, an aeroplane, a motorbike and a train). Leave a pause for your child to fill in the noise:

  I am driving in my little motor car – brum brum
  I am flying in my little aeroplane – zzz zzz
  I am riding in my great big choo choo train – choo choo
  I am driving on my great big motorbike vrum vrum.

- Make a babble bag (see page 92) and a sound sack (see page 95).
- Think laterally about what she might be trying to say (for instance, 'ba' instead of 'ball' or 'wawa' for 'flower'). Through no fault of your own, you might be missing some of her attempts and then not rewarding them with a repetition or some praise.

- Don't worry about the clarity of your child's words at this point – count all attempts, no matter how far removed from the target, as real words. I can't tell you how many times a parent tells me their child is saying nothing and, when I visit, I see the child attempting so many words that the parent isn't cottoning on to.
- If it's difficult to pin her down to concentrate and listen to language, do more listening activities (see page 96 for suggestions) to help your child's ability to focus. Remember – good listening leads to good understanding, and once a child can understand, she will begin to try to talk.
- Try not to question your child all the time, however tempting this might be. It is better that you say the word so she can hear, remember and understand it.
- If your child has a dummy, get rid of it and try to limit bottles to bedtime or begin to use a beaker or open cup instead.
- Keep in mind that early walkers are exploring here, there and everywhere and, therefore, aren't staying close to the adult in order to hear a model for language. Try to follow her when she plays.
- Try not to compare your child to others. Remember – only the brilliant talkers will stand out to you and not the children who are similar or worse! You need to get advice if your child isn't making any noise (he may not be hearing), or not showing any interest in other people, or if air is coming out of his nose when he speaks – you will hear a blow of air coming out when he speaks, but you'll need to listen carefully to detect this.

If you're at all worried, talk to your health visitor or telephone your local speech and language therapist for advice.

SPEECH AND LANGUAGE DEVELOPMENT MILESTONES: 12–18 MONTHS

Children develop skills at different rates but, by 18 months, usually children will:

- enjoy games like Peek-a-boo and Pat-a-cake and toys that make a noise.
- start to understand a few simple words, like 'drink', 'shoe' and 'car', and also simple instructions like 'kiss Mummy', 'kick ball' and 'give me'.
- point to things when asked, like familiar people and objects, such as 'book' and 'car'.
- use up to 20 simple words, such as 'cup', 'Daddy' and 'dog'. These words may not always be easily recognized by unfamiliar adults.
- gesture or point, often with words or sounds to show what she wants.
- copy lots of things that adults say and gestures that they make.
- start to enjoy simple pretend play, for example pretending to talk on the phone.*

---

* These milestones have been provided by the website www.talkingpoint.org.uk and are reproduced with kind permission.

CHAPTER SEVEN

Combining Words Phase (18–24 months)

Fasten your seatbelts and adjust your safety goggles because during this 18 to 24-month period, most parents will encounter a language explosion or surge in their little one's speech development. Let's talk numbers. At 18 months, an average child would have approximately 20 to 50 recognizable single words but, at two years, the average child could have approximately 200 words and even be using two words in a sentence.

Don't panic if your little one is way off this average because the range of what is considered to be normal during this six-month phase is massive. At the top end, you might expect a boom of words and have a child who is saying two or even three-word sentences at 24 months but, at the other end of the scale, children with only 50 single words at 24 months are considered to have perfectly normal language development, too. If this is the case, you might have to wait until your toddler's in the next six-month phase for his language explosion to arrive.

In this chapter, I'll show you how to broaden your toddler's experiences and verbally bombard him in order to bring on the explosion. We'll think about the *types* of words he is using – such as family names, social words and verbs – and I'll explain how, once he has a collection of about 50 words (covering as many of the different categories of words as possible), he'll start to join two words together, for instance, 'No yoggie', 'Bye Stu' or 'Monkey eating'.

At the start of this phase, your toddler's words will probably use the same syllable repeated (for example, 'baba' for 'baby'; 'nana' for 'banana'; 'bibi' for 'biscuit'; 'gan gan' for 'granny') and much of what he says will be difficult to understand because his consonant sounds aren't quite right. The first consonant might be incorrect ('dat' for 'cat' or 'dacda' for 'tractor') and the last not there at all ('u' for 'up' or 'bu' for 'bus'), but the vowels should be almost perfect by now, which will help you to work out what the target word is.

Some of your child's attempts at words will make you crease with laughter. (I've often heard 'Winnie the Pooh' spoken as 'ne dah poo' by little ones, or heard 'cock' for 'clock'!) And because of the way your toddler says a word in such a unique and cute way, your whole family might take on that word and use it for years to come. For example, we may sound bonkers to strangers but, in our house, we all say 'tupatupatea' for 'cup of tea', 'coo me' for 'excuse me' and 'nin nins' for 'raisins'.

My friend's father was so keen to have a unique word for 'Grandad' that he didn't refer to himself as anything and waited to see what his grandson would come up with. He's now known as 'Geedad'.

Your toddler's speech may be slightly unclear but you'll understand most of it because, hopefully, you're so tuned in to his favourite toys and games and the experiences he has that you'll know what he's going to say even before he says it. Strangers, though, won't be quite so au fait with his lingo so you'll probably end up doing a fair bit of interpreting – when a toddler is two years of age, strangers are thought to understand their chatter only about 50 per cent of the time.

For this reason, we'll start thinking about how you can encourage your little one to improve the clarity of his speech by teaching him to listen to the sounds that make up words. You have to listen to and decode a speech sound before you can have a chance of saying it. This is known as phonological awareness and phonological processing.

As you'll see, there's a lot that goes on during this phase of language development and, by two years, your toddler should be able to:

- **Understand** *two* words together (such as 'Mummy's biscuit' or 'naughty doggie')
- **Remember** *two* words in a sequence ('give me brick and dolly' when he packs away, for instance)
- **Express** *two* words together (such as 'want toast' or 'no coat').

So, in this chapter our aim is to hit the speech therapist's target that, at two years, 'two is the magic number'. Think about it – that's quite an incredible leap forwards from the 12-month-old baby in the last phase. So, let's get started and create some talking toddlers!

YOUR TODDLER'S VOCAB COUNT

Most children aged two have a vocabulary of 75–225 words, but if your child has 50 words or fewer, he would be considered to be a late talker. Professor Leslie Rescorla, Director of the Child Study Institute at Bryn Mawr College in Pennsylvania, reported that the most popular 25 words spoken by two-year-olds are: Mummy, Daddy, baby, milk, juice, hello, ball, yes, no, dog, cat, nose, eye, banana, biscuit, car, hot, thank you, bath, shoe, hat, book, all gone, more and bye-bye.[1]

EXPANDING YOUR TODDLER'S LANGUAGE

As we've established, during this phase you're likely to see a massive boom in language development and, virtually every day, your toddler will copy you like a pint-sized parrot in order to learn as many new words as possible. At the peak of his language explosion, one report says, you may hear him say a number of new words every single day.

This is when you and your partner will have to become that parenting cliché and spell out the words you don't want your child to copy from you. (For example, 'How was your day, dear?' 'Darling, it was C-R-A-P! Please take him to the P-A-R-K so I can have a glass of wine.')

Initially, your child will learn the names for his own belongings – take 'shoes', for example. He will know his own shoes as 'shoes', and then will learn that yours are also called shoes. He will then spot shoes on the TV or in a book and realize that even though they may be different colours, shapes and sizes, they too, are called shoes. It's a very intricate process – first of all, you have to familiarize your child with the object, then help him understand its name and then, finally, encourage him to say it. You cannot expect your child to say the word until the first two stages are complete.

Although, to some extent, the language explosion will happen naturally as your child processes and copies all the words he hears, you can help him to expand his vocabulary by working through the Small Talk Time tips below.

Small Talk Time Boom boosters!

Staying one step ahead

Always try to stay one step ahead of your baby's language. I heard a lovely story recently. Hugh knew that his son Oliver said 'dog' for every four-legged animal he saw and 'duck' for every bird, as he couldn't name any others. So, thinking that he was making it easier for his son to understand the world around him, Hugh did the same. It wasn't until Oliver's mum heard her husband pointing out 'dog, dog, dog' when they were reading *The Gruffalo* that she asked, 'Why are you saying dog when there are no dogs in *The Gruffalo*?'

Hugh explained that because these were the only animals Oliver knew, he didn't want to confuse him by stirring more into the mix. But how could Oliver's language ever expand if he didn't ever hear the correct name for each animal? By talking at the *same* level as Oliver,

Hugh wasn't extending his understanding at all. If you want your child's language to *expand*, you have to provide a language model at the right level – only saying 'dog' and 'duck' was too low a level for Oliver and therefore wouldn't encourage him to move on.

In order for a toddler's language to expand, you need to model the words over and over again before you can expect him to say them. By now you should know that a better way to expand Oliver's language and extend his vocabulary would be to use the Say What You See technique – so, label all the animals, and then, once your child is able to say them, copy and add a word each time, so 'duck swimming', 'Gruffalo looking', and so on.

Copy and add

Every time your child says a sound or a word you should copy the word and add another word. So, Fion says 'grapes' and you say 'I want grapes'; Ardil says 'car' and you say 'driving car'; Noah says 'Mummy' and you say 'Mummy eating' and so on. Try doing this whenever your child utters a sound, a word and, later, when he says a sentence.

Explore and encounter a range of experiences

The majority of words are learnt through everyday experiences, so allow your child to have a wealth of different experiences. I love this quote from Professor Elizabeth Crais from the Division of Speech and Hearing Sciences at the University of North Carolina: 'A child's knowledge of the world will be demonstrated in their word knowledge.' What she's getting at is that learning to talk underpins learning and social development. The words a child uses tell us what he knows about the world. Therefore, if you can expose your child to a range of experiences and talk about them in an elaborate way, this will help him to experience the world in more detail, consequently helping him to learn more. A child knows about 4,000–5,000 words when they start primary school and several thousand one year after that; the faster you learn language, the more knowledge you acquire.

Use the Say What You See technique (see page 17). Remember – the more you say, the more they'll learn. Notice what your child is interested in, what he is looking at, pointing at and walking towards, and talk about what he is motivated by. Don't try to 'teach' him too much or dictate what he should be interested in. Instead, keep it natural and just chat and explain what you are doing as you unload the washing machine, make the lunch or go upstairs to fetch something. Talking about everything you do will expose your child to lots of lovely new words. Remember to allow him to participate in the conversation and leave gaps for him to reply. Don't hog the conversation!

Develop conversations as you go about everyday life, whether you are chatting about doing the shopping as your toddler sits in the trolley, or telling him that Mummy is running the bath, Grandpa is cutting the grass, or Daddy is cooking. Remember to reduce your language to the right level for your child. Parents worry that they shouldn't lower their language level too much and they try to speak in proper sentences with proper grammar. This is where being a Tuned-in Parent (see page 9) is crucial; you need to know what level your child is expressing himself at by listening to him and pitching your language level slightly above. When a child reaches four and five years old you can pretty much go for it, but at this age, a child is still learning and you need to be in tune with the level he is at.

Expand your child's language and thought, ensuring you continue to encourage new words rather than simply repeating the words you know he can say. Have high expectations of what your child can understand and the stories he likes to hear and you will see (and hear!) the rewards.

Play Where's the . . . ?/Where's your . . . ? games

Games like this (see page 136) will help your child to understand that he must remember the name of the object you are saying so he can try to say it for himself. Generally, speech therapists are very anti parents who continuously question their children because they feel it puts children off communicating altogether (for instance, my mother-in-law continuously asked my daughter to kiss her and Jess point-blank refused to, instead smothering Rosa, the dog, in kisses!). So make the games light-hearted and fun. Give lots of praise and physically prompt your child to point at the right object if you're not sure he knows.

Arrange play dates

The more you expose your child to other children, different toys and new experiences, the more he will have to talk about.

Have ten minutes of Small Talk Time every day

This should be uninterrupted, focused time spent being a Tuned-in Parent. During this time, observe what your child does or says and what he likes to play with and use Say What You See (see page 17).

Create a Small Talk Time Tool Kit of resources

Fill your kit with books, pictures, toys and treasures that your child likes. Open it each day and try to elicit language using verbal prompts. For example, you could say, 'Ooo, let's see what's inside our Small Talk Box . . . you'd like to see the beach photos today. Look! You built a . . . with . . . and you put beautiful shells on the top. Then we ate an . . . and had a lovely swim in the . . .'

Collect treasures

When Jess was little, I bought one of those drawers that you put on the wall that has lots of boxes to put treasures in. Jess and I filled it with a bird's feather we found in the garden, a bracelet that Granny gave her for her birthday, an Easter chick, a pine cone we found in the woods, a little rugby ball Grandad gave her when Wales won the Grand Slam, and so on. She loved listening to me telling her the stories that were associated with the objects ('Yes, this is the ball Grandad gave you.

It's a lovely ball. It's a little ball with a dragon on it'). I made sure I repeated the object name over and over again – 'ball', 'ball'. Then, when I pointed to the objects, she tried to say the words.

Toys in the bin
Take a range of objects that belong in a particular category (e.g. animals, vehicles, etc.), say the name of the object and drop it into a bin or a saucepan, so it makes a very rewarding clunking sound. Encourage your toddler to do the same.

Books
Use a 100-first words book and take turns to point to the things that interest your child. Joel, a little boy I am working with, loves the *Thomas the Tank Engine* first words book – *Thomas's Really Useful Word Book* – because, on every page, Thomas goes somewhere different (Joel's favourite page is the wildlife park!). I teach him the vocabulary by using his finger to point to the pictures at the side of the page, name them, then point to the same object in the busy picture. I then pause to allow him to copy me. His love of Thomas has hooked him in and encourages him to talk and exclaim with delight every time we look at the book.

Another book I highly recommend is *You Choose* by Pippa Goodhart and Nick Sharratt, which is fantastic for developing speaking and listening skills. It begins sentences like 'My favourite food is . . .?' 'If I went on holiday I would go to . . .', then there are options for the child to choose from. There are also much harder statements, like, 'When I am big I would like to be a . . .' with pictures of people working to pick from, and 'I would like to wear . . .' and then a range of different types of hats and so on. It's a real favourite in my clinic for this age upwards. The amount of language you can entice for all levels is endless.

Repeat, repeat, repeat

Read the same stories and sing the same songs over and over again. You may get sick of the same story, but I'm certain your toddler won't. He will be bombarded with the vocabulary in the story and, therefore, will start to remember the words in order to use them himself. Also, if a child learns a set phrase by rote, from a song or a book, he learns to extend his memory and learns the grammatical structures needed in sentences (we'll learn more about this in the next chapter).

Posting games

Make up a few sets of flashcards using pictures from catalogues or Google Images stuck onto cardboard; perhaps laminate them, and keep them in your Small Talk Tool Box. Possible topics to focus on are:

- food (can be further divided into fruits/vegetables)
- animals (can be further divided into zoo/farm/wild/pet)
- clothes
- furniture
- toys
- shapes
- things in a house (can be further divided into things in the bathroom/kitchen/lounge)
- things in a school
- things at a birthday party

Encourage your child to name them, for instance, 'It's a . . . bed', before he posts them into an old shoe box. He'll love it.

Other flash card games

Get hold of a simple pack of flashcards – they can be useful in lots of word games, such as the following ideas:

- **Skittles** – Stand your flashcards up against skittles (or old toilet rolls) and take turns to instruct each other on which picture to knock down.
- **Stepping stones** – Lay the cards on the floor and tell each other which picture to jump on.
- **Clothes line** – Hang your pictures on a clothes line together; this will help develop fine motor skills, too. Just string a line between a couple of chairs.
- **Hunt the picture** – Hide the pictures around your room and hunt them out. Find them and then say what they are.
- **Fishing game** – Find a magnet and tie it onto a string. Put a paper clip on each picture. Now fish for the cards and then name them.
- **Memory games** – Show two of the cards to your child, put them face-down on the table in front of you and say, 'Where's the cow?', 'Where's the pig?' Then extend the number of cards your child has to remember to three. Another idea is to find objects that fit within a particular category and match one object to another, then an object to a picture. You could do this using a plastic milk carton cut in half – stick the picture of an object on the outside and then get your child to place the real object inside the milk carton. When he has mastered this, move on to matching a picture to a picture, such as finding all the pictures on flashcards that are animals, all the pictures that are food, and so on, and drop the matching pictures into the milk carton.

Other games that encourage word combining

- Take two sets of objects or pictures, mix them up and then sort them. For example, try food versus animals – put the food into a toy shopping trolley and the animals into a barn.
- Make a scrapbook of pictures of objects cut out from a magazine, with a different set of objects on each page.
- Make a slideshow of photos for your iPad that fall into a particular topic, such as garden words, nursery words or food words.

Praise every effort

Remember – praise every attempt and *don't correct*. If your toddler says 'jamas' instead of pyjamas, say, 'Yes, your pyjamas,' and reward his efforts. Don't say, 'You can only have a banana if you say it properly.' Instead, try saying, 'Say banana and you can have it!' Accept any approximation of the word and give praise. If your child says 'ba' when they leave the house, you say 'Bye bye house.' If you continue to correct him, you will affect his self confidence and his motivation or eagerness to want to try to communicate.

I am often asked by parents if they should encourage number, shape and colour learning at an early age. My answer is that these concepts are too abstract for toddlers. Colours and numbers will come in their own time and words that carry meaning are far more useful for little ones at this age. How many times do adults use a colour's name in their language? ('What a lovely pink top', or 'what a beautiful red sunset.') Hardly ever – so bear that in mind. Knowing colours seems to be a gauge of how clever you are, and I totally disagree with this.

You'll know your efforts are working when . . . (Spotting progress)

At some point, your child will no longer use an approximate word for something (for example, 'duck' for bird, parrot, robin and penguin) and he begins to spontaneously say the specific words in the correct situation, widening his vocabulary.

SIMPLIFYING LANGUAGE – FROM 'GAAA' TO 'WATER'

MIT (Massachusetts Institute of Technology) researcher Deb Roy wanted to understand how his infant son learned language. So, in 2005 he wired up his house with video cameras to catch every moment (with exceptions!) of his son's life, then studied 90,000 hours of home video to watch his utterance of 'gaaa' slowly turn into 'water'. The Speechome project[2] is the largest ever study of child language development in a natural or clinical environment.

By collecting each instance in which his son heard a word and noting the context, Roy and his team mapped all 530 words the boy learned by his second birthday. In doing so, they uncovered a surprising pattern, which was that when caregivers used simpler language, the closer the boy got to grasping a word. At the point they sensed he was on the cusp of getting it, all three primary caregivers – Roy, his wife and their nanny – simplified their language to guide him to the word, then gently guided him towards more complex language once he had grasped it.

Roy says, 'We were all systematically, and I would think subconsciously, restructuring our language to meet him at the moment of the birth of the word and then bringing him gently into more complex language.'

Roy says this provides evidence that caregivers modify their language at a level never reported or suspected before. It's not just that his son was learning from his linguistic environment; 'the environment was learning from him,' says Roy. (Perform a Google search for 'Deb Roy: The Birth of a Word' to watch Roy's fascinating talk on his findings.)

GETTING SOME CLARITY

It takes time to master the ability to string a bunch of speech sounds together to make a word. As we've learnt, vowel sounds are the easiest sounds to make, and then there's a developmental pattern to how consonant sounds develop.

We take our speech and language skills for granted (speech being the sounds that make up words, and language being the words that make up sentences) but can you imagine how difficult it is for a toddler to talk? Every single new word that passes his lips is like one tremendously challenging tongue-twister. So you won't be shocked when I tell you that clear speech will take time and a lot of practise – and some people never manage it! (Take Jonathan Ross, for example.)

Your toddler probably misses off the ends of words, the beginnings of words and uses alternative consonant sounds. You may not notice this so much as you'll be tuned in to the way he talks, but if you try writing down a few of his words, you'll start noticing the mistakes, and some may even make you giggle.

Don't worry – this is your toddler's very clever in-built editing system. It's essentially his way of simplifying the words down to their most basic form so he can try to say them. In time, with lots of word modelling from you and practise and repetition from him, he will hopefully start to say the word more clearly and unfamiliar adults won't look to you to interpret for him.

It is important to applaud your child for his efforts and revel in his wonderful attempts at tongue-twisting challenges, like 'animal', 'helicopter' and 'hospital', which will probably sound more like 'aminal', 'topter' and 'hopital'!

Your toddler will probably simplify language in the following ways . . .

- **Reduplication** – This is repetition of the same syllable to make a word, for example, 'daddy' becomes 'dada', 'water' is said as 'wawa', 'Iggle Piggle' becomes 'big big'.
- **Weak syllable deletion** – In a word there is always a weak syllable, for instance, 'guitar' where the 'gu' part is weak and, a child will delete it, saying 'tar' instead, or 'getti' for 'spaghetti', for example.

- **Final consonant deletion** – For example, 'bu' for 'bus', 'u' for 'up'.
- **Cluster reduction** – Many words have two consonant sounds that are positioned next to one another. This is called a consonant cluster, and 'blending' two sounds into a consonant cluster is very difficult for a young child to do and, therefore, he might drop one of the sounds completely, for example, 'FLower' = 'fower', 'GRanny' = 'gan gan', 'SPoon' = 'poon', 'STar' = 'tar'.
- **Fronting** – Some sounds are articulated with your lips (p, b, m) and others with your tongue. Some use the tongue tip (t, d, n) and others use the back of the tongue (k, g). The sounds articulated with the back of your tongue are harder to say and it is very common for children to misarticulate these sounds. Instead, they tend to replace them with the tongue tip sounds. So, cow will be 'tow', 'car' will be 'tar' and 'gate' will be 'date'.

CASE STUDY: WAYBAJEA! – TRACEY AND MINNIE

When my co-writer Tracey's daughter Minnie was around two years old, she began shouting, 'Waybajea!' whenever she was excited or something good had happened. Tracey was a bit bemused, but thought it might be something that was said at nursery, or a lyric from a song that she didn't know. This went on for quite a few weeks (possibly even months) before Tracey was watching *Something Special* with Minnie on TV and noticed that the presenter Justin Fletcher (aka Mr Tumble) was encouraging the children to 'wave or cheer' when they spotted a fountain. Minnie shouted, 'Waybajea!' when she saw the fountain and the penny dropped ... she was saying her interpretation of 'wave or cheer'. Tracey said, 'Yes, the fountain, let's wave or cheer!' speaking very clearly to model the words correctly, and after a few repetitions Minnie had it nailed.

- **Gliding** – This refers to replacement of the consonants 'l' and 'r' with the consonants 'y' and 'w' so 'lion' is pronounced as 'yion' and 'rabbit' as 'wabbit'.
- **Assimilation or consonant harmony** – The child uses the same consonant twice to make the word easier to say, so 'dog' becomes 'gog', 'biscuit' becomes 'bibib' and 'yellow' becomes 'lellow'.

It's a job to wonder how any child ever gets the word right when they have all of these 'processes' to contend with! But rest assured, over time, your child's speech will get clearer and clearer, the more a word is modelled for him.

AND, ACTION! HELLO, VERBS

The first set of words your toddler will learn to say are the nouns – the objects and the people he is motivated by, like Dada, Nana, car, dog, biscuit, ball, and so on. The next set of words he learns are the actions – so verbs, such as drink, eat, jump, carry, look. And, once he has a selection of each (about 50 words in total), he starts to add the noun to the verb to build a small sentence – 'Mummy sleeping', 'teddy walking', 'brushing teeth', and so on. This will be even more prevalent in the next six-month period.

Some children need to be encouraged to use verbs once they have a stream of nouns, and may use very general words that they apply to everything, such as 'get' and 'do' in place of more specific verbs. So, your toddler might say 'doing bricks' rather than 'building bricks' or 'get up' rather than 'climb up the ladder'.

(Small Talk Time) **Helping your child to learn new verbs**
A child needs to understand the meaning of a verb before he'll say it, so these games use repetition, simplified language and real-life

experiences to cement his understanding and encourage him to vocalize his growing list of action words. And you won't even have to make
a conscious effort to 'learn' most of them because they just revolve
around daily life.

Say What You See

Think about your child's daily life and what he actually does. A typical
morning probably goes something like this . . . get up, snuggle in
bed, change nappy, carry downstairs, drink milk, get dressed, watch
TV, eat breakfast, and so on. This is where my Say What You See technique is invaluable – repeat as many of the action words as possible
– 'changing nappy', 'drinking milk', 'getting dressed', etc.

When watching TV or reading books, point out to your child what
people/animals are doing 'Look – Zachary's jumping', 'Mummy's
cooking', 'Mr Tumble is dancing', 'Spot's eating', and so on.

You can use the same technique while playing with your child:
'Teddy falling', 'Dolly crying', 'dog drinking'.

Scrapbook

Make a scrapbook of family members doing things, or collect magazine pictures of people doing things – painting, laughing, kicking,
eating – and say each action as you look at the pictures.

Naming games

Collect pictures from magazines of people, carrying out animals or
toys doing activities, then create a game where your child tells you
what they are all doing. You could even make a postbox out of an old
shoe box (simply cut a rectangular letter box hole in it) so your child
can post the pictures into it. I often use this game at my clinic because,
at this age, children love trying to cut, sticking and posting games and
it makes learning verbs fun for them.

Hide the pictures around the room and ask your toddler to find a
particular one: 'Where's . . . sleeping?' – do the sign to help. (It is always

useful to go back to signs when you are teaching your child new words, particularly verbs and prepositions [positional words]. Signs provide visual information to back-up the spoken word making it easier to retain.)

Act up

Act out as many of the actions as possible and encourage your toddler to copy you to help him understand the meaning of the verb.

Embarrassingly, when my daughter is in a tizz – particularly when waiting for her breakfast – I often find myself leaping around the kitchen performing actions for her and saying, 'Mummy dancing, Mummy kicking, Mummy singing, Mummy spinning!' while trying to butter her toast at the same time. Slightly bonkers, but very effective for language development and for avoiding meltdowns!

PHRASES

A phrase is two words that we always say together. 'All gone', 'what's that?', 'in there', 'no more', 'coat on', 'shoes on', 'get down' and so on are considered to be phrases rather than two-word sentences because a child learns the whole phrase and doesn't necessarily have the ability to conjugate a two-word sentence for themselves yet.

Basically, a child will first learn to say single words, then some phrases appear, followed by two-word sentences that he has had to construct himself, like 'Bye-bye, Kei'. So, try to encourage little phrases like 'tea time!' to help your child expand the number of syllables he can put together and to guide him towards making sentences.

Small Talk Time **Helping the words to just pop out**

Use phrases throughout your daily routine and, to help the second word of the phrase 'just pop out' of your child's mouth, leave a pause after the first word. For example, 'It's time for . . . [tea]',

'Coat . . . [on]', 'Open the . . . [door]', 'Peek-a . . . [boo]', 'Ready, steady . . . [go]'.

TWO-WORD SENTENCES

At two years some children are only using single words, but others have started putting two words together – that's why I've included this subject in this chapter. Again, don't worry if your child is not making two-word sentences yet. At this age there is a huge range in what is considered to be normal development. Your child might not start pairing up words for a few more months, and if that's the case, here's what you have to look forward to.

Once your child has at least 50 words covering a range of different types of categories – names of people (Mummy, sister); names of objects (favourite toys or food); social words (hello, bye-bye, night-night); action words (running, eating, sleeping); describing words (hot, cold, dirty, big), he is ready to being joining words together. Exciting!

WRITING A WORD LIST

It's obviously hard to keep track of how many words your toddler knows so it might be an idea to start keeping a list – don't just write down the word, but write down the way your toddler says it. This will help you to keep one step ahead of him and it's also really rewarding for parents to see their child's progress! (And it's fun to look back and reminisce about them later on too.)

From one word to two

Two-word sentences usually contain words from two different categories and that's why, during the language-boom phase, it's very important to encourage your toddler to become familiar with sets of words from a range of different categories. Furthermore, a child has to fully understand what each single word means before he will attempt to put two words together. You need to be sure that your child understands you speaking to him in two-word sentences before he has a hope of saying a two-word sentence himself. For example, does he understand 'hot' and 'cup' separately? If the answer's yes, then he will probably understand 'hot cup' together. (To test this out, see the Small Talk Time below.)

During this phase, your toddler will probably attempt stories and songs using gibberish interspersed with real words. The gibberish will increase in length when your toddler cannot think of the right word. For instance, I spotted my 19-month-old saying a stream of gibberish and then clapping her hands and saying 'up' and I knew instantly what she was trying sing – the 'Sleeping Bunnies' song with the 'wake up' line.

Toddlers in this phase will also try to combine two quite clear words. The word order should be consistent, but there won't be any grammar (the grammar usually appears in the next phase, between two and three years). We call this kind of speech – that uses only the key words and leaves out all the grammar – telegrammatic speech because it is constructed in the same simplified form in which telegrams were written in the olden days. Examples of this type of speech are 'go home' meaning 'I want to go home', 'no get down' for 'I don't want to get down' and 'where mumu?' meaning 'where's mummy?'. It's another way your child has cleverly learnt to get his message across by simplifying his language in his own way (see page 167).

How two-word sentences appear

There is a loose developmental pattern relating to the order in which two-word sentences appear. This is listed below:

1. 'That' *plus* object: 'that car', 'that duck'
2. 'More' *plus* action or object: 'more hide', 'more splashing', 'more book', 'more cake'
3. 'No' and disappearance/non-existence *plus* object, person or action: 'no sleep', 'Mummy gone', 'no raisins'
4. Person *plus* object: 'Daddy cake', 'Harry shoe'
5. Concept *plus* object/person: 'little flower', 'dirty feet', 'cold yogurt', 'hot potato'
6. Possessive pronoun/'belonging' word *plus* object or person: 'my grandad', 'Mummy plate'
7. Object or person *plus* action: 'baby cry', 'Daddy dig', 'bird up', 'cat meow'
8. Action/object/person *plus* location word: 'climb in', 'go down', 'fall out', 'on nose', 'cat in'
9. Question word *plus* object or person: 'where Mummy?', 'who that?'

Small Talk Time **Understanding two-word sentences**

Once our children start to talk, we are desperate for them to say more and more, seeking to get inside their minds and draw out their thoughts and feelings about the world. The first step towards this is to encourage your child to understand two-word sentences. Once he has achieved this, he'll attempt to say them. Try the techniques below.

- Gather the following objects – apple, banana, biscuit, teddy and dolly (or use two favourite cuddly toys). Sit the teddy and dolly down in front of your child with the apple, banana and biscuit. Ask him to 'Give teddy the biscuit' and 'Give dolly the apple'. If he does not understand, repeat the instruction and demonstrate the activity for him.
- Find a sponge, a teddy and a doll. Give the sponge to your child and ask him to 'Wash teddy's leg' or 'Wash dolly's hair'. As above, if

your child does not understand, repeat the instruction and demonstrate the activity for him.

- Find a box and a basket, or a barn and a house, and gather some objects, animals or people. Ask your child to 'Put cow in barn', 'Put dog in basket' and 'Put spoon in house'. Now swap roles and see if your child will direct you to hide the objects.

- Make a postbox out of an old shoebox. Make some flashcards of people doing things from pictures from a catalogue, for example, man sleeping, girl running and so on. Say the sentence out loud and see if your child knows which picture you are talking about. Encourage him to describe the picture by starting him off with 'It's a . . .'

- We have talked a lot about giving choices, so now begin to give choices at a two-word level. When your child is reaching for more raisins and you know exactly what he wants, plead ignorance and say, 'More orange or more raisins?' Don't always anticipate your child's needs – make him work a bit harder to communicate what he wants or needs by talking.

- Try to ensure that older siblings aren't doing all the talking. Give your younger child an opportunity to speak, even if he says nothing. (For more advice on dealing with siblings, see page 281).

- Use the 'Copy and Add' technique (see page 159). If your child says 'dog', you say 'dog sleeping'.

- Play enjoyable games with your child – bubbles are always fun and I make sure I always have a bottle of bubble mixture at my clinic, and in my handbag for that matter! Blow some bubbles for your child and let them pop. If he says 'op', say 'bubbles pop' or if he says 'bubble', you say 'more bubbles' or 'I want bubbles'. Make 'big bubbles', 'small bubbles', blow 'bubbles up' or 'bubbles down' in order to expand his understanding of two-word sentences. It's simple to do and yet it can have such a positive effect. Other fun games will also elicit a request for more – 'more slide', 'splash again', 'more balloons' and 'tickle again', for instance.

- At 18 months old, if Jess ever saw someone go or heard someone say 'bye', we played a turn-taking game where she said 'bye' and I added a name on the end. It goes like this:

  > Jess: 'Ba.'
  > Me: 'Bye Lyn.'
  > Jess: 'Ba.'
  > Me: 'Bye William.'
  > Jess: 'Ba.'
  > Me: 'Bye Uncle Stevo.'

  As you can imagine, this game goes on for quite some time – it's nearly as popular with Jess as Peek-a boo!
- Practise greeting people and things – take things out of the toy box and say, 'Hello, teddy,' 'Hello, book,' 'Hello train,' and so on. And when you see people, encourage your child to say hello, too. This is good on the telephone.
- If you have one of those pop-up games in which animals or people pop up when you push a button, say 'farmer up', 'cow up', 'sheep up', and then say, 'sheep down', 'cow down' as you push them down.
- Post objects into a shape sorter and say 'bye, red circle', 'bye, blue triangle', etc.
- Play hiding games – get a teatowel and hide things under it, then say 'teddy's gone' or 'car's gone'.
- Make a 'gone' book – a book that has an object on one page and nothing (a blank page) on the next. So you can say 'ball', then 'ball gone' and so on. Encourage your child to say 'bed gone' and not just 'gone' as you would've expected in the previous phase.
- Involve your child in simple chores like loading the washing machine and explain what you are doing – 'socks in', 'tights in', and so on.
- Point to parts of the body and say 'Cari's nose', 'Cari's tummy'. Labelling body parts is a good way to start introducing two-word sentences.

- Your child should be able to hum and sing, so encourage him to sing two words at the end of a sentence rather than just one, for example, at the end of 'Twinkle, Twinkle . . . ' your child might sing 'little star'. (See page 46 for tips on how to encourage words through song.)
- Your child will also be learning how to express pain verbally, so model sentences like 'hurt finger' or 'sore bottom'. You can role play this with cuddly toys falling over or going to the doctor. Consider purchasing a doctor's kit, which is a great learning prop.
- Watch TV together and talk about and act out the programmes using two-word sentences, such as 'Peppa Pig crying', 'George Pig cuddling' and 'Jess lost, where's Jess? In the box.'
- Use role-play scenarios involving appropriate two-word comments, So, if you were playing shops you might say, 'Buy bread'. If you were pretending to be at the dentist's, say, 'Open mouth,' or, if you're pretending to give dolly a bath, say, 'Wash neck.'

PLEASE AND THANK YOU DILEMMAS!

Don't worry too much about teaching your child to say 'please' and 'thank you'. I know British people love to be polite but, when you have only 50 words, it's far better that they are functional words that carry a message. Only once your child can put a short sentence together should you then add the social niceties.

When my daughter Jess was about one she started saying 'Ah' and pointing at everything she wanted. When I picked her up from Granny's house one day, Granny said 'I'll encourage her to say "please" instead.' I had to tell her that this is a real no-no. We didn't want Jess to say 'please' thinking that please is the word for drink, book or outside, because she'd then end up saying 'please please!'.

I discussed this issue with one of my speech therapy friends, Katie, who had taught her 18-month-old daughter Clara lots of single words and signs, and was not worried about 'please' and 'thank you'. She said it was quite embarrassing when Clara would go up to an adult and say 'drink!' because she was too young to say the two-word sentence 'drink, please'. This left Katie worrying about whether or not other people thought she was a terrible mother for not encouraging Clara to say please and thank you. I'd still argue that there's plenty of time to learn the niceties and that, for now, it's far better to have functional words that will help your child communicate his needs.

While we're on the subject of please and thank you, I have been asked on a number of occasions if it's a good idea to encourage the use of 'ta' for 'thank you'. My answer is no. This might sound contradictory to my advice about turning a blind eye to 'doggie' or 'horsie' as mentioned earlier (see page 42), but the difference is that the word 'doggie' clearly derives from the core word 'dog' and, therefore, we are not detracting from the good model for language. Because 'thank you' is a long word that has difficult sounds to articulate, a child will shorten it to something like 'angkoo', which is a much better attempt at the real word than 'ta'. So, if you get a 'ta', simply model back the correct words: 'Yes, well done, you are saying, "Thank you!"'.

LISTENING FOR SPEECH SOUNDS

We are hearing and listening continuously, but is the brain actively engaged in what it is listening to? Possibly not and, consequently, some children need help to learn to listen to the sounds that make up a word before they can learn to say the sound in order to speak clearly.

Hearing is a passive process that involves the ear simply hearing sounds. On the other hand, listening is an active process that involves tuning in, decoding and responding to sounds in the environment. It sounds rather daft, but you need to train your ear to hear in order to listen – which is pretty difficult in a world that often involves continuous background noise like the TV and radio, or constant chatter at nursery. The ability to listen to speech sounds is fundamental to speech and language development and, in the speech therapy world, this is known as phonological awareness.

Not only must your brain listen to and process the single sounds that make up a word, it also has to decode a whole word to determine if it recognizes the pattern of sounds together and the sequence in which that word appears (its context within a grammatical sentence). It is said that we retain the whole sentence in our working memory before we process it. This whole system is known as auditory processing.

As we've already learned, you can expect a range of different mistakes in your child's speech during this phase that are perfectly normal (see page 00 in chapter seven). But by two years, your child should have the sounds p, b, m, d, h and n in place at the beginning of a word ('pig', 'bee', 'milk', 'dog', 'house' and 'no'), while the sounds k, g, t, n, ng will be inconsistently used. The use of all consonants at the end or in the middle of words will be erratic. Therefore, your child will have to listen to these sounds when you model them within words. If he is not using one of these sounds, he may need to be encouraged to listen to the sound in order to help him say it.

The tips in the Small Talk Time, below, will help you to fine-tune your child's listening skills without pressurizing or criticizing him, in order to help him to say a sound correctly.

THE 'FIS' PHENOMENON

It's proven that the ability to hear the difference between sounds comes way before a child is able to articulate those particular sounds. This is illustrated by the 'fis' phenomenon. The name comes from an incident reported by J. Berko and R. Brown in 1960.[3] A child referred to his inflatable plastic fish as a 'fis'. However, when adults asked him, 'Is this your *fis*?' he rejected the statement, shaking his head. When he was asked, 'Is this your fish?' he responded, 'Yes, my fis.' This shows that although the child could not produce the sound '*sh*', he could perceive it as being different from the sound '*s*'.

Small Talk Time **Honing those listening skills**

The games below are designed to be fun and entertaining, and to help your toddler focus his attention on the sounds that make up words. By encouraging your child to have excellent phonological awareness (see above) you will be preparing him for reading and writing, so whatever level your child is at – whether it be the top end of what is expected during this phase (saying about 200 words), or the bottom end 50 words – there's no harm in having a go at these exercises. Some of the games may seem familiar, which is because they are games I've suggested previously, but they are taken on to the next level. Always remember that if your child says the sound incorrectly, reward his attempt, then simply model the correct target for him (see page 125 for a full explanation on how to model words for your child).

Create a sound sack

Make up a bag of two or three objects that start with one particular sound and encourage your child to pull them out and name each one. Why not make a sound sack for a range of different sounds? Initially focus on the sounds that you know your child should be able to say by the end of this phase – p, b, m, h, n and d. So, in a 'b' sack you would put a ball, toy bed, boy, bear, bus, brick or book and in a 'm' sack you would put a monkey, money, man, moon or mouse. Move onto the sounds your child is struggling with.

Read, Read, Read!

One of the best ways to help children develop an awareness of speech sounds or phoneme awareness naturally is through the use of children's books, so look out for stories that rhyme, use alliteration or have some sort of predictable pattern. This type of awareness is a very important milestone in the development of early literacy.

Being aware of rhyme is important when learning to read and spell because it can help children appreciate that words that share common sounds often share common letter sequences. So, if you can spell 'hat', you can also spell 'bat', 'rat' and 'mat'. This also applies to reading: if you can read 'call', you can read 'ball', 'tall' and 'fall'.

Being able to recognize rhyming words helps the child develop the ability to break down longer words into smaller parts and then recognize those smaller parts (for example, 'call' then 'calling' and 'called'). Again, this is an important skill for reading and spelling. Re-read stories over and over again, allowing children to occasionally 'fill in the blanks' with an appropriate rhyming word.

Get rhyming

Make up some rhymes of your own and try to act them out. You could make an airplane fly in the sky, for example. Leave pauses so that your child can add in the missing word. Below are some ideas to get you started:

- fly in the . . . (sky)
- sheep is . . . (asleep)
- mouse in a . . . (house)
- duck on a . . . (truck)
- a bee in the . . . (tree)
- sing on a . . . (swing)

Remember that singing songs makes language stick, so perhaps sing these sentences in a song. Try using the tune to 'If You're Happy And You Know It' for 'there's a fly in the sky, way up high', for instance.

Make up rhyming nicknames for friends and family, such as Stevie Weavie, Sally Mally, Cam Wham or Pat Cat. Why? Because children love to do this! One child I worked with said, 'Listen to my song,' and came out with a list of rhyming words.

Hit the mic!

Use an echo mic from a toy shop or a real microphone to practise saying some individual speech sounds or rhyming words. You could say, 'What is the next word?' then hold the mic next to your child's mouth. For example, with 'Humpty Dumpty', sing: 'Humpty Dumpty sat on a wall, Humpty Dumpty had a great . . . [hold up the mic to your toddler].'

Or try singing nursery rhymes and alter them so that your child can learn to tell the difference and discriminate the first sounds of the word, then correct you. For example, try 'Little Bo Peep has lost her jeep', 'Jack and Jill went up the mill', and 'Hickory dickory dock, the mouse ran up the rock'.

Play puppets

Make a puppet say a sound and ask your child to copy it, for example, try 'furry Fred says "fff". Can you say it, too?'. Make the puppet ask for things but get it wrong so your child has to correct him, for instance, 'I want my chook' (book) and 'give me a dink' (drink). Your child can use the context to determine what furry Fred means. Then have the puppet repeat the rhyming words (and maybe even add one more), for example, a puppet that can only say words that sound like 'drink' – 'think', 'wink', 'sink', 'mink', 'link'.

Domestic noises

Listen to household noises and make them into speech sounds. Your child may be able to name the object, but he may need to be encouraged to broaden his use of speech sounds. For instance, he may say 'bish' for 'fish', so if you encourage him to say the 'f' sound away from the word 'fish', he should begin to transfer the skills he has learnt in order to say 'f' correctly. This will help him to recognize and listen to the sound and provide him with a means to say it. You would say, 'Can you hear the hoover? It says "v v v".' Some more examples are: rain = t t t; kettle = f f f; wind = w w w; dishwasher = sh sh; washing machine spin = m m m; bouncing ball = b b b.

OTHER ISSUES THAT MAY ARISE AT THIS AGE

My child won't sit still

This is quite a common problem, but a problem that you do need to try to work on, as being able to sit still – along with other skills like knowing your name, holding a crayon or pencil, being able to open a book, take your basic clothes off or being potty-trained – are desirable skills needed to start Foundation 1 (otherwise known as reception class or pre-school).

A good way to encourage sitting and listening is to look at books so try the following suggestions. Remember – don't put too much pressure on your child or he may refuse to play with you if he doesn't think it's going to be fun.

- First, ensure your toddler has access to several colourful board books (so that it is easy for him to turn the pages himself). Try to look at them together but allow your child to lead the flow and turn the pages, so that he is actively partaking in the activity. If he won't sit with you, flick through the book and comment on interesting pictures at a distance and let him play with it or look at it whenever he wants. Initially, you could just aim to get him to sit for two or three minutes and then work towards five minutes.
- Help your child make his own book – a scrapbook that has things that interest him, such as photos, wrappers, artwork, stickers, and so on.
- Read bedtime stories with your child, even if he seems to be expressing more interest in carrying on playing or his beaker of milk. Making the effort to read him a story reinforces the idea that storytime equals bedtime. Let him choose a book to read, and suggest cuddling up together. If he has a tendency to become distracted or is tired, read just one book together or say that if he comes and sits down, you will read another one. Ensure the story is at the right level for your child. (See page 283 in chapter ten for tips on how to find the right book for your child's stage of language development.)
- During the day, pick a time when your child isn't too busy – perhaps after a sleep – and just sit down on the floor and begin reading out loud. Don't worry about making him sit still on your lap – let him run around and play while you read, if that's what he wants to do. He may or may not become interested, but he is hearing you and becoming accustomed to the idea of you reading to him.

Remember – just as we adults all choose to read different books, children have different tastes, too. Why not take your child to the library and see which books interest him? If he chooses a book that seems too high a level, go with it, but don't read the text, just talk about the pictures in a way that is one step ahead of your toddler's language level. So, if he is saying single words, read the book using two or three-word sentences.

Focusing your child's attention

Another reason that your child may not be able to sit still is if there are too many toys about. It can be difficult to focus when there is too much on offer. (This often happens to me in a cake shop – I get over excited and want everything!) Help your toddler focus by putting away excess toys and, each day, bring out no more than two or three games. If he is sitting at a table to read, ensure there's nothing else within reach/in his eyeline – it's always best to clear the decks.

If your child moves on to another game too soon – for example, he was doing a puzzle and moved onto the cars before finishing – quickly put most of the puzzle pieces in yourself and leave the last one or two. Then say, 'First puzzle, then cars,' and divert his attention back to his original choice of activity. Use phrases like 'one more go', 'one more minute' and 'finished now' so that it is obvious that the game is complete.

Mealtimes can be another difficult time for sitting still. It's all tied in with eating avoidance – which, as you know, is a fairly normal part of a young child's life. My only advice here is to try not to distract your child with the TV – it's so antisocial. If things start getting frisky, give goals to work towards – for example, say, 'Eat one more mouthful and then finished.' If he then eats one more mouthful, don't push any more onto him unless he reaches for more. Saying 'Just finish your peas/carrots/potatoes' could be another thing to try.

If your child has a tendency to get down and run about at mealtimes, insist that he must sit for at least a short period. Remember that you must have high expectations! If he never sits for a meal, insist he sits for 30 seconds and then extend it. Using distractions like books or Skype (!) can be good for one mealtime, but they will usually become a vicious circle and the level at which you will have to distract your child will continue to increase to unsustainable levels. I used to encourage dolly to eat with Jess, which helps symbolic play, or you could try a one-minute or two-minute egg timer and say, 'You must sit for one minute and then you can get down.' Give lots of praise for any attempts to sit still.

Saying naughty words

My friend's 20-month-old started speaking clearly at a very early age and was able to repeat entire sentences. The problem is that she'd learnt a few embarrassing expressions (like 'shut up') and she used them with strangers when they went out. My friend had tried everything to get her to stop using them – from reasoning with her to threatening to punish her – but nothing seemed to work.

If your child is using inappropriate expressions, firstly, ensure you are not modelling them. You may not think you are but, like me, with the b**ger word, it wasn't until someone pointed it out that I realized how much I was saying it, so it was no wonder that Jess was saying 'bu-gah', too.

Consider what might be triggering your child to say the phrase. Is it when someone unfamiliar talks to him or just when there's general noise? I met a two-year-old child who said very little except 'dit'. When I asked his mum what he was saying she was embarrassed to admit that he was saying 'sh*t'. She explained that he'd heard her say 'sh*t' when she dropped one thing and now said it every time he dropped something, or fell over. I explained that she'd have to make a big deal of falling over at home and then to replace the expletive with the word 'sugar' using exactly the same tone as she would normally. Before long, her son would change 'sh*t' to 'sugar'!

The main advice is try to ignore the phrase. Responding to it – and repeating it – will only make it worse. Children might be swearing to get attention (it's hard not to laugh when your child effs and blinds, but try to remain poker-faced as smiles and chortles will only encourage him – remind friends and family of this too!). Children swear to feel grown-up. They don't understand that it's not ok. Try to reset their rude words by coming up with some more interesting words altogether that won't offend but can still be used to express anger or surprise. I'm rather fond of 'blithering blackbirds!' and 'heck and double heck!' You may sound like a rather crazed character from an Enid Blyton novel, but wouldn't you rather your child was saying these harmless phrases instead of the f-word?

I'm concerned – my child is way behind his peers

I see lots of parents who are panicking because their child is falling behind. I always tell them that, at this age, toddlers really become individuals – you'll notice that your little one might be at a different level to his or her peers (whether it's behind or ahead) when it comes to a range of things, including speech, eating and confidence. You'll see that some children love being outside, some are sociable, some are shy and others like nothing better than scootering and trampolining all day long and don't want much to do with sitting down and enjoying a conversation. This is when the differences between boys and girls can become more obvious, too (for more on this see page 277).

The trouble is, you just can't help but compare your child to others, no matter how much you tell yourself that everybody's different. I always tell my anxious parents that the children their eye will be drawn to – who will stand out – will be the children who are doing exceptionally well and not the children who are at the same level as or behind their own.

My advice is to just accept that your child's individual differences will be noticeable. Some children will be going hell for leather and saying a number of new words every day while others will be going much slower. At two years your child could be saying 75 single words and attempting a few two-word sentences, or he could have 200 words and be speaking in two and, sometimes, three-word sentences.

Remind yourself that by two and a half years most of the children whose words were slower will have caught up and you won't notice so many differences.

SPEECH AND LANGUAGE DEVELOPMENT MILESTONES: 18–24 MONTHS

Children develop skills at different rates but, by 24 months, usually children will:

- concentrate on activities for longer, like playing with a particular toy.
- sit and listen to simple stories with pictures.
- understand between 200 and 500 words.
- understand more simple questions and instructions, for example, 'Where is your shoe?' and 'Show me your nose'.
- copy sounds and words a lot.
- use 50 or more single words. These will also become more recognizable to those not familiar with the child.
- start to put short sentences together with two to three words, such as 'More juice' or 'Bye, nanny'.
- enjoy pretend play with their toys, such as feeding dolly.
- use a limited number of sounds in words – often these are p, b, t, d, m and w. Children will also often miss the ends off words at this stage. They can usually be understood about half of the time.*

---

* These milestones have been provided by the website www.talkingpoint.org.uk and are reproduced with kind permission.

CHAPTER EIGHT

Language Expansion (24–36 months)

If your child didn't go through the 'big boom' in the previous six-month phase, then you'll certainly see it between the second and third year. In fact, your toddler's vocab should *double* during this phase. And, by the end of their fourth year on the planet, many children will have about 500–600 words and some could have as many as 1,000 – that's a 500 per cent increase from the average of 100–200 or so words that is expected at two years of age. At some point between the second and third year, you may see your child effortlessly learn as many as nine or ten new words a day!

Let's remind ourselves just why language is so important. You need language for remembering ('why is Daddy putting me to bed tonight? Oh yes, because Mummy's gone to the cinema'), thinking and reasoning ('why won't that shape fit into that hole?' or 'why has my daddy got to go to work?'), for self-control ('I'm not allowed to climb the stairs so I won't', or 'don't have another chocolate biscuit' in my case!), and planning ('shall we go swimming or to the swings today?'). We also need language for dealing with emotions and worries, making friends and, of course, communicating.

In this chapter we'll be covering three key areas:

- **concepts** – Such as hot, cold, clean, dirty, long, short, fat, thin.
- **grammar** – Your toddler will develop the intricacies of her word and sentence structure to make longer and more complex sentences

('dog bark' might change to 'the dog is barking'), and use more advanced grammar such as correct word endings and appropriate pronouns ('me go' becomes 'I'm going'), plurals (cats, horses) and others.

- **memory** – This evolving skill is crucial for further language development.

Once your little one has begun to master and combine these three core elements, you'll notice that she will suddenly want to start telling *you* stories. So, we'll also learn about narrative skills and look at how you can create many elaborate tales to tell.

Lastly, we'll look at smoothing out your toddler's speech sound errors. It's when she starts chatting away, telling made-up stories, that you may begin to notice that she is getting certain sounds or words a bit wrong. She might say 'foots' for 'feet', or 'goed' instead of 'went', because she's still trying to work out how language works and master the rules behind it. You'll still have words that are mispronounced, such as 'busgeti' (spaghetti), 'wimmin' (swimming) and 'trouserers' (trousers) – which you'll 'ploberly' find totally endearing! I'll show you how to gently correct these mistakes without knocking your child's developing verbal confidence.

So, all of the Small Talk Times in this chapter are geared towards achieving these impressive milestones. Won't it be lovely to sit back and have your toddler tell *you* a story?

CONCEPTS

Let's consider the concept of a 'tree'. Although there's an extraordinary array of different types of tree in the world (different sizes, shapes, colours, textures, fruits, seasonal changes, life-spans, and so on), they all fall under the single concept of 'tree'. So, your child at two years should be able to say the word 'tree' when she sees an oak, for example, but will not have a sense of the concept of a tree. But as her ability to think develops, she will become interested in finding out what a tree essentially is – or what the concept of a tree is: she'll begin to notice the features that make this oak a tree and not a plant, a flower or a piece of timber. Therefore, the true definition of a concept is an idea, a thought or notion – a mental category that helps us to classify particular objects or events that share a set of common features or attributes.

At two to two and a half years, a child begins to understand the size concepts, such as 'big' and 'little', and the quantity concepts, such as 'all' or 'none'. Then, during the two-and-a-half to three-year stage, there is a massive expansion of the understanding of more complex concepts – such as those of location (for example, in/on/under) and time (today/tomorrow).

Alongside this expansive interest in things, your child will start to ask a barrage of questions – at two to two and a half years, you will hear 'what' and 'who', and from two and a half to three years, 'where', 'when' and 'why?' will be added to the list (at which point, parents may begin struggling to provide the answers). After all, why is a tree not a plant? For those of us who aren't biologists or keen gardeners, the answer isn't always obvious.

Our daily language is full of concepts and we have to teach our little ones to understand them and to use them. Below, we look at ideas for how to do this.

Teaching your child general concepts

Remember that a child must have a good understanding of a concept before using it expressively. Therefore, there are two stages to learning any new concept – firstly, helping your little one to understand the word and, secondly, encouraging her to use it.

The concepts likely to catch the eyes – and the imaginations – of children of this age are the more distinctive/obvious ones. Understanding of the more subtle concepts comes later. So, 'fat' is likely to come before 'thin', 'large' before 'small', 'tall' before 'short' and so on. I laughed and cringed when my co-author Tracey told me when she knew that two-and-a-half year old Minnie had obviously grasped the 'fat' concept. They were shopping in the supermarket and wheeled their trolley past a couple, when Minnie said very clearly, 'That was a fat man, wasn't it?' Yikes.

You might have to develop a thick skin as your toddler begins describing the world around her using these new concepts without a care for social etiquette, but I can assure you that you'll probably laugh more than you'll blush. And, of course, the most embarrassing gaffes will become part of your child's oral history, just like those first words!

Below are examples of the concepts to try to incorporate into your daily life and during your ten minutes of Small Talk Time while playing. Below them are some Small Talk Time games that will help you to practise them. The goal is to get your toddler familiar with the label of a word, and then understand the concept of it and the context in which to use it. Here are the key concepts:

- on/off
- same/different
- happy/sad
- full/empty
- loud/quiet
- old/young
- up/down
- more/less
- top/bottom
- big/little
- all/none
- front/back
- old/new
- long/short

- hard/soft
- over/under
- hot/cold
- smooth/rough
- forwards/backwards
- above/below

Small Talk Time **Teaching your toddler concepts**

Remember – language develops through play so be aware of what is happening in your toddler's play during this phase, so that you can find as many opportunities as possible to develop her use of concepts as she potters about.

- Mealtimes give you a great opportunity to teach concepts. First, name all the food to extend your child's vocabulary, then talk about the concepts. Fish fingers are 'rough', but the fish in the middle is 'smooth'. That yogurt is 'cold' because it has been in the refrigerator. By doing this you are helping your child to understand concepts by talking about the object and thinking about how it fits into her world.
- Share books and if the illustrations lend themselves to teaching a variety of concepts (for example, big/little, happy/sad, long/short), point them out. Believe it or not, *Thomas the Tank Engine* books are really good for teaching emotional concepts – the trains have the most exaggerated facial expressions, which are great!

  You can buy opposites books that have concepts in them: we have a book called *Opposites Peek-a-Boo* by Eric Hill at my clinic. I also like *The Baby's Catalogue* by Janet and Allan Ahlberg, which is full of everyday pictures from family life and is good for learning concepts. There is a page of garden objects, a family page, a breakfast page, etc. The book contains pictures of things to describe as soft, hard, hot, cold, prickly, smooth, big, little and so on.

- Collect from around your house objects that are big and little, or the same and different, or soft and hard. Talk about these objects with your child.
- Play the game I Spy . . . using attributes to describe the chosen object, for example, 'I spy something that is soft.'
- Play the game I Went To the Shop and Bought . . . When you take turns to add something new to the end of the list, introduce a concept. For example, you could say, 'I went to the shop and bought a big cake,' and your child says, 'I went to the shop and bought a big cake and a new hat,' and so on. Also try, 'I went to the zoo and saw a tall giraffe,' then 'I went to the zoo and saw a tall giraffe and a thin snake.'
- Try drawing, painting or moulding with play-dough things that are fat/thin (for instance, a fat cat or a thin cat, the top of the mountain or the bottom of the mountain, a happy or a sad face) and talk about them. Talk about your creations and ask your child to explain them to another adult.
- This age group loves 'container play' – filling and dumping objects into containers, handbags, baskets, etc. Give your child a pile of objects that are hard/soft, rough/ smooth, heavy/light and so on, to put into their containers.
- Children of this age often have a strong desire to dress themselves and be independent, so let your child choose her clothes and describe the clothes as she puts them on (for instance, 'Oh, you've found something with long sleeves/a thick jumper/a pretty shirt').
- Engage in symbolic play and act out household activities with a running commentary involving concepts, for example, 'We're wiping the dirty table – now it's clean,' or 'We're vacuuming the soft carpet and then the hard wood.' Talk to your toddler about the activity as she makes the house look shipshape – you can't go wrong on this one!
- Your child should also be able to imitate vertical strokes on paper, so say 'down' as the brush goes down and encourage her to say

'up' as the brush goes up. You could try painting 'fast' or 'slow' or with 'thin' or 'thick' stripes.

- Get your child to tear up some paper, then talk about 'big' pieces and 'small' pieces. She'll love sticking them down, too.
- Lastly, try categorizing a range of objects in play. For example, 'Let's put all the noisy farm animals/all the summer clothes together,' and 'Let's tidy all the big books into this box and all the small puzzles onto the tray.'

COMPARATIVES AND SUPERLATIVES (-ER AND –EST)

Once your child has grasped some of the concepts listed above, why not use these words to compare and contrast things with each other? So, when your child can say 'big tractor', show her that we can be even more specific about its size and explain that even though this tractor is big, that one is even bigger, but the one over there is the biggest. What excitement that'll bring on!

Small Talk Time **Bigger, biggest and best!**

- Line up a range of objects in order of size. Size differences are visual and are therefore easier to grasp. Jumble them up and line them up again. Ask which is the biggest, then go along the line and say, 'This car is bigger than that car, this car is bigger than that car and this one is the biggest.' Make sure your child understands the words bigger and biggest.
- Again, use food at mealtimes to talk about size comparisons. First, use two objects, for example, 'I have a big cup, but your cup is bigger,' 'This potato is big, but that one is bigger,' or 'Your hands are big, but my hands are bigger,' When you say the word 'bigger', sign it to emphasise the size by stretching your hands apart. Once

you think your child understands this concept, try three objects to go through the same format, for instance, 'My cup is big, your cup is bigger but this cup is the biggest!'

Go through the same format with other tangible objects. For instance, use the comparatives and superlatives as you load the washing machine using sock length, smelliness or dirtiness – this should appeal to a toddler's sense of humour! Make sure you use only regular forms at this stage (which are those ending in the regular –er and –est ending, for instance, hot/hotter/hottest, happy/happier/happiest, quiet/quieter/quietest and soft/softer/softest.

Later, you will find that your child generalizes this pattern and applies it erroneously to irregular forms, so she'll use 'badder' rather than 'worse' or 'worst', 'good', 'gooder' and 'goodest' rather than 'good', 'better', 'best' and 'beautiful', 'beautifuler' and 'beautifulest' rather than 'more beautiful' or 'most beautiful'. There are many other irregular patterns, so you will have to sensitively model the correct form back in a positive way.

TEACHING YOUR CHILD PREPOSITIONS

Prepositions are words (or spatial concepts) that describe a location, such as 'in', 'on', 'under', 'in front', 'behind' and so on. First, your child will learn to understand these words and then begin to use them herself. For instance, during the two to two-and-a-half-years phase, your child should understand 'in', 'on' and 'under' and, during the two-and-a-half to three-years phase, she should start to say them.

So, before embarking on prepositions, make sure your child can say two-word sentences and understand three-word sentences. Start with putting a preposition into a two-word sentence, for instance, 'It's under blanket'.

Prepositions are crucial for your child to learn as they will help her to expand her sentence length, enable her to answer a 'where' question and retell a story or an event in greater detail. Let's think about some Small Talk games that will help your child to learn prepositions.

Small Talk Time **Getting into space, man!**

In order of difficulty, below is a list of the prepositions your child needs to master:

- in/out
- on
- up/down
- under
- behind
- in front of
- on top of
- at the bottom of
- over
- near/next to
- beside
- between

The games below are listed in order of difficulty, so progress through them in sequence (as far as possible). They involve your child physically putting herself into a position, then putting a toy or an object into a position and, lastly, using the word without any visual information to help her.

1. Begin with a physical demonstration, like standing ON the chair or sitting UNDER the table – say what you are doing. Then help your child perform the same actions whilst you describe what she does. This will help her to understand the prepositions. Why not take photos so that you can talk about them later?

To make this game more fun, play Hide and Seek – leave the room and tell your toddler to 'Hide UNDER the cushions!' Or make up an obstacle course out of furniture, enabling you to both climb over, under, on top, beside and between things.

2. There are a number of nursery rhymes that use prepositions (see the list, below). Sing these and act out the prepositions, then talk about them.

   - 'Ring a Ring O' Roses' (we all fall down)
   - 'The Grand Old Duke of York' (up/down)
   - 'The Hokey Cokey' (in/out)
   - 'Roly Poly' (up/down)
   - 'Jack and Jill' (up/down)
   - 'Hey Diddle Diddle' (over)

3. Hide a small toy in, on or under a box and direct your child to find it, telling her that it is 'in the box', 'under the box' and so on. Model the words for her so she learns their meaning.

4. Try to incorporate prepositions into your daily routine. For instance:

   - When tidying up, ask your child to put things in specific places ('Put your pyjamas under your pillow', 'Put bunny on the chair').
   - When you're loading the washing machine, say, 'Put your trousers in the machine.'
   - When wiping the table, say, 'Here's the cloth, wipe under your plate.'
   - When in the bath, say, 'Wash in your ears, under your chin, next to your tummy button.'

5. Read books that have prepositions, such as *Where's Spot* and *We're Going on a Bear Hunt* (in which the repetitive line is 'we can't go over it, we can't go under it . . .').

6. Once you feel your child is able to understand these concepts, move on to tabletop activities. Draw pictures of people or animals in, on,

under, in front and behind things. Also, cut out pictures from magazines of people in, on, under, in front of and behind things.

7. Ask your child to help you with some basic cooking. Use this opportunity to talk about what is going 'in' the mixing bowl, what is 'on' the table, and where items are (for instance, 'The spoon is *under* the lid').

MASTERING SIMPLE USE OF GRAMMAR

The introduction of grammar will come after your toddler's language boom, and after she has started using two key words in a sentence (see page 171 for tips on how to encourage two-word sentences). It is said that a normally developing child needs to understand 200–250 words before she understands grammar, and be able to say the same number of words before spoken grammar appears.

Picking up grammar isn't easy. Grammatically, English is a killer as there are so many irregularites. But the daunting task of absorbing all these grammatical rules and their exceptions is what the brain of a three-year-old does without flinching. Even more incredible is the fact that toddlers don't just know the rules, they truly understand their logic. In a famous experiment by Jean Berko Gleason in 1958, children were presented with a fantasy creature rather like a bird and were told it was a 'wug' – an invented word – and then shown a second wug. The English-speaking toddler invariably said 'two wugs', demonstrating that he had learnt the grammatical rule of plurals and could transfer this knowledge to a completely new word.

The mistakes toddlers make also show us how deep their understanding of grammar is and how they apply it. 'We swimmed' is a great example of a toddler applying a perfectly logical rule to the past tense of the English language; it just happens that this is one of our many irregular verbs. This overgeneralization of the rule persists until the child has sorted out the instances in which the general rules apply and those in which they are overruled by the irregular verb. Amazingly, children are likely to have grasped most of these irregularities by the age of three and a half to four years (use of the past tense is discussed in the next chapter.

The norms of grammar development

You may want to know a bit more about which grammatical rules are picked up and when (and do a bit of revision yourself on possessive pronouns and the like – most of us have no idea what all these conjugations are called; our brain just automatically arranges the grammar correctly for us). In his book *A First Language* (1973), researcher Roger Brown outlined the developmental stages in grammar. This model is still used by speech therapists today to predict the path that normal expressive language development usually takes.

Stage 1 (at about two years)

A child learns to put two words together. She should have just about conquered this at the age of two years.

Stage 2 (between roughly 24–36 months)

A child will learn to:

- use the possessive 's', so phrases like 'man's book' appear, and she begins to use her name when talking about herself.
- introduce pronouns, such as 'my', 'mine', 'you', 'me' and 'he' and 'she'.
- put 'ing' on to the end of a verb ('I am running').
- use plurals ('one banana, two bananas').
- use negatives ('no', 'not', 'can't').
- raise her intonation for a question.
- begin to use the past tense.

Stage 3 (between roughly 36 and 42 months)

A child will learn to:

- inconsistently use the present tense auxiliaries 'can' and 'will', for example, 'I can swim,' or 'I will come.'
- overgeneralize the past tense, for example, 'goed' instead of 'went' or 'writed' instead of 'wrote'.

The Small Talk Time games below focus on the areas of grammar that should have been mastered by the time a child reaches three to three and a half years of age.

Small Talk Time Putting '-ing' on the end of a verb

Here are some regular verbs to start you off: play, kick, jump, cry, wash, walk, brush, push, paint, cook, dance.

- Take pictures of your child or someone else doing these actions and combine them in a slide show. Ask your child, 'What is happen-ING?' Remind her to listen to the question, particularly listening to the '–ing' ending. Make sure she uses a matching '–ing' ending in response to the question, for instance, 'The girl is jumping,' or 'Mummy is dancing.' Toddlers often start by saying 'girl running' and miss out the 'is', but this is fine and you can simply model the correct phrase by saying, 'Yes, well done, the girl is running.' Print off your photos and make up some flashcards to practise with.
- Play charades. Take turns to act out an action, then guess the action using the '–ing' form. Afterwards, you can talk about the game in the past tense to get your child thinking about the next phase, saying, 'First you jumped and then you danced,' for instance.

Small Talk Time Plurals

When we want to signify that there is more than one of something, we make it plural by adding an 's' to the end of a word (for instance, 'one cat, three cats'). However, some words are irregular and don't follow this rule. If your child is having difficulty with this, help her by first practising regular plurals where you simply add 's'.

- If your child misses the 's' off the word (by asking for a 'raisin for Erin', for instance, give her one raisin, then model, 'Erin wants raisinSSSSS. Raisins for Erin.' Or if your child says, 'Dan shoe on,' put on one shoe and look puzzled. Model the phrase again, 'Dan shoessss on,' before putting on the second one.
- Draw some pictures of objects. On one page, put one object and, on the other, put many (one flower and three flowers or one pig and two pigs, for instance). Talk through the pictures with your child, emphasizing the 's' ending on the plurals.
- Play I Spy, choosing plural objects to spy. For instance, you might pick 'booksssssssss' as there are lots of them in the room.
- When your child is talking, remind her of plurals by saying things like, 'Was there one chip on your plate or lots?' and, when she says 'lots', remind her that she needs to say 'chipssssss'.
- Try finding groups of objects to talk about – on a dinner plate, separate one pea from a group of peas and say, 'One pea, lots of peas.' This works with everything from bricks to animals.
- Think of things that come in pairs (socks, shoes, Noah's ark animals). Practise the singular and plural forms for each word, for instance, 'glove' and 'gloves'.
- When your child has mastered regular plurals, introduce the irregular plurals (for example, mouse/mice, sheep/sheep, fish/fish, child/children, foot/feet) using the methods above.

Small Talk Time Negatives

At two years, 'no' and 'don't' tend to become rather popular negatives! You'll hear things like 'no juice' and 'no want bedtime'. Use the following tips to help your child understand negatives.

- Draw pictures of three people – the first two wearing a hat and the last, not. Say, 'Hat, hat, no hat.' Shake your head to make it more understandable. Try this again using faces and a nose ('Nose, nose, no nose'). Encourage your child to join in.
- At the end of a meal offer 'More?' If she says no, say, 'No more.'
- Open the refrigerator and play the following game: 'I like yogurt, I don't like curry paste. I like butter but I don't like tomato purée.' Look at the toy section in a catalogue and say, 'I like Ben Ten, I don't like Peppa Pig,' and so on.

At two and a half to three years, the 'not', 'none' and 'nobody' words appear. For example, a child might say, 'Do you want more or not?' Use the tips below to encourage this development.

- Look through picture books and take up opportunities to use these words. For instance, you might say, 'Crocodile is hiding under the bed,' then turn the page and say, 'Monkey is not hiding under the bed, monkey is in the wardrobe. Who is hiding under the table? Nobody is hiding under the table.'
- The most common use for the word 'none' is in answer to the question 'Can I have a sweet?' – 'No, there are none left'! Emphasize the word 'none' as your child absorbs the impact of the concept of an empty sweet jar!

Small Talk Time **Pronouns**

Essentially, pronouns relate to how we refer to ourselves and others. Between 19 and 24 months, your toddler's grasp of pronouns will probably begin when she starts talking about herself in the third person, for instance, 'Anabelle drink'. This is rather more charming than what comes next – 'mine', a word you are likely to hear all too frequently (usually accompanied by a toy clutched in a fist and a frowning face!).

At two to two and a half, this develops into 'my', 'me' and 'you', so you'll probably begin hearing, 'My can do it!', 'Me do it!' and then, 'I', 'mine' and 'yours'.

At 30 months, your toddler should be able to distinguish between a boy or girl and begin using 'he', 'she' and 'they'. Children often become muddled between 'he' and 'she' – you might hear your child say 'that one' instead!

Use the ideas below to help your child practise pronouns:

- Play at dealing cards, saying, 'One for me and one for you . . .'
- When you are sorting clothes, say 'Daddy's top', 'your trousers' and so on, and encourage your toddler to pick something up and say 'my jacket', 'your socks'.
- Take photos of yourself and your child doing things and discuss these with her, saying, 'I am swimming,' and so on. Take her hand and encourage her to point at herself when she says 'I'. Then show her a picture of you doing something and take her hand and point to yourself and say, 'You are drinking.'
- Before a child can use 'he' and 'she' we have to be certain that she knows the difference between a boy and girl. So ask, 'Is Daddy a boy or a girl?', and so on. Point at pictures in books or people on the TV and ask, 'Boy or girl?'

When you are certain that your child knows the difference between male and female, start to practise 'he', 'she' and 'they' using the following tips:

- Collect old family photos or cut out pictures from magazines of boys, girls and groups of people together. Say corresponding things, such as, 'What is *she* doing?' or '*She* is wearing a hat'. Reverse roles, so your little one has to ask the questions using the correct pronouns.

- Use Playmobil or Lego characters to make up a simple story, for instance, make the characters play Hide and Seek. Retell the story using the correct pronouns ('He was hiding in the car', 'They were under the bed,' and so on).
- Talk about everyday experiences as they happen ('*He* is eating,' or 'They are happy'),

Later try 'his', 'hers' and 'theirs', expected at around three and a half years:

- Use pictures of a boy, girl and a group and select some real food. Ask your child to close her eyes and then allocate a different piece of food to the boy and girl. When she opens her eyes ask her, 'What's for *her* dinner?' Encourage her to respond with a pronoun in a full sentence (you may have to model the sentence type you want several times first), e.g. '*Her* dinner is fish.' Reverse the roles.

Auxiliaries

Omitting auxiliaries like 'can' and 'will' is very common as, when they are left out, the meaning of the sentence usually remains intact (I suppose the sentence is grammatically correct and therefore just sounds more grown-up and 'prettier' when the auxiliaries are used).

The earliest form of auxillary you'll notice your toddler using will probably be 'is' and 'am' – basically, the verb 'to be'.

Is

People usually say 'he's' rather than 'he is' but it is easier to hear the latter form and therefore we tend to practise this and wait for a child to naturally shorten it. So, you would model 'he is running' or 'my sock is wet' and over time, your child will shorten these sentences to 'he's running' and 'my sock's wet'.

Am

Here are some examples of a child missing 'am' out of a sentence: 'I in sandpit,' 'I cold,' and 'I bubbles in my eye, but I upset and cry'.

Have

Again, we usually say, 'I've done a picture,' rather than 'I have done a picture,' so if you hear your child say, 'I done a picture,' model the correct sentence back using 'have'.

VERBAL REASONING

You'll find it easier to reason with your two-and-a-half to three-year-old as her language and understanding reach a higher level and she understands sentences along the lines of, 'If you don't put your puzzle away I'll call Louise's mum and tell her not to come and play'.

Of course, the result is that parenting can feel rather like a high-level negotiating role at the United Nations, but there is something thrilling about being able to reason with your toddler – and her reasoning back. She is becoming a little person, with her own logic and ideas (even if her logic is sometimes a little out of left field!).

Small Talk Time **Possessives**

Children can get terribly confused between plurals and the possessive 's' (for instance, 'the ladies' or 'the lady's house') so we need to encourage them to think about the words carefully.

- Use real objects (clothes are good) to practise using possessives. Say, 'Whose sock is this? It's Daddy's,' or 'Whose book is this? It's Fabian's.'
- When you are going out, get your child to sort out all the coats, saying, 'That's Freddie's coat/Tom's shoe/Daddy's glasses,' and so on.

- Take photos of your child with belongings, and discuss the pictures with her, saying, 'It's Ella's tractor,' and so on.
- Cut out pictures of toys from a catalogue and gather pictures of your child and people she knows. Stick them into a book, with the picture of a person on the left-hand page, and an object on the opposite page. Then look through the book with your toddler, modelling 'Adam's jeep', 'Lola's fairy wings' and so on.

HOW YOUR TODDLER'S GRAMMAR WILL DEVELOPS

At two-ish, a child will still use overextension (see page 130). A child at this age also uses underextension (the opposite of overextension). For example, a child may only call black Labradors – and no other dogs – 'dog', or call her own boots 'boots', calling other boots 'that' or 'shoes'. But, over time, this will change and your child will even learn to request clarification.

MEMORY

It's only natural to focus on the parts of language you can hear – the talking – and dismiss the aspects of language development that aren't so apparent, such as concentration, memory and understanding. But, as I keep reiterating, you need to be able to focus, remember and understand words before you can say them. So, in this section, we will think about memory and its importance in the language-development process.

There are three types of memory that are crucial for language development. These are the long-term memory (LTM), short-term memory (STM) and the working memory (WM). To explain this, I can use the example of a telephone conversation I had with my mum to arrange what to do on Mother's Day.

When my mum mentioned Mother's Day, my long-term memory enabled me to remember our plan from last year – to have a family lunch. It was a disaster. All the children were tired (it was their nap time) so they grizzled throughout the meal. Because my mother and I could remember this, we could describe and explain why we shouldn't do the same this year. During the discussion, as each sentence was being spoken, it was processed and retained momentarily in our working memory, but then forgotten (meaning that, after the call, I wouldn't have been able to retell the conversation word for word). The finer details of times and plans were stored in my short-term memory for a brief episode of time – to get me to the venue or until I wrote the details in my diary! And, because the details were not rehearsed over and over again after the event, they weren't stored in my long-term memory, so they have been forgotten.

Your memory systems work together so that what is said can be immediately processed by the working memory, taken into your short-term memory and then, when the information is stored and understood, it will either be linked with existing knowledge in the

MEMORY NORMS

- At 18 months, a child should be able to echo or repeat the last word or the most predominant word in a sentence.
- At two years, a child should have a working memory (also known as auditory memory, as she is remembering what she has heard) of two objects.
- At two to two and a half years, a child can sequence two pieces of information in order, so she should remember two key elements in a longer command (for instance, 'Pick up the brush and give it to Daddy').
- At three to four years, a child should remember three key objects.

long-term memory, or forgotten. This is how our toddlers learn everything, from new words and sentence structure to what their routine is at breakfast and how they play with building blocks.

There's nothing worse than forgetting a name when you see someone or forgetting a word you want to use in the heat of the moment, so start training your child's memory now!

WHY IS A GOOD WORKING MEMORY SO IMPORTANT?

Experts say that if you test working memory in pre-school, you can predict academic success three years later. So a good working memory is the key to successful learning and goes hand-in-hand with speech and language development, and a good verbal working memory can be an indicator of intelligence.

Small Talk Time **Memory Boosters**

A child's memory is assisted massively by her ability to sit still and listen – a seemingly impossible feat for some two- to three-year-olds. So ensure your child has excellent listening skills (see page 96 for tips on improving them) so she can listen for language.

- Learning to sing the words to your child's favourite song is a great test for her memory and something that she will love to do. Encourage her by providing actions or props to help her visualize the words in the song (for example, the actions in the song 'Wind the Bobbin Up'). When a word or a message is attached to a tune you can remember it more easily (see page 100), so don't just stop at singing songs – sing a message, too! If you feel uncomfortable singing, just make your voice as sing-songy or as rhythmical as possible so that your toddler can tune into it and remember it more easily.

- Ask your little one to remember a message and deliver it to someone in a different room (for instance, 'Can you ask Louis if he would like a snack?' or 'Tell Daddy Mummy wants a G'n'T.').
- Take a set of musical instruments. Play one shake of the tambourine, followed by a ting on the triangle and one clap of the hands – see if your child can copy the sequence. Change the sequence.
- Encourage your child to remember an item of food from the shopping list as you go around the supermarket. Can she remember two things that you need to buy?
- Try the following simple repetition memory games:
  - **Noises** – Do one noise first and get your child to copy, then add another to make two noises, then another to make three. Ask your toddler to copy you in sequence.
  - **Words** – Place some pictures of objects that fall within one category (for instance, food, toys or vehicles) on the floor facing upwards. Encourage your child to remember, then repeat, then post a range of pictures either into a postbox or into a puppet's mouth, saying 'Give the puppet the car/bus/train.'
  - **Sentences** – Give your child an instruction. Encourage her to say it out aloud before she carries it out (for instance, 'rub your tummy' or 'touch your nose and jump').
- Play pairs with some cards and encourage your child to remember where a particular card is when it is placed upside down on a table.
- Hide objects around the room, then have a treasure hunt to find them. Or encourage your child to hide an object, then tell you where to find it.
- Place five or so objects on a tray, take one away and ask your child to name the object that has disappeared.
- Assemble a few groups of objects and pictures and sort them into categories. Mix them all up again and see if your child can remember which item fits into a particular category.
- Your toddler will enjoy listening to familiar stories, so leave a key word out and see if she can fill it in. The next step might be to

purposefully say the wrong thing to see if she notices and corrects you. You could also encourage her to stay tuned in by telling her 'Every time I say "lion", you must roar like a lion.'

- Read a story to your child and encourage her to repeat it back (see below, under Telling Stories, for more information).

VERY ACTIVE BRAIN ALERT!

The brain of a three-year-old is two and a half times more active than an adult's. Forming all those neural pathways is a time-consuming task!

TELLING STORIES

So, your toddler's vocabulary is increasing, her memory is improving and she is beginning to master concepts and grammar. And, when all these things start to click, children also begin to talk about absent objects to start a conversation. In other words, they move away from only referring to the here and now and their imaginations begin to run riot . . .

Here's a story my daughter tried to tell me at 22 months:

Jess: 'Granny hat.'
Me: 'Yes, Granny's hat blew away in the wind.'
Jess: 'Granny run.'
Me: 'Yes, Granny ran after it!'

Your child will also talk about things that have happened during the day. With some prompting, she might be able to sequence things into a simple story – for example, 'Me go outside.' 'And what did you do outside?' 'Collect bugs.' By age three, she might be able to tell a simple made-up story based on her own experiences or books she's read. She'll probably leave out lots of detail and rely on the listener to ask questions or interpret a meaning from the odd sentence or two (for example, 'Luke at the shops,' after reading a book about Topsy and Tim at the shops or, 'Balloon in tree. Stuck,' when, a few days before, her balloon became stuck in a tree).

That's why narrative skills (being able to sequence a chain of events into a pattern so that they have some kind of significance) are a good indicator of how a child thinks and demonstrate her understanding of the experiences she has encountered.

If you want to boost your toddler's narrative skills, follow my Small Talk Time tips below. Hearing your Small Talkers take on the day's events is certainly a great motivator. A child's observations and quirky eye for detail never fail to be entertaining.

Small Talk Time Telling a story

First of all, your child must listen to you retell stories over and over again, and learn a framework, to be able to retell her story. Try the ideas below:

- The easiest way to achieve this is retelling things that you've done using the 'first, then and last' model – a simple Small Talk technique. For instance, 'First you sat in the dentist's chair, then you opened your mouth and then you had a sticker.' Or try using the same format to explain how to make a piece of toast, how to get dressed and what happened when you went shopping.
- You can show your child a familiar photo and talk about it. Who is in it? Where were you? When was it? and 'What happened next? Help her to answer these questions, then retell the story, for instance, 'Mummy and Frankie went to the seaside on my birthday. Then we built a big sandcastle and then the sea washed it away.'
- You can also make up stories about toys or people you know using the 'first, then and last' framework. Try to act them out as words are much easier to learn when they are brought to life.

- Try using a talking ted – you take teddy out on an event with you and retell what teddy did once it has happened. This technique is very popular in nurseries and schools.
- Try giving your child two objects, then make up a story. For example, for a dolly and a box, 'Dolly said "I'm tired", so she made a bed in a box and then went straight to sleep.'
- Act out familiar stories such as *Rosie's Walk*, *Who Sank the Boat?*, *The Gruffalo*, *Five Minutes' Peace* and *Farmyard Tales* – my nephew loves this game.
- Cook together and think about the sequence of events that occurred as you gobble up your culinary delights. For instance, you could say, 'First we measured the butter and flour, then we mixed them up with the egg, then we put it into the cake tin and last, it was ready!'.
- Fuzzy felts or misfits games are quite good for telling stories, or you can buy jigsaws that enable you to tell a story (all the pieces fit together so that you can put random pictures together).
- Read a familiar story and, before you turn the page, ask, 'What happens next?' or 'What happens at the end?'

MAKE A STORY SACK

The idea of story sacks was first created by Neil Griffiths, an ex-head-teacher-turned-children's writer, in 1997 (see www.storysack.com for more information). You read a story, then find objects that can help to bring the story to life (a teddy that resembles a character, props that can be used to represent scenery, noises or settings and so on) and put them all in a bag. This is the ultimate visual support – by finding the real objects to talk about and learn about, your child can try to retell the story to you. Using this game is a lovely way to encourage your little one to tell stories, then listen to her imagination run riot. Try to nurture and develop this skill as much as you possibly can.

- Colour photocopy a favourite book (or I tend to buy a second copy of a story classic from a charity shop) and cut out the pictures of the most significant events in the story. Then read the full book and ask your child to put the cut-up pictures into the story sequence.

THE NORMS OF STORYTELLING

Between the ages of two and a half and four years, a child begins to listen to stories with increasing attention and, at three years, she will be able to sit and listen to a story for about 15 minutes. She will also be able to retell a short story, managing to describe the story setting, the basic sequence of events and the central characters. The same information may be repeated and she may get fixed on a particular part of the story, adding more and more information about it (which may or may not have been part of the original story!). She may then lose track of the plot altogether.

SMOOTHING OUT THE TRICKIER SPEECH SOUNDS

It's when your child begins to 'freestyle', chatting away about anything and everything, (whether it's in the here and now or a creation from her imagination) that you may start to notice some quirks in her speech. After all, she is still fairly new to speech, so it's only natural that she is still refining her sounds and words.

For example, when Minnie was two and a half, Tracey noticed that she had a bit of an issue with saying the 'l' sound after another consonant, and was using 'w' instead. So 'clock' was 'cwock', 'play' was 'pway' and 'flag' was 'fwag', despite the fact that she could pronounce the 'l' sound (she could say 'lion' and 'lemonade').

This is perfectly normal for a child of two and a half. Try not to become too panicked by a speech sound error as all sounds have a developmental pattern and the error your child is making may be completely normal for her age. Look at the guidelines below to help you to decipher whether your child should have a particular sound or not at a particular age. With Minnie, we knew that she *could* say 'l' so, in time, she would manage to blend two consonant sounds together (such as 'cl', 'pl' or 'fl') so that her speech would sound perfect!

Although Tracey initially feared that Minnie was going to end up talking like Jonathan Ross, I was able to reassure them that this is totally normal – and temporary.

Common speech sound errors

In order to offer the same reassurance to as many parents as I can, here's my list of common speech sound 'bumps' that become apparent at around this time. See which ones you recognize from your little one's chatter:

- Your child may be mixing up her 'd's and 'g's and her 't's and 'c/k's, so you might hear 'dog' as 'gog', and 'car' as 'tar'. This should improve at about three years of age.
- 'Sh', 'ch', 'j' and 'jz' will be difficult at this age (sh = shoe, ch = chocolate, j = jam and jz found in television). You will hear 'shop' as 'sop', 'chip' as 'tyip' and 'jelly' as 'delly'.
- 'R' will be articulated as 'w', so 'rabbit' becomes 'wabbit'.
- 'L' is likely to be articulated as 'y', so 'lion' becomes 'yion'.
- Your child will definitely not be able to say 'z', 'th' and 'v', so 'zoo' becomes 'soo' or 'doo', 'three' becomes 'free' and 'van' is 'ban' or 'fan'.
- At two years, a child will regularly leave the final sound off a word (so, 'bu' for 'bus' or 'u' for 'up', for instance), while at two and a half years, a middle or final consonant might be inserted, but it will

often be incorrect (so, 'but' for 'bus' or 'ub' for 'up'). If the target sound has been achieved at the start of the word, then it is only a matter of time until that sound appears in the middle and the end of the word.

- You will also hear many muddled words, such as 'hopital' for 'hospital', 'aminal' for 'animal', 'elemy' for 'Emily' or 'diccifult' for 'difficult' – all normal!
- If you have any concerns about any of the above, below are some Small Talk Time games that aim to tackle each common issue.

Small Talk Time **Let's sort the speech sounds**

Young children learn words as a whole and are not generally aware that a word is made up of a sequence of separate sounds. It's only if a child has pronunciation difficulties that we have to break down the word into each component to make it easier for her to become aware of the sounds. This has to be done through firstly discriminating between the target sound and the articulated sound, and then rebuilding the target sound into the word by articulating the single sound, then saying a sound with a vowel, then that sound in a word.

By focusing on one target consonant speech sound at a time, her speech sounds will improve. Let her take her time and learn slowly, and keep practising the target sound, even after she has learned to say it, so she can fine-tune her new speech sound into a word.

The kit

Invest in a set of picture sound cards that represent a whole range of sounds. (There are many varieties – Jolly Phonics is probably the most well known.) These are sets of cards, each with a picture and possibly a letter on it. The picture is usually something that represents the sound (for instance, a snake for an 's' sound or a baby sleeping for the 'sh' sound). Use these cards to encourage your child to say the sounds she finds tricky. Remember – if the letter is written on the card, always use the sound and not the letter name (so for the letter 's' you would say 'ssssss', not 'es').

Stage 1: Listening to the difference in sounds

Your child needs to be able to distinguish between the target sound and the incorrect sound. For example, if she says 'dun' for 'sun', you'll use pictures that represent 's' and 'd' to check that she can hear the difference between the two sounds. You will say those sounds randomly and encourage her to point to the corresponding sound card (she should manage this from a selection of four or five soundscards at about two-and-a-half years, maybe earlier). You could vary this activity by encouraging your child to stick a sticker on the correct sound card or throw a beanbag onto it.

You have now established whether or not your child can discriminate between the incorrect and target sounds. She cannot move on to the next stage until she can. Once you know your child can make the distinction, help her to cement this understanding. For instance, in the 's' example above, in which the child replaces an 's' sound with a 'd' sound, you could emphasize the fact that the 's' sound is a long sound and the 'd' sound is a short sound.

If your child is unable to discriminate between the sounds, have her hearing assessed – if she can't hear sounds, she certainly won't say them. If her hearing has been checked, play the listening games listed on page 96 in chapter five to help her improve her listening skills.

Totally immerse your child in the sounds she is finding tricky. This is known as auditory bombardment and involves saying the target sound almost continuously during everyday experiences to help the child to hear it. So, using our 'sun' example, you'd find as many opportunities as possible to say 'sss'. So if you're threading beads, say 'sss' as the beads are whizzing down the string; say 'sss' when you are sizzling sausages on the stove; 'sss' when a baddy comes on TV; and 'sss' when wiping the table as you make a snake shape with the cloth.

Some sounds are particularly hard, such as 'k' or 'c'. When this is the case, it is very important not to put pressure on your child to say the sound. Instead, play a range of listening games to let her hear the sound while you say it – over and over again, until you're blue in the face!

Stage 2: Producing the single sound

In this stage you help your child to practise saying the target sound on its own – using our example, it would be the 's' sound. This will be very easy for some children, but others will need lots of adult help before they can do it (see pages 250–57 for tips).

You could try to:

- draw the sound and the picture that represents it
- make a play-dough model of an object associated with the sound 's', for example a snake or a snail
- say 's' as you post the 's' sound card in a home-made posting box
- place a number of 's' sound cards against skittles and knock them down
- use the 's' sound cards as stepping stones and say them out loud
- play I Spy . . . choose anything beginning with 's'

Stage 3: Blending the target sound with a vowel to make a 'silly' word

This is the pre-real-word stage. So you might try blending 's-oo'/'s-ee'/'s-ah'. This is all done using picture sound cards to represent the consonant and the vowel sounds, e.g a snake for 'sss' and a mouse for 'ee', or a ghost for 'oo'. I usually place the consonant sound card next to the vowel card and blend them – 's' and 'ooo' (snake + ghost sound cards) make 'sooo'. The aim is to get the two sounds blending smoothly but, to begin with, there might be a gap between the target sound and the vowel – this is ok.

You could also try stacking vowel cards next to skittles and asking your little one to throw the ball at them. Whichever skittle she knocks down, take the vowel picture and match it to the tricky consonant – I place the consonant next to the right side of my mouth and the vowel next to the left and move my head from right to left as I say the sounds 'sss' and 'ooo' so that the child is directed to look at the pictures and can see how my mouth moves at the same time.

At this age, children enjoy playing with language and words, for example, whispering and copying varying intonation patterns, so you could find a puppet and make it say all of these rather random words as you blend the target consonant sound with a vowel.

Stage 4: Saying really short words!

When a child is able to blend the consonant and the vowel sound together really smoothly (as in Stage 3), she is ready to try short words. Use pictures of objects that begin with the target sound (following our 's' example, this could be sea, sock, sun, sand, Sam and sad). Play the games below to practise saying these short words. Avoid words that have a two-consonant blend at the beginning, such as spider, slide, swim and star, as these are much harder to say than words in which there is a consonant followed by a vowel. Always remember to reward your child's efforts and model the word correctly if she says it wrong.

Go around the house and collect objects that begin with your sound. Put them into a sound sack (see page 95) as you encourage your child to say the words.

- Make two identical sets of picture cards using two identical cata-logues. Pick out the cards showing objects beginning with your target letter. You could play a pairing game or Snap.
- Play the the Tray Game game, in which , you have a number of objects or pictures of objects starting with the target sound on a

tray, then you cover them and take one away. Your child has to remember which object or picture has been removed and try to say the word.

- Make a slide show of pictures starting with a particular sound using Google Images and go through them with your child using your laptop or iPad.
- Write a list of foods starting with the target sound and go shopping for them together. Working with the 's' example, you could look for sausages, steak, salami, cereal (think first *sound*, not first letter), swede, satsuma, celery, sandwich, salad and squash.
- Hide 's' pictures around the room and ask your child to find them and encourage all of your child's efforts to say the words as she identifies the pictures she has found.
- You can also tweak games from your toy cupboard to suit your purpose. There's a great board game called Leap Frogs (available from the Early Learning Centre) in which a frog jumps on a trampoline, and you could then make it land on one of your previously made picture cards. Or there's Springy Spiders where spiders dangle from a springy piece of elastic and bounce on a bug that has a piece of Velcro on it (you can also buy this from the Early Learning Centre) and you can paper clip your picture cards to the bottom of the bug or try a shark attack, where you press each tooth down when you say a word, waiting for it to bite your finger.
- Finishing a word or phrase in a storybook works really well, too. Go the library or just raid your own books to find stories with characters whose names start with the target letter. So, for our 's' example, *Where's Spot?* would work well, as would *Fireman Sam*.
- Make a scrapbook of pictures that begin with the target sound – 'My "s" book' – using pictures from magazines and catalogues. Or choose a range of sounds and have a page for 's', a page for 'd' and so on.

If your toddler is struggling with a word, say it with her and emphasize the target sound – 'ssssock'. Don't get her to try too many times if it's really difficult for her – it creates a real sensse of negativity. In such a case, it's useful to go back to Stage 3.

Stage 5: Short phrases

When your child is able to say short words, we move on to putting the words into a short phrase (it's better when the word starting with the target letter is the second word in the sentence as this is representative of how the target word would appear in a longer sentence, i.e. next to another sound. So, with the 's' example, you could try phrases such as 'big sun', 'blue sock' and 'red saw'.

You could draw a number of socks on a page, colour each one in a different colour, then practise saying 'blue sock', 'red sock' and so on. This is more difficult than it sounds and your toddler will often need help to know when she needs to say the target sound at the beginning of the second word. Sometimes, a child will say the target letter at the beginning of both words (so, using the 's' example, 'sssblue sssock'). If this happens, encourage her to listen carefully to establish which of the words starts with the snake noise, and ask, 'Does "blue" start with "s"? No, it starts with "b". Let's try again. B-lue sssock.' (I often use the snake sign to visually prompt the child into saying 's' in the correct place.)

Stage 6: Putting the target word in a sentence

When a child is able to use short phrases with target words, encourage her to then think of a sentence to use the word in, for example, 'The sun is in the sky.'

- This can be done using storybooks, particularly if they revolve around a character whose name begins with the target letter (so, working with the 's' example, Fireman Sam) or around a subject that starts with the target letter (so, for 's', it could be a story about swimming, sun, sea and sand or school).

- When you go out, look out for things that begin with the target letter and talk about them (for instance, 'Let's tell Daddy what that naughty seagull did').

- Use the target letter in general conversation, too – this can be difficult because it's hard for children when they are trying so hard to tell you something and are in a rush to remember to use that blasted 's' word. Remember that the words that have been spoken incorrectly for the longest time (the earliest and possibly most frequently occurring words) will be the last to change – old habits die hard. My advice is tell your child, 'From now until we get to the shop (no more than five minutes) we're going to try really hard to say the "s" sound.'

- You can also ensure that a high-frequency word, such as 'sock', is always spoken correctly, so correct your child every time. If this works, focus on another three or four words starting with that sound. If one word is consistently spoken correctly, others will also slip into place. Your child should be able to say this word correctly within a sentence before you move on to the next stage.

- Get your child to try tongue-twisters to develop speech sounds at a sentence length. My favourites include:

    Red lorry, yellow lorry

    Cooks cook cupcakes quickly

    Flora's freshly fried flying fish

    Purple paper people

    She sells sea shells on the seashore

    I scream, you scream, we all scream for ice cream!

Peter Piper picked a peck of pickled peppers,
If Peter Piper picked a peck of pickled peppers,
Where's the peck of pickled peppers Peter Piper picked?

I thought a thought.
But the thought I thought wasn't the thought I thought I thought.
If the thought I thought I thought had been the thought I thought,
I wouldn't have thought so.

I saw a saw that could out-saw any other saw I ever saw.

Stage 7: Using the sound in other places or in different positions within words

When your toddler has mastered the above stages and can say the target sound at the beginning of the word, it's more than likely that, given a bit of time, the sound will be spoken correctly across all positions in a word. If this doesn't happen, you need to go back to Stage 3 and work up to Stage 7 again, putting the target sound at the end of a word, or within a phrase, as in Stage 5.

Stage 8: Blending two consonants together

Blends are difficult to articulate and may need a lot of practice. Generally, we do not worry about whether a child can say blends until they reach four and a half or five years of age.

You will need some new pictures of words that begin with your target consonant sound blended with another consonant. So, working with the 's' example, these will be 'sl', 'st', 'sm', 'sn', 'sw' and 'sk'. Make each blend the new target sound and start back at Stage 2, getting your child to say the blend on its own, and progress from there.

Points to remember

If your child is not saying the sound correctly after two or possibly three goes (you know your child's limits better than I do), keep praising her and back off (this is the case from Stage 2 onwards). After this number of attempts, she is probably not ready to say the sound or word correctly.

- In general conversation, again, allow your child two or three attempts and then give up as, after this many attempts, you are unlikely to understand the word she is attempting to say. Try to take the pressure off by encouraging her to show you or somehow give you a clue. If it becomes too frustrating for her, distract her by changing the subject completely (for instance, 'Did I tell you I saw Bob the Builder in Oxford today?').
- Don't correct a child all the time – it's too intense and your child will get annoyed and may not want to play with you anymore. Choose a five-minute slot in your day to practise or choose one single word that you are going to focus on.
- Always keep in mind that your child is doing her best, not being lazy (I hear this complaint *a lot*). As a speech therapist I know that children always communicate to the best of their ability at that particular time – if a child could do it better, they would.

If you're struggling, contact your local speech therapist.

MASTERING TALKING AND PLAYING – AT THE SAME TIME!

By three years, your child will be able to play and talk at the same time, for example, by giving voices to the dolls she's playing with. She'll begin to play in groups with other children, sharing toys and taking turns.

She will also be able to focus on what you say at the same time as she plays, so she won't have to stop what she is doing in order to listen to what you are saying. (The inability to do this is the reason why your child sometimes appears to completely ignore you!)

OTHER ISSUES THAT MAY ARISE DURING THIS TIME

How to react when children say the wrong thing in public

The other day, my friend Jane was walking home with her toddler, Grace, nearly three, and a man walked past them. Grace said very clearly, 'Mummy, that was a dirty old man, wasn't it?' He heard and turned around and said something. Jane was mortified and also concerned about where this phrase may have come from. Hopefully, it was just because the man's trousers were a bit muddy and Grace obviously had no idea that what she was saying had another meaning.

So, what can you do in these situations? Apart from growing a very thick skin – and a good line in apologies – I would say that it's just a case of accepting that at this age your child has no inhibitions and hasn't yet become au fait with our politically correct culture. For now, all you can do is say, 'We mustn't say that, because you might make that man sad.' And if you get asked a series of 'why' questions about it, answer as best you can, then try to change the subject!

My child's speech has regressed since we had another child – what can I do?

Alison has a 24-month-old daughter and a five-month-old son. Until her son was born, her daughter was learning new words all the time, but after his arrival it seemed that she went back to baby talk. Alison came to see me at my drop-in clinic because she was concerned and wanted to know what she could do get her daughter's speech back up to speed.

This is very common when a new baby arrives and the parents' attention is suddenly divided. In toddlers and pre-school children (under five), the resulting 'jealousy' may be exhibited by speech regression, and attention-grabbing 'watch me' moments during potty-training or play.

Your toddler is likely to experience a temporary regression of her development in response to the stress of the change in her family.

If you think of development as a set of uneven stairs that children climb as they add on new skills, most children progress forwards in a predictable sequence. But it's possible to take a step backwards as well, usually when stressed.

Try not to worry too much. The best approach is to not become angry or frustrated with your child, but to reward her for using her language skills and give her praise as the older sister. Time spent around her peers at a playgroup will help model more appropriate language skills, but be careful not to rock the boat again by taking her away from the family. Try to spend some one-to-one time with her every day so that she feels special. It will be difficult to divide your time equally, so don't try, or you will feel added pressure and strain, which your children will pick up on.

EARLY LANGUAGE TESTING

When educational psychologist Jean Gross left her two-year tenure as the government's communications advisor in January 2012, she published a report saying that language checks on two-year-olds should become routine. She revealed that children with poor speech at two are 'doomed to a lifetime of failure unless they receive help'.

Testing them in school is too late as children who are inarticulate at five have little chance of catching up with their peers. They are twice as likely to be unemployed in their thirties, and at greater risk of ending up in prison.[1]

'Recent research showed children's language at two predicted how ready they would be for school,' she said. 'By that age, children are on the path to success or failure at school. Their path is set if this isn't picked up early.'

Honestly, what a way to scare you off at the end of a chapter! The good news is that if problems are recognized and treated early, most children tend to improve quite quickly. Just remember to seek help if you ever feel concerned.

SPEECH AND LANGUAGE DEVELOPMENT MILESTONES: 24–36 MONTHS

Children develop skills at different rates but, by three years of age, usually a child will:

- listen to and remember simple stories with pictures.
- understand longer instructions, such as 'Make Teddy jump' or 'Where's Mummy's coat?'
- understand simple 'who', 'what' and 'where' questions.
- use up to 300 words.
- put four or five words together to make short sentences, such as 'Want more red juice' or 'He took my ball'.
- ask lots of questions – she will want to find out the names of things and learn new words.
- use verbs (action words, such as 'run' and 'fall') as well as nouns (naming words).
- start to use simple plurals by adding 's', for example 'shoes' or 'cars'.
- use a wider range of speech sounds. However, many children will shorten longer words, such as saying 'nana' instead of 'banana'. She may also have difficulty where lots of sounds happen together in a word, e.g. she may say 'pider' instead of 'spider'.
- often have problems saying more difficult sounds, like 'sh', 'ch', 'th' and 'r'. However, people who know her can mostly understand her.
- now play more with other children and share things.
- sometimes sound as if she is stammering or stuttering (stuttering is the American term for stammering). She is usually trying to share her ideas before her language skills are ready. This is perfectly normal. Just show you are listening and allow plenty of time for your child to speak.*

---

* These milestones have been provided by the website www.talkingpoint.org.uk and are reproduced with kind permission.

CHAPTER NINE

Complete Sentences (36–48 months)

By now you'll notice that your three to four-year-old loves to talk. It was probably only 18 months or so ago that you wondered when you'd ever hear your child's needs and wants being spoken aloud and now you probably don't ever get a minute's peace, having to explain everything you do and continuously answer why you're doing it! Think how much your child has changed in such a short time – it's quite an incredible achievement.

But, as usual, with a new phase of development comes new challenges. Between the ages of three and four, most children will start talking in longer sentences, use grammar correctly and begin to master our many irregular patterns. They'll become much more eloquent when it comes to expressing their feelings and emotions, and will begin to develop stronger friendships with their peers.

This is also the year when you will think about which primary school your child will go to, so in this chapter we'll look at gearing up your child's language skills in preparation for this momentous step. You'll encourage your child to chat confidently, to listen to and follow complex instructions, and you'll be scrutinizing his phonology (speech sound) skills to check that he can be understood in preparation for learning to read and write.

With this amazing expansion of language comes a child who thinks more deeply and will tell the most compelling stories about his world and how he views it. And, to top this all off, there'll be a sense of humour eruption! I can't wait – let's get started!

EXPANDING SENTENCES AND TELLING STORIES

I'm sure by now you won't have to encourage your child to chat and talk, but remember to stay one step ahead of him – help him to connect his thought to word, talk to him about his day and expand his vocabulary and grammar. Encourage him to talk about everything and anything – to reflect on past and present experiences, plan future events and predict what might happen, anticipate new experiences, use his imagination to create a fantasy land, and speculate about what he may or may not encounter there.

With so much to talk about, you should expect much longer sentences now, of three or more key words, while your child tries to retell stories of his day or describe his innermost thoughts. His sentences should be made up of nouns and verbs, sometimes used in the correct tense, and a range of different concepts, all articulated in good sequential order.

In chapter eight we looked at encouraging your child's emerging narrative skills (see page 212) and here, we'll learn how to expand them further, in line with the wider range of experiences he is enjoying, the storybooks he is thinking about and the vivid imagination he is developing.

Small Talk Time
Expanding sentences and telling stories

- It's quite hard to retell a story, but even harder to make one up, so start with sequencing a story your child has just read from a familiar book – *The Three Little Pigs* is a good story for this purpose because it's very predictable and has a repetitive phrase in it that makes it easier for a child to hook on to. Read it through together, then allow your child to hunt through the house for objects that tie into the story. Using the props you collected, go through the book again, talking about each page and each prop. Then take the book away and encourage your child to retell the story once again without any visual support. This will encourage him to retain the new words and attempt to increase his sentence length as he tries to retell it.

Next, encourage your child to talk about something that has happened during the day, then something that he experienced in the past and then something completely made up – this will be progressively harder for him. If he seems to be struggling, help him by expanding his thoughts and words by prompting him to remember key information and modelling the correct versions of his sentences back, fine-tuning the details, adding new words and concepts and correcting grammar.

Continuously encourage your child to tell stories (see pages 211–14 in chapter eight) and be increasingly more detailed about the people, places and times he includes in his stories.

- I'm a big fan of show-and-tell, which involves children bringing something in to nursery or pre-school to show to the other children and talk about. It can be almost anything – it might be a picture from a newspaper, a feather you found in the park or a stone from your garden under which you found some woodlice! If your child has to take something in for show-and-tell, make sure you practise what he'll say at home using the 'first, then and last' technique (see page 212). If there is no show-and-tell planned, why don't you do a show-and-tell for Daddy or Granny?
- Talk about problems and find different solutions with your child, for instance, 'Mummy has lost her keys, let's think about what we can do . . . phone Daddy, look for them, remember when we last used them, try and pick the lock,' or 'Oh no, we've run out of milk. Let's think about what to do . . .'

- Encourage your child to give you a sort of presentation. For instance, you might say, 'Tell me all that you know about football/Lyn's house/Teletubbies.'
- Look at textless storybooks such as Raymond Briggs' *The Snowman* and encourage your child to tell the story.
- If you usually read a story while sitting in a particular chair, why don't you swap with your child so that he can sit in the storytelling chair.
- Put together some old photographs in a line on the floor and see if, together, you can make up a story.
- Talk about things that happened to you in the past and retell those stories – how lovely it'll be to have a pair of ears to listen to stories from your life. Minnie is always asking Tracey to tell her the story (again!) of when they first got their rescue cat Keith because they had so many mice in their old house.
- Create a storytelling box. Put three or four objects into a box – try an object, a picture of a person and a picture of a place or an object that represents a place (such as a spade for the beach), then add any other random object, such as a key, a piece of pasta, a ball or a clothes peg. Try to get your child to make up a story using the contents of the box as inspiration and props. You go first to model the idea for him.
- Buy a photo album from a charity shop and fill it with things you like to talk about – a postcard, pictures of dogs or dinosaurs, the foil wrapper from an Easter egg, a bus ticket, a leaf . . . You could make another one to fill while on holiday or fill one with pictures involving your child's favourite theme (perhaps Transformers or whales and dolphins, for example).
- Encourage your child to tell stories using puppets (puppets can be quite expensive, so why not take the stuffing out of an old cuddly toy and use it as a puppet?). Teddy could entertain his audience with stories about his visit to the shops, the park or the swimming pool.

Is my child turning into a liar? The make-believe boom

Children often start telling 'lies' at about three years old, when they discover that their parents cannot read their minds and that they can cover up the truth (for example, 'Did you just eat Mummy's Easter egg?' 'No', says little Sophie, with a chocolate-covered mouth).

And it's not just when they've done something wrong and they don't want to admit it. When my niece Eleanor was three, she was always making up stories about what had happened during her day or week. When you asked her a question, she told the truth. It was when she ran out of things to say that she carried on with a pack of lies. My brother was getting increasingly nervous that she was turning into a compulsive liar so he asked for my advice.

My response was that Eleanor was definitely not turning into a liar. She just enjoyed the adult attention and responses to the stories of her day and week so, when she got to the end of the real story, she was so keen to carry on that she made up things rather than end this Small Talk Time.

Children at this age and stage are absorbed in fantasy play and imaginary language, and often blur the lines between reality and fantasy when telling a story. The best thing to do is to say, 'I really enjoyed it when you told me about what happened at Creation Station – you are so clever to remember that story. And it was funny when you added that extra bit and pretended that the monkey came – it made me laugh.' Once you give a child permission to be creative in telling pretend stories, you can always remind him of the distinction between truth and tale, and he can continue with the same amount of engaging enthusiasm.

There'll come a time when your cheeky monkey pretends his tales are real. Sometimes, it's just too irresistible for a three-year-old not to exaggerate. You can decide how far you let him go with this, but try not to come down and squash his story too early.

If the lying gets out of hand, you might have to clamp down a bit – try not to worry too much, though, because this *is* a normal stage of language development. Let your child's imagination run riot and his language skills blossom. And don't forget to enjoy the fun – I bet you'll struggle not to laugh at some of the porkie pies!

DEVELOPING GRAMMAR

At the same time as listening to a wonderful drama unfold from the mouth of your chatty child (hopefully the kind Steven Spielberg will want a piece of one day!) you must also try to notice his grasp of grammar.

By three years of age, the start of grammar development should be well under way. A lot of the basics will have been acquired during the two to three-year period, such as the pronouns (I, you, me, he, she, they); some question words; a basic understanding of the past and future tenses and auxillaries 'he *is* running'; prepositions (in, on, under); and possessives ('the dog's bone'). Gosh, he has been busy! But there's still a way to go and between the ages of three and four, your child will:

- learn more prepositions – behind, in front, beside, between (for example, 'It's *between* the two books').
- expand his use of when and why questions (for example, '*Why* are you called "Daddy"?' and '*When* are you going?').
- expand his use of the regular past tense (for example, 'He played outside.') This begins at two and a half to three years.
- learn the irregular past tense (for example, 'She *lost* the ball.')
- learn the future tense (for example, 'She *is going to* ride a horse' or 'She *will* ride a horse') at about three to three and half years
- expand his use of possessives – his, hers, theirs – and object pronouns – him, her, them (for example, 'That's *his* garden, let's go and see *him*.')

A lot of these aspects of grammar we've already discussed (see pages 199–207), but we haven't yet thought about how we encourage our children to talk about the past or the future. Look at the advice in the Small Talk Time below for some ideas.

Small Talk Time **Talking about the past**

- After you and your child have done something, immediately ask him to tell you what happened. For instance, as soon as you've washed his face in the bath, say, 'What happened?', then model the answer 'Mummy washed Jess's face.' Just after your child has painted a picture, ask, 'What happened?' and wait for the answer – 'I painted a picture.' If it is not spoken correctly, model it back correctly.

- Find the flashcards you used to illustrate verbs like running, jumping and eating (see page 201). Show your child a flashcard and say, 'What has happened?' instead of 'What's happening?' Model the correct past tense, for instance, 'The girl jumped,' or 'Mummy danced,' then encourage your child to have a turn.

- Retell your day or a familiar story using the past tense. Also, act out a story and then retell it again using the past tense.

- Watch what your child is doing – yes, it's my Say What You See technique again (see page 17)! When he has just done something, ask, 'What did you kick?', 'What do you play with?' or 'Where did you wash?' and encourage him to answer in a full sentence: 'I kicked the ball,' 'I played with the doll,' or 'I washed my face.'

Small Talk Time **The future tense**

- Again, it's easier for children to learn this tense in the here and now, so use the Say What You See technique. For example, just before you make yourself a drink, as you have a cup held up to the tap, ask your child, 'What is going to happen? Mummy is going to make a drink.' Just before your child picks up his favourite toy, say, 'Stu is going to play with the Lego.' Then ask what he is going to do next. If he uses 'gonna', don't worry – we all say this and it makes our language flow more easily.

- Do some cooking and, before you start, talk about all the stages. For instance, you might say, 'Let's make some lunch – what about beans on toast? What shall we do first? Next? Then? Brilliant, we've got a plan so . . . Ready, steady . . . cook!'

- Sequencing cards can be a good prop for talking about the future tense. I like the 4-Scene Sequencing Cards available from Early Years Resources (see the Resources section on page 301). Start by using two or three cards, then add more. You can look at the pictures and comment about the sequence of what's taking place in them, for instance, 'First she climbs the ladder, then she sits down at the top – what's going to happen next?' Alternatively, make your own sequencing cards by taking photographs, say, of your child going down a slide – the first picture when he's at the top, the next when he's reached the middle and the last when he's at the bottom of the slide. Then ask him to put the cards in the correct order.

- At bedtime, talk about what will happen tomorrow. For instance, 'We've got a big day tomorrow – let's think about what we will do. In the morning, we will buy a birthday present for Zac, then we will come home for some lunch and then we'll go to Zac's party at the swimming pool – yay!'

QUESTION WORDS – UNDERSTANDING WHY CHILDREN SAY 'WHY'

Asking questions is a vital way of obtaining information. Even knowing that a question needs to be asked is quite a step forward for your child – he is acknowledging that he doesn't know something and would like to know about it. A child needs to recognize that there is a gap in his knowledge and that he has the ability to ask for help, seek information or ask for an explanation about something. It's another step in his voyage of discovery – his way of exploring and understanding the world around him.

During the two to three-year phase, your child should have learnt to use the question words 'what', 'who', 'why' and 'where' (see page 191). During this three to four-year phase, he will need to practise these words some more – hence the quick recap, below – and begin to use some new question words such as 'when' and 'how'.

Small Talk Time   Question time!

This Small Talk Time is about encouraging our children to *ask* general questions as well as improving their ability to ask general questions.

- Bring out an object that your child has never seen before and encourage him to talk about it. You could model this by doing a role play with your partner, with one of you asking the other questions about the object, for instance, 'What is that? Where did you find it?'
- Look at holiday photos together and ask questions about them, such as, 'Where did we go?', 'What did we do next?', 'Why were we laughing?' or 'Where was Daddy?'
- Give your child a question to ask someone in another room – like a little messenger! For example, you could say, 'Ask Daddy where you are going today?' or 'Ask Nanny what is in the fridge?' He will enjoy having the job of asking a question and relaying the response.

What?

By the age of three (and often way before), your child should successfully be able to understand what's meant when asked the question

'What's that?' – whether or not he can answer it will depend on the level of his vocabulary.

Previously, I've advised not asking your child too many questions, but in order for him to start using question words correctly, he will have to hear question words being modelled for him. He is older now, so is likely to be able to cope with a few questions. Try the ideas below.

- Talk about what you are eating for dinner. You could say, 'What are you eating? You're eating [point to your child's food to cue him in] . . . potato, chicken and peas.' Encourage him to ask you the question back. This may work particularly well on the telephone – if your child is talking to Grandma, who is eating her breakfast or cooking her lunch or dinner, you can whisper to him, 'What's Grandma having for dinner?' Hopefully, he or she will ask Grandma the question and relay the answer back to you. When the phone is hung up you can ask the question again, 'What was Grandma having for dinner?' and encourage your child to ask Daddy, 'What are we having for dinner?'
- Read books like *The Very Hungry Caterpillar* by Eric Carle or *Handa's Surprise* by Eileen Browne. Both have lots of opportunities for 'what' questions, for instance, 'What did the caterpillar eat next . . . ?'

Why?

The barrage of whys usually commences at any time from about two and a half years of age, but often enters a whole new league of persistence (and irritation!) when your child reaches three. I imagine every parent of children around this age has had a conversation rather like the following . . .

Child: 'Why are you in front?'
Adult: 'Because I'm driving.'

Child: 'Why are you driving?'

Adult: 'Because we are going to nursery.'

Child: 'Why?'

Adult: 'Because we can't walk to nursery, it's too far away.'

Child: 'Why?'

Adult: 'Because we live in Oxford and your nursery is in Kennington.'

Child: 'Why?'

Adult loses the will to live . . .

I know it's tempting to turn the tables and ask, 'Why do you keep asking me why?' But that will be a bit too advanced for your little one at the moment so, for now, you'll have to go with it!

'Why' questions are very often answered with a response beginning 'because', so it's important that your child knows how to answer a 'why' question appropriately, which you can model for him using the ideas below.

- Talk about your day and use the 'why/because' format. For example, you could ask, 'Why is there a plaster on your knee? Because you scratched it.' Then, a few minutes later, act dumb and ask, 'Why *did* we put that plaster on your knee? Oh yes . . . [pause], because . . . [pause] you scratched it.' If your child doesn't reply in the pause, add the word in for him.
- Make some 'why/because' cards – the idea is that they come in pairs to help practise 'why' and 'because' questions and answers. For example, the first picture might be of a baby crying and the second is of a bottle of milk. You ask, 'Why is the baby crying?' and the question, hopefully, prompts the answer shown in the second picture (which starts with 'because . . .') – 'Because he wants his milk.'

If you don't have time to create cards, just show your child a picture from a magazine or a book and ask a 'why' question, for instance, 'Why is the girl's dress dirty?' – 'Because she fell in the mud.'

Who?

'Who' is one of the easier question words as it's answered with people's names or animal names, which children generally learn before object names (there are some exceptions to this, though, such as job titles, which are pretty tricky to remember).

- Talk about who is in your family and who is in a friend's family.
- Describe something, for example, 'I have two long ears and a fluffy tail and I love to jump and I eat carrots,' then ask, 'Who am I?' Encourage your child to then do the same back to you (reverse the roles).
- Talk about characters your child likes from books or TV, then ask questions about them and model answers. For example, you could ask, 'Who drives a red van? Postman Pat,' or 'Who's not in bed? Iggle Piggle's not in bed.'
- Use the board game Guess Who? Flip up all the characters' frames and ask, 'Who has got blue eyes, brown hair and a big nose?' Take turns to do this.
- Read books and ask who questions about the characters. For instance, if reading *Who Sank the Boat* by Pamela Allen, you could keep asking, 'Who sank the boat?' or, with *The Gruffalo* by Julia Donaldson and Axel Scheffler, you could ask, 'Who lives in the wood?' If you're reading *Dear Zoo* by Rod Campbell, ask, 'Who was too grumpy?' and so on.

Where?

At about three years of age or slightly earlier, your child should be able to answer 'where' questions. This important development will allow him to begin to think about places. When retelling a story, you would naturally have the *when* (the time frame), then the *who* (the person/animal/key character), then the *where* (the place) and then the *what* (what happened). A simple example of this is as follows: 'This morning, Auntie May went to the shops and bought an apple.'

- First, ask your child questions to model the question word 'where' in context so he can learn how to ask 'where' questions himself. For instance, you could ask, 'Where does a frog live?', 'Where does a bird live?' or 'Where does Granny live?' Then say, 'Now you ask me?'
- Play Hide and Seek, or Hunt the Thimble and choose such a difficult hiding place so that your child has to ask you, 'Where are you?' or 'Where is it?'.
- The *Where's Wally?* series by Martin Handford is great for practising taking turns to ask the 'where' question.
- Read the book *You Choose* by Pippa Goodhard and Nick Sharratt, which asks questions such as 'Where would you like to go on holiday?' and 'Where would you like to live?' Prompt your child to ask you the same questions, too.
- Go through a book with your child, simplifying the story by asking questions about it. For example, with the book *We're Going on a Bear Hunt* by Michael Rosen and Helen Oxenbury, you could ask, 'Where are the family now?' and encourage him to answer, 'In the grass/mud/cave/river.' Then reverse the roles so he asks you the 'where' question and you have to answer. Other books that are good for this activity are *Peace at Last* by Jill Murphy, *Where's Spot?* By Eric Hill and *The Smartest Giant in Town* by Julia Donaldson and Axel Scheffler.

When?

This question word is much more difficult for a child to grasp because, in order to do so, he needs to understand the concept of time. That's why being able to answer 'when' questions comes much later, at approximately three and a half to four years. Use the tips below to encourage this development.

- Ask 'when' questions and answer them yourself to create a good language model for your child to copy. For example:

  Q: 'When do you need a toothbrush?'
  A: 'When you brush your teeth.'
  Q: 'When do you need a warm coat or a scarf?'
  A: 'In the winter.'
  Q: 'When would you wear these sunglasses?'
  A: 'In the sunshine.'

- Talk about your day and ask your child questions such as, 'When do we have breakfast? Before or after we brush our teeth?'
- Ask your child, 'When is your birthday?' and answer for him, for instance, 'It's in March.'
- Read books like *Owl Babies* by Martin Waddell and Patrick Benson or *What't the Time Mr Wolf?* by Annie Kubler and ask 'when' questions (and give the answer, too) whenever a time has been referred to, for instance, 'When did Mr Wolf get up? At 7 a.m.'

I FEEL . . . EMOTIONAL CONCEPTS

It's really important that we teach our children the words they need to express their feelings but, of course, at the age of three, they are only just learning what a 'feeling' actually is. And yet, the emotional highs and lows a three-year-old experiences in any ordinary day are likely to be as unpredictable as sailing the Irish Sea.

Even if they can't yet control or understand their emotions, children at this age definitely have strong feelings about wanting a particular book, not wanting to go to bed, not wanting to get dressed and not wanting to turn off Peppa Pig. They get frustrated when they can't reach something that they want to play with, or have to wait for something that they want instantly (milk, for instance!). And, if you tell them after the eighth bedtime story that that is the last one, you risk a full-scale meltdown. No wonder temper tantrums are rife.

Even making choices or decisions can be quite overwhelming for your little one. I get in a flap about petty things such as deciding what to wear in the morning, so imagine how your child feels about this sort of issue.

To make matters even more complicated, toddlers cannot control their impulses, so when you say, 'Don't do that again!', all they want to do is do it again, either to test your boundaries or to see what the consequences are if they do do it again. I often tell parents to be careful with such phrases. When you say, 'Don't run,' all your child might hear is 'run'. Instead, tell him what he *should* do, for example, say 'walk!' This is called positive parenting.

There are ways in which you can help your little one to understand his emotions, and learn to express them in a way that won't involve him turning bright red and kicking and screaming on the floor. Work through my Small Talk Time games below and you will hopefully have a calmer, more contented toddler . . .

Help your child understand his emotions

Feelings are a bit harder to understand and to learn to say than the other concepts we discussed previously (see page 189 in chapter eight). They are not as tangible as prepositions and, therefore, appear a bit later, towards the three-year mark. The following games focus on common emotions for young children: happy/sad, cross/angry and frightened/scared and anxious/worried. Understanding of feelings such as being bored, excited, surprised, and so on comes later.

Always verbalize and label your child's emotions for him. When he is sad, tell him how he is feeling, for instance, 'You are sad because Sarah has gone home but we'll see her again soon.'

Give your child a warning when something he is enjoying is about to end, such as, 'In one minute the toys are finished and it's time for bed.' But even with advanced notice children will usually protest. Explain the feeling your child is having for him by labelling his emotions, for instance, 'You are cross because you had to stop playing with Lightning McQueen.'

Many children cry and shout when they have to leave a playground, for example. This is normal for a child, yet distressing for parents and can often take the shine off a lovely play session. I'd advise mums and dads to put their child's thought to words in such a situation, for example, 'You are cross because we had to go home and I am sad because you kicked me.' Try to remember that your toddler was having fun doing things with you, so don't stay away from playgrounds. They are fun and good places to learn skills such as climbing and running – and, in this phase, exploring emotions!

Remember, on this note, to emphasize the positive feelings that the park inspires, too, for instance, 'Going down the slide made you laugh!' or 'You are so happy on the swing!' When the subject of leaving comes up, you can put a positive spin on that as well by enticing your toddler with something else interesting, for example, 'We are going home to see Daddy and we will be happy when we see Daddy.'

If all else fails, get creative with some storytelling that suits your purpose. I have one friend who has invented a tale about a 'park man' who comes to lock up the park at the end of each day. If Robert is refusing to leave, they simply spot a man in the far distance of the park and say, 'Quick, the park man is coming – we'd better leave before he comes or he'll be cross and we'll be sad.' Little white lies like this can be the easiest way to diffuse a situation without causing a meltdown.

Small Talk Time
Getting to grips with feelings and emotions

Try the following ideas to encourage your child to grasp emotional concepts:

Act out feelings

Get your child's favourite dollies or teddies and act out different emotions, such as falling over and feeling sad, then getting cross because I wanted a plaster and then getting bored while Mummy looks for a plaster.

Pull faces

Pull faces that represent a particular emotion in the mirror, saying, for instance, 'Let's do a worried face! Now an angry face!' There are some lovely facial expression books available that will help with this – try *Funny Face* by Nicola Smee, which I think is great.

Seek out examples

When you read books and watch TV with your child, explain and describe how people are feeling. For example, you might say, 'Oh dear, Postman Pat has lost his parcel and he's sad,' and 'Woody is frightened because Buzz thinks he can fly and he might hurt himself,' or 'Thomas is surprised because the signal has fallen.'

FEELINGS – BOYS ARE DIFFERENT TO GIRLS

In his bestselling book, *Raising Boys*, author Steve Biddulph, describes how boys are born weeks behind girls in their emotional development, and may be a year behind when they start school. Biddulph argues that, aged three, a little boy may only be able to express happy and cross, while a girl has the words to describe a range of emotions.

This is why I believe that parents should make a real point of describing emotions to boys and playing the Small Talk Time games mentioned here. Talking about their feelings just doesn't come as naturally to boys!

PLAYING WITH LANGUAGE – RHYMING AND JOKING

Now that your child is pretty clever at getting his thoughts and feelings across verbally, it's time to have some real fun! You've had a giggle at his very cute language mistakes, such as, 'Mum, it's soaking hot,' or 'Peel your ears open,' but now he's really able to make you laugh with some attempts at making up silly jokes, songs and rhymes. Rhyming and joking demonstrates that your child understands the intricacies of language at a much higher and more abstract level. Here are some ways to encourage your child to play with language.

Small Talk Time **Playing with words**

Mess around with words in the following ways:

Play word-association games

Some of you may remember Mallet's Mallet, a feature in a children's TV show from the late 1980s called *Wackaday*, hosted by Timmy Mallet. If not, I will explain: he used to play a word-association game in which you mustn't pause when replying and, if you do, you get a bash on the head with a giant foam mallet! Take turns with your child to say words that somehow relate to each other, for example, brick/house/garden or trampoline/jump/hop, until someone can't think of another word to say – at which point you get a bonk on the head.

Talk about language and how it sounds

Mention onomatopoeia to your child. You needn't use the actual word 'onomatopoeia', but talk to him about words that sound like the object they describe, for instance, 'zip', 'splash', 'roar' and 'pop'. Then put them into practice and make the words come alive by zipping a zip (and stretch out the 'zzzzz' sound), making a splash in the water or popping a bubble. Your child will have to think really carefully about this in order to understand the concept.

Try a story rap

Choose a fairytale your child knows, find some rhyming words to do with the narrative and away you go. For example:

> *Once I knew a girl and she had some golden locks*
> *She broke into a house and wore a pretty frock*
> *She ate from some bowls and sat upon some chairs*
> *Then she realized it was a house that belonged to bears!*

Adding a rhyme

Take turns to add a rhyming word to a line or made-up sentence, such as – 'the big fat cat sat on the mat and played with a bat' or 'the friendly frog sat on a log in a bog and met an ugly hog'.

Add on silly rhyming words to basic, everyday objects as a game – your child will probably take great delight in correcting you. So say, 'Can you finish your drinkie winkie?' and your child will probably say, 'No, Mummy, it's not a drinkie winkie, it's a drink!' Or say, 'Can you take off your bib-a-dib-dib?' and you'll be told it's a bib.

Learning idioms

Teach your child some idioms, which he will probably find highly amusing because the phrases are quite odd when taken literally. See what he thinks of the following:

> *Don't cry over spilt milk*
>
> *Many hands make light work*
>
> *Too many cooks spoil the broth*

Pull your socks up

Keep your eyes peeled

Chant rhymes

This rhyme is very popular with most children:

Oh dear, what can the matter be?
Two old ladies stuck in the lavatory
They were there from Monday to Saturday
Nobody knew they were there!

Also try tongue-twisters (see page 222–3), and make some up yourself.

Joking around

One of the best things you can do to develop your child's sense of humour is to use your own. Make jokes, tell funny stories, laugh out loud, laugh at little catastrophes – children love a bit of drama, and tend to respond well to outbursts along the lines of, 'Oh dear, I've chipped Daddy's favourite mug,' or 'Crash, bang, whoops! I've dropped all the baking trays on the floor!'

Having a sense of humour helps children on an emotional and social level, and research shows that people who laugh a lot are healthier because they're less likely to be down in the dumps, which makes them more resistant to illness. And the list goes on – people who laugh more experience less stress, have lower heart rates, pulses, and blood pressure, and have better digestion. Laughter may even help humans better endure pain! So, what can we expect our little ones to laugh at?

At three years of age, your child is likely to have a slapstick sense of humour (he'll love seeing a man with a bucket on his head, a fish wearing sunglasses or a dog that says 'meow') and won't yet be ready to enjoy what we would consider to be a 'real' joke.

But what children of this age laugh at the most is toilet humour. Who would have thought bodily functions could be so funny? You have been warned – during this period, an entourage of 'pooey', 'stinky', 'wee-wee' and 'fart'-type words will appear . . .

Gently discourage bathroom humour, or at least try not to participate too enthusiastically (I find that it's the dads who often seem to enjoy it more than the children!). The problem is that, once your child works out it's funny, he won't realize that it's not appropriate in certain circumstances – at Great-Aunt Nora's 90th birthday party or on the pre-school visit, for example. But allow him to laugh a bit – it's harmless and, honestly, my husband who's 38 at the time of writing still thinks a good 'poop story' is hilarious – he assures me it can lighten anyone's mood!

Small Talk Time **Playing the joker**

- Encourage your child to find things funny and ensure you laugh heartily at his attempts at humour, too, whether it's drawing 'funny' pictures or telling 'funny' jokes. Praise him for trying to be funny and be open to surprise – the first time your child makes you laugh is one of life's great pleasures.

- Make humour a part of your day-to-day interactions. Encourage your child to share funny observations or reactions, even when you're around other adults.

- Enjoy funny books and websites, TV programmes and films together. Most children of this age find *Mr Bean* hilarious, enjoy the TV programme *You've Been Framed* and love watching Daddy Pig from the TV programme *Peppa Pig* fall into the duck pond or walk into trees. They'll often look to you first to see if they are right that it's funny, so if you giggle, they will inevitably follow suit.

- Teach your child some jokes and encourage him to take centre stage and be a comedian. Here are some simple jokes to help:

Why did the banana go to the doctor?
Because he wasn't peeling well!

What do you call a three-legged donkey?
Wonkey!

Knock, knock
Who's there?
Lettuce
Lettuce who?
Lettuce in, it's cold out here!

Knock, knock
Who's there?
Boo
Boo, who?
It's ok, you don't have to cry

What did the policeman say to his tummy?
You're under a vest!

CASE STUDY: MINNIE'S FIRST JOKES

When my co-writer's daughter Minnie was about two and a half, Tracey invited my husband, Jess and me over for a roast lunch. Minnie started showing off her counting, trying to get up to ten, and then, out of the blue, created her own joke, saying, 'One, two, three . . . chicken!' before collapsing in hysterical giggles. We laughed with her and the more we all laughed, the more encouraged she was to come up with more 'jokes', for instance, 'One, two, three . . . cup!', 'One, two, three . . . potato!' and 'One, two, three . . . dog!'. This went for on at least ten minutes and we were all weeping with laughter by the end. It was a real joy to witness a toddler begin to experiment with her sense of humour.

OTHER ISSUES THAT MAY ARISE DURING THIS TIME

Speech sound mistakes

By this age you should be able to see which sounds your child is having difficulty with. If you can't, use a simple picture book and ask him to label simple pictures. Write down how he says the words and see if there's a pattern.

Once you've established which speech sounds your child is struggling to say, try the following tricks to help him say that sound. Below, I've listed the sounds that most commonly cause problems and suggested games that may help. It's a good idea to practise these exercises in the mirror, so that your child can see what his mouth is doing. Remember to encourage him, even if he doesn't say the correct sound. Don't let it become a negative experience for him – it's supposed to be fun!

Small Talk Time **Finessing speech sounds**

Firstly, have a quick recap of the speech sound section in chapter eight (see pages 214–21) to refresh your memory, then look at the list of commonly mispronounced sounds, below, to find your child's specific speech sound error, and follow the advice given.

'P'

'P' is often replaced with 'b' or 'd' – for instance, 'pig' is spoken as 'big' or 'dig', or it may simply become 'ig'. At my clinic, I usually take a rectangular piece of paper and cut strips up the long side, not cutting the strips off completely. Hold the strips next to your mouth and say 'p, p, p' – you will notice that the paper 'jumps'. Then hold it by your child's mouth and encourage him to say 'p, p, p'. The jumping paper will motivate him to want to say the sound again. Once he can say 'p', keep the paper by his mouth and say other words that start with 'p' (for instance, 'paper', 'pea', 'purse' and 'Peppa Pig'). You could then encourage him to use minimal pairs, which are pairs of rhyming words using the incorrect and the target sound (for example, 'pea'/'bee', 'Po' [Teletubby]/'bow'/'dough' or 'pig'/'dig').

'B'

This is a lip sound and very similar to 'p' and 'm'. Try using a straw to drink, which can improve all three of these sounds because this exercises the lips into a closed position. 'B' is often replaced with 'd', so encourage the 'b' sound on it's own, then use minimal pairs work (see above, under 'P') to encourage your child to hear the difference between the rhyming words (examples are 'bug'/'dug' and 'boo'/'do').

'M'

I often practise this with the help of some lip salve. Rub it on your child's lips and encourage him to rub his lips together and then say 'mmm'. Next, try replacing the 'brum' noise of a motorbike with 'mmm', and eating chocolate, saying 'mmm' everytime a piece goes in his mouth (I should be saying 'delicious apple' but, honestly, chocolate will work better). Once he has got the sound right, try again and encourage him to say words beginning with 'm' (for instance, 'mum', 'moo' and 'milk').

'K'/'c'/'g'

Open your mouth, put your finger on your tongue so that your tongue tip stays in the base of your mouth and say 'k, k, k'. The same technique applies for 'g'. These sounds are often replaced with 't' and 'd', for instance, 'car' becomes 'tar', 'gate' is said as 'date' and 'leg' becomes 'led'. You could also try minimal pairs (see above, under 'P') (for example, 'Kate'/'gate' and 'key'/'tea'). If the above doesn't work, try to make the angry goose noise (that rather disgusting noise when you're trying to clear phlegm from your throat), which achieves closure of the back of the tongue against the roof of the mouth to make the sound. This should be in place by three years.

'Qu'/'x'

'Qu' (as in 'queen') is a blend of the consonants 'k' and 'w', and 'x' (as in 'exciting') is a 'k' and 's' sound blended together. So these sounds are blends, which are difficult to say before the age of five years. In order to say both of these sounds, a child would need to be able to say 'k' first, then add the second consonant.

'F'

The 'f' sound is often replaced with a 'b' sound, so 'four' becomes 'bour'. To encourage your child to make this sound correctly, ask him to bite his bottom lip and blow out – like a rabbit's teeth. In fact, as a rabbit has no noise, I've taught my daughter to say 'ff ff' when I say 'What does a rabbit say?' in preparation for the start of her trying to say 'f' words when she is about two and a half to three years. You could also try placing a piece of breakfast cereal on your child's bottom lip and encouraging him to remove it with his top teeth. This will encourage him to move his mouth into the correct mouth shape.

'V'

This is a tricky sound – you might hear 'DVD' as 'DBD' or 'van' as 'ban'. The 'v' sound comes much later at about four and a half years, so don't worry too much about it now – it's articulated in the same way as the 'f' sound (see above).

'S'

This sound is often mistaken for 't' or 'd', so 'sun' is said as 'dun'. 'S' should be spoken correctly by three and a half years. Also, 's' can be lisped in three different ways:

1. A dentalized lisp, in which the child's tongue pops out between their teeth.

2. A lateral 's' which sounds like the Welsh 'll' sound.
3. A palatal 's'. Say 'y' and feel the middle of the tongue lift up towards the roof of your mouth. Keeping your tongue in that position, say 's' – that's what a palatal 's' sounds like.

Lisps are very common and, at three to four years, we don't worry massively about them so long as the child has an approximation of an 's' sound. A trick that I use to help children find the sound is to encourage them to say 't t t t t t' as fast as they can, so that the sound turns into an 's' sound. Try it. Have a play around with this technique before you introduce it to your child.

If you want to describe to your child how to say 's', say, 'Put your tongue behind your teeth, bite, smile and blow out – "s s s s"'.

Be aware that it is unusual for air to come out of your child's nose when they say 's'. If this happens, hold your child's nose and see what happens. Does a perfect sound come out? If so, you need to go and see an ear, nose and throat specialist because this indicates a problem with the palate and needs further investigation. Otherwise, this speech-sound error is a placement problem and the usual tricks should work.

Use the technique above for each of these lisps mentioned, but you may need some extra guidance for the lateral 's', which is particularly difficult to conquer. I would suggest you see a speech therapist who will try to achieve a good sound in the first session. Depending on this and the motivation of the child, the therapist may tell you to go away until the child himself notices and or wants to change it. You'll have to consider this wisely. If you battle on with a sound that is very difficult to achieve, you will potentially run the risk of causing a lot of angst (rather like forcing a child to play a musical instrument) and making him less cooperative, which could affect your relationship with your child.

'Shh'

This is commonly thought of as a tough sound to master. 'Sh' is often replaced with 'd' in the early stages and then, later on, 's', so 'shoe' becomes 'du' and then 'sue', for example. Close your teeth, push your lips forward in a circle and blow out. Encourage your child to do the same and put his finger by his lips so that his lips can reach for the finger when they are protruded. Once he's got it, go outside and say 'shh' to any noise you hear! 75 per cent of children aged four years should say this sound correctly.

'Ch'

This sound is often replaced with 't' or 'd' and, later, with 'ty' or 'ts', so 'chair' becomes 'dair', 'tyair' or 'tsair'. It is articulated in the same way as the 'sh' sound (see above), so a child must try to achieve a 'sh' sound first. Once he has, encourage him to put a little 't' and 'sh' together. You might need a picture of a dripping tap, to represent 't', and a mummy saying 'shh' to a baby to help achieve this.

Start practising this exercise if a child isn't saying the 'ch' sound correctly by approximately four years.

'J'

The 'j' sound comes as a pair with the 'ch' sound, so once your child has cracked 'ch', 'j' should follow naturally by four and half years.

'L'

A child will usually replace this sound with 'w', so 'lemon' becomes 'wemon', for instance. The easiest way for a child to see the correct position for his tongue is in a mirror, so encourage your child to lift his tongue up onto the ridge behind his top front teeth, then say 'l', as he looks at the shape both his and your mouths are making in the mirror.

Start practising this if a child isn't saying it correctly by approximately four years.

'Th'

This sound will usually be replaced with 'f', so 'three' becomes 'free'. To produce the sound, encourage your child to bite his tongue and blow out – try it yourself. Once he has mastered this, encourage him to say 'thin', 'the', 'thing' and other words beginning with 'th'.

Start practising this exercise if your child isn't saying it correctly by approximately six years. If your child is struggling with this sound now, please don't worry.

'R'

This is quite a difficult sound to explain to a child. Most children replace 'r' with 'w'. The main difference between the two sounds is the position of the tongue. Try it. I usually encourage a child to practise saying the two sounds after each other so he can hear that he is saying 'w' for both sounds. If you hear two 'w' sounds, you will have to teach your child how to say 'r' by telling him to lift his tongue tip up towards the roof of his mouth, then smile and blow out for an 'r' sound and curl his lips into a circle for the 'w' sound. Once this is achieved, tell him to say a vowel and then 'r', for example, 'eeer' or 'aaaar', so he can feel his tongue moving upwards after the vowel. Try this for a couple of days, then try adding the same vowel to the end of the 'word', too, for example, 'eeereee' or 'aaaraa'.

Start practising this exercise if your child isn't saying this sound correctly by approximately six years and, until then, don't worry about it.

Blends

The following consonant blends might be tricky for a child of this age to achieve:

- 's' blends – 'sn', 'sm', 'sl', 'sw', 'sk', 'st', 'squ'
- 'l' blends – 'fl', 'cl', 'sl', 'gl', 'pl', 'bl'
- 'r' blends – 'cr', 'fr', 'dr', 'tr', 'gr', 'br', 'pr'

It's difficult for children to blend two consonant sounds together. Usually, a child will drop one of the sounds or change the blend altogether, so 'snake' becomes 'nake', 'clock' is said as 'cock', 'blue' becomes 'bue', 'train' becomes 'dain' and 'princess' is said as 'bincess'. So you might hear, 'A pider [spider] followed me to the twings [swings] and down the side [slide].'

Before you practise these blends with your child, you must ensure that he is able to say each consonant in the blend individually. So, if your child can say 'f' and 'l' clearly, he's ready to try to say 'flower'. Encourage him to listen to each sound. For instance, you might say, 'Let's say the sounds for train – "tr-ai-n". Can you hear "tr"? It's a "t" and a "r" together. Let's say it: "t" then "r" is "tr tr tr".' Then add the rest of the word –'tr-ain'. Ensure you don't say 'tuh' and 'ruh', because the word 'train' does not sound like 'tuh-ruh-ain'. (See my explanation of page 214 about my daughter Minnie.)

It is always a good idea to practise these as minimal pairs (see page 250, under 'P'), for example, 'peas'/'please', 'gate'/'great' and 'stick'/'tick'.

Start practising these sounds if your child isn't saying them correctly by approximately six years – until then, don't worry about it.

I have missed out 't' and 'd' purposely as it is unusual to not be able to say these sounds. If your child can't say these sounds by the age of three years, I would suggest he needs to see a speech therapist for some guidance. Difficulty saying them is associated with dummy sucking – if this is the case, ditch the dummy as soon as possible.

It might just take a few simple sound games to master these sounds, but very often it takes longer. If this is the case, you will need to go back to the eight-step process in chapter eight (see pages 217–23). Just be patient. I often say to worried parents that there are very, very few seven or eight-year-olds that don't speak clearly – most children have sorted out their speech sound mistakes by this age.

Be aware of the sounds your child can and can't say and try to encourage him in a fun and motivating way, so you don't make him feel self-conscious or negative about the way he speaks. Seek help if you are worried. Generally, speech therapists worry more about language problems than speech-sound problems (this, of course, depends on the severity of the speech-sound error).

CASE STUDY: MY CHILD WON'T TALK AT NURSERY

'My three-and-a-half-year-old daughter Elina has been attending nursery five mornings a week for three months and has not uttered a word to anyone while she is there (even the teaching staff). She went to playgroup (one where I left her) two mornings a week the year before. No speech there either, although I didn't know this until recently – they just thought she was shy. I had no idea about any of this as she speaks normally when she's at home or anywhere other than nursery! As she starts full-time school in a few months, this is now becoming worrying. What can I do?'

This sounds like a fairly classic case of selective mutism. It can be pretty tricky to overcome, unfortunately, so it is important to try to crack it early in Elina's school career, so her parents need to get the right people involved as soon as possible. Below is my advice on how to handle this issue:

- Firstly, take all pressure off the child to talk and tell the nursery staff to do so, too. Saying things like 'You can't have a drink until you say drink' or 'I'll be cross if you don't talk,' won't improve the situation.
- Start by placing a person she will talk to (maybe the key worker – parents are often too emotionally involved with the situation and this can sometimes be noticed by the child) in the setting with her, everyday if possible, even if it is just for a short period of time. If it can't be the key worker, try another sensitive member of staff that Elina seems to respond to.
- Ask the adult to take the child to a quiet area somewhere in the nursery or, ideally, in a separate room attached to the nursery.

Let them play together using a non-verbal game, for example, Connect 4 or Pop-up Pirate, for about ten minutes every day. Don't ask any questions or give any reaction if she speaks. If she whispers, don't encourage her to say it more loudly. Do this every day until she has started to talk.

- Then allow either another member of staff or another child to join in and play games. All play the game together. Once spoken communication is established in the side room with a number of children, encourage Elina to play the same games back in the main nursery, then build up to a group dynamic again.

- If a side room isn't available, allow Elina to whisper to the key worker and then slowly extend the distance away from the talk partner so that Elina can be overheard by others, although she isn't talking to them. Gradually, expand the number of talk partners and others allowed to overhear until she is able to speak freely.

- Sometimes, an inanimate talk partner (such as a teddy or other soft toy) can be used at first, so that Elina is talking in the setting into a soft toy's ear, albeit that the teddy doesn't respond! This would need to be on Elina's agenda and she would probably need to want to speak, or she won't be motivated to break this situation.

- To help motivate her, talk to her about how lovely it will be when she is able to speak at nursery, without pressurizing her. Just put the idea into her head that one day she will be able to speak in nursery and how great that will be. Don't ever talk about how she doesn't talk while she's in earshot.

- If these strategies don't help, an educational psychologist would be a good next step. The true definition of a selective mute is a child who speaks in one setting but not in another. If the child doesn't speak well across the board, this is not selective mutism.

So the problem isn't that a child can't speak, it's that the child won't speak – an educational psychologist can help to try to work out what the root of the problem is.

SPEECH AND LANGUAGE DEVELOPMENT MILESTONES: 36–48 MONTHS

Children develop skills at different rates but, by four years of age, usually a child will:

- listen to longer stories and answer questions about a storybook he has just read.
- understand and often use colour, number and time-related words, for example, 'red car', 'three fingers' and 'yesterday/tomorrow'.
- be able to answer questions about why something has happened (in the past tense).
- use longer sentences and link sentences together.
- describe events that have already happened, for instance, 'We went park.'
- enjoy make-believe play.
- start to like simple jokes.
- ask many questions using words like 'what', 'where' and 'why'.
- still make mistakes with tenses, such as saying 'runned' for 'ran' and 'swimmed' for 'swam'.
- have difficulties with a small number of sounds – for example 'r', 'w', 'l', 'f', 'th', 'sh', 'ch', 'j' and 'dz'.
- start to be able to plan games with others.*

---

* These milestones have been provided by the website www.talkingpoint.org.uk and are reproduced with kind permission.

CHAPTER TEN

· · · · · · · · · · · · ·

Common Parental Concerns

Whether I am seeing patients at my clinic, visiting families through my NHS work, or am off-duty on playdates with my daughter, mums and dads always seem to quiz me about the same issues. Parental hot topics, which often result in me getting a good grilling, are dealing with dummies, how to pick a nursery that promotes good communication, stammering, bilingualism, glue ear, how siblings can impact on speech and how to get the best out of a storybook.

So, in this chapter I'm sharing my expert advice on these testing topics with you . . .

DITCH THE DUMMY

The general rule is that, once a child starts attempting words at about 8 to 12 months, you should start to think about ditching the dummy. So, if your child reaches roughly 18 months and is showing signs of being hooked on her dummy, my advice would be to go the whole hog and take the dummy away completely rather than trying to reduce the number of hours the dummy is used, which is what some parents try at first. At my clinic we find that parents have a good success rate when they tell children to leave their dummy out on their birthday or at Christmas for the fairy or Santa, who will leave them a present in return. Another trick is to visit a young baby and persuade your child to give the dummy to the little one, saying, 'You are so kind, well done, he needs it much more than you.' Every time she asks for it after that, you say again, 'What a kind girl you are, you gave it to baby Toby.'

Dentists agree that dummies have a significant impact on the development of children's teeth. When choosing a dummy, a dentist would suggest, aside from not having one at all, that you go for an orthodontic design, with a hole in the teat, which is supposedly better

CASE STUDY: FOUR-YEAR-OLD DUMMY USER WITH SPEECH PROBLEMS

When a child comes into the clinic I can see immediately by the shape of the mouth if the child uses a dummy. I recall one four-year-old boy who kept the front of his mouth completely still while talking – even his teeth were stunted in growth due to dummy interference. Parents tend to whip out the dummy as they walk into the health centre but I knew instantly what the problem was. To be technical, he was using the back of his mouth to talk, getting into a habit of saying 'k' and 'g' instead of 't' and 'd' ('t' and 'd' are tongue-tip sounds, while 'k' and 'g' are made using the back part of the tongue) and he had a lisp (see page 146). He would say 'key' instead of 'tea' and he would use the Welsh 'll' sound (as in 'Llanelli') instead of 's', so 'sausages' would be spoken as 'llaullagell'. He was beginning to be aware that he didn't sound like his friends and was getting frustrated. It was no surprise to the mother when I told her to ditch the dummy immediately and, within a couple of months, his speech was almost perfect. His mum explained that letting go of the dummy involved a couple of nights of crying but had been a lot easier than she ever expected.

for the teeth. But for speech, they are all equally as restrictive to the movements of the mouth, so neither one nor the other is better.

Through my work, I have met lots of families who use the dummy as a noise dampener or a plug for noisy babies. If your baby is being noisy, under no circumstances be tempted to use a dummy as a gag. If she is intolerably vocal, this might be annoying when you can't hear a conversation or the TV over the din, but it is good news that she is making lovely noises and it's best to encourage her 'speech', not restrict it. Babies from large families or generally noisy environments will babble loudly to compete. So if you have a noisy baby, check whether or not the environment is too loud for her before muffling the sound with a dummy.

PICKING A NURSERY OR CHILDMINDER

One of the (many!) difficult decisions parents are likely to have to make in the early years is choosing a nursery or childminder. You are likely to be fraught with guilt and insecurity about going back to work, and the stress of finding the right person to look after your precious little one while you aren't there, and the right setting for her, is enormous.

Unfortunately, I can't help you make the tricky choice, but having been grilled by lots of friends about what questions to ask and what to look out for in terms of finding a positive speech and communication environment for babies and toddlers, I do have some pointers. Below are my observations and recommendations.

Nurseries

- The most important thing in the early years is for a child is to feel special to many people, but to one person in particular, so that they know that *that* person is *their* special person. Who will your child go to when they need a cuddle or when she's upset if you're not there? Ideally, your child will have a key worker with whom she can form a strong bond in this new environment. By two and a half to three years of age, a child is more sociable and independent and, therefore, has more confidence to be an independent person in a nursery setting.

A friend of mine has a little boy who didn't settle into his nursery at all well, even though it had a glowing reputation. When my friend asked what happened when he cried, the manager said they all took it in turns to look after him. That didn't allow him to build a strong bond with one adult in particular and made settling in more difficult. The nursery told my friend that they waited for a child to find their own key person – but what would happen if every child formed a strong attachment to the same person? This is one of the main ways in which childminders and nurseries differ – a childminder has specific children to look after in her home, so she is automatically the child's key person.

Every nursery, meanwhile, should have a policy on key workers, and you should definitely ask about it. Will your child be handed to, and collected from, the same person every day? Will your child's key person have an opportunity to spend individual time with her every day to make her feel special and to nurture her? Will your child's key person have a chance to think about and discuss your child with you if there is a problem?

- You should ask about the staff-to-child ratio. The government standards differ slightly across authorities but ballpark figures are as follows: the ratio for nought to two-years-olds is 1:3; for two to three-year-olds, it is 1:4; and for three years and older it is 1:8 or 1:13, depending on staff qualifications. So anything better than that is going to be better for your child and her communication skills as she'll have more adult contact.

- I'm not a fan of nurseries that have a baby room and a toddler room, splitting up children of different ages. In terms of boosting speech, it's far better for toddlers and babies to mix, as it creates a more typical family environment. The little ones pick up new words from the older ones, while the older ones learn to tell stories to the younger ones, help them to wash their hands and generally nurture them, giving them an opportunity to use the language they have been exposed to by their parents. This is called a family group, and it tends to work well for both older and younger children.

- Think about how the layout of the nursery works – I'm not keen on large, open-plan nurseries because I suspect a child gets far less adult contact in such rooms and, of course, they need an adult to provide them with a model for language. So look out for cosy areas in which your child can be in close proximity to an adult who can model language and expand her language skills as she plays. A good nursery will also have little adult-free areas. These child-only spaces are designed to encourage confidence at peer level for social and verbal communication.

- I know you should think about the people more than toys, but do look at the resources the nursery has. For instance, have the puzzles got all their pieces? Has the toy kitchen got some food in it and a spoon? This is a good indication of whether the profits of the nursery are coming back to the children or staying with the management.

- When you visit, watch the nursery staff to see how they interact with the children. Ideally, they will be:
  - talking to the children and kneeling down to their level.
  - using simple language, backed up with signs and gestures.
  - supporting the children's play, not taking over or being passive.
  - helping children extend their play by one level (so that, if your child is playing with the trains, a member of staff will bring another element into the game, for instance, by saying something like, 'Toby's come off the track – how can we help him?'
  - trying to find out about your child, her likes and dislikes and what she is motivated by.

- Consider the atmosphere of the nursery – have the staff created a good atmosphere or does it feel clinical? Are they warm and welcoming? If they don't make an effort in this way when they're trying to win your custom, they're certainly not going to when you've walked out of the door.

- The environment should be as visual as possible – there should be lots of artwork by the children up on the walls, pictures on the drawers showing what's inside, and short vocabulary suggestions for the staff to say and repeat visible in each area of the nursery (for instance, 'splash'/'pour'/'wash' by the water tray). The story and song time should also be visually supported with props (for example, a story sack [see page 213] with the food that the Very Hungry Caterpillar eats and a selection of objects that represent songs, such as a tractor for singing 'Bouncing Up and Down on the Big Red Tractor').

- Ask the staff about the outside-play activities they engage the children in. Ideally, some of these should revolve around learning as well as playing. This is referred to as play-based learning. So they might have pets to look after, play sorting games in paddling pools where they have to sort items that float or items that don't; on a hot day they might have to put 'suncream' (usually toothpaste) on dollies; they might do nature hunts, visit a mobile library, and so on. My sister-in-law runs a nursery called Free Rangers where they run a forest school within the nursery, so that, every day, the children have outdoor play-based learning rather than just a breath of fresh air.

- At mealtimes, do the staff eat with the children? This provides a good model for fussy eaters and a staff member will be able to encourage communication, as mealtimes are one of the most social times of the day.

- How and what do they communicate to you about? Do they provide daily summaries in a nursery book – ideally filled in by your child's key person – in which, occasionally, some sentences are written in red to show what the next developmental step would be?

Childminders

The difference between a childminder and a nursery is that a child has a closer contact with, and feels special to, one – and only one – person. And this is one of the reasons people tend to choose nurseries – they cannot stand the thought of their child becoming too close to another adult. Jess loves our childminder and rather than feeling jealous about how attached she is to Lyn, I feel thankful and relived that I have chosen the best childminder I could have for her.

When looking for a good childminder, many of the factors that should inform your choice of nursery (see above) also apply, along with the further tips I give below:

- One thing to be careful about is the number of school and nursery pick-ups and drop-offs your childminder has to do. Will your child be spending much of her day in a car or outside a school gate?
- Find out if the childminder will take your child to a local toddler group. If so, will she be communicating with her while they are there? A work colleague of mine collected her son for a doctor's appointment from a toddler group that the childminder took him to most days. She said that many of the childminders were chatting on their mobile phones while the children were playing, so you should ask where your child will be going and find out the reputation of that particular place, and visit it, too.

I think that I've covered the basics here. Just don't forget the most important thing – trust your instincts. If you want to feel confident you've made the right choice for you and your toddler, look at many different nurseries and childminders in your area with my pointers in mind and one is bound to stand out to you as being the best fit.

STAMMERING

Learning to talk, like learning to walk, is never a completely smooth journey, and does not happen overnight. Young children often stop, pause, start again and stumble over words when they are learning to talk. Not even adults have perfectly smooth speech. We often find ourselves getting stuck with our words.

Between the ages of two and five years, it is normal for a child to repeat words and phrases, and to hesitate with 'umms' and 'errrs' when she is trying to figure out what she wants to say. These are known as word-finding difficulties.

However, about 5 in every 100 children stammer for a time when learning to talk. They experience sound or word repetitions, for example, 'sh sh sh shop' (known as part or whole-word repetition), they might stretch out a sound, for instance, 'shhhhhop' (called elongation), or they might try to say a word but nothing comes out of their mouth (known as a block). In approximately 75 per cent of these cases, the stammer will resolve, but it should always be handled very carefully, especially if the stammer has been present for longer than six months or if there is a family history of stammering.

Many children find it easier to talk fluently as they get older. Others continue to find talking difficult, often getting stuck and feeling as if they can't talk properly. Whatever the situation, I would advise that it is always better to get them some help.

What is stammering?

A child is thought to be stammering when she:

- puts extra effort into saying words.
- talks in a tense or jerky style.
- has trouble getting started, so no sound comes out.
- stretches out words, for instance, 'I want a sssstory.'

267

- repeats the first sound of a word or part of a word, for example, 'm.. m.. mummy' or 'mum mum mum mummy'.
- stops and gives up trying to speak.

How is fluency affected?

Stammering may come and go. The child's speech may be fluent for several days or weeks, then the speaking may become difficult again. Fluency can be affected by:

- an increase in complexity of language (it's as if the child's brain is thinking too quickly for her mouth).
- growth spurts, which lead to clumsy movements in general, then the body tends to readjust and right itself.
- difficult or unusual situations at home or at nursery; busy times when turn-taking in talking; exciting or rushed moments.
- talking to different and new people – adults or children, family or strangers.
- how the child is feeling – unwell, tired, anxious, excited or confident.

What can help stammering?

If your child has a stammer, consult a speech and language therapist as soon as possible. The therapist is likely to see your child as soon as possible and give you the following advice:

- Slow down your own rate of speech to make it easier for your child to follow what you are saying, and help her to feel less rushed. She will, hopefully, copy you and slow down, too. This can be more helpful and less intrusive than telling her to 'slow down', 'start again' or 'take a deep breath'.
- Use the same sort of sentences your child does – keep them short and simple.

- It may help to pause for one second before you answer or ask a question. This is for two reasons – firstly, taking a pause will slow down the rate of the conversation and, secondly, your child might copy you and learn to take a pause before she answers a question, giving her a split second of extra thinking time to put her thoughts together and form a sentence.
- Show your child you are interested in *what she is talking about* rather than *how she is talking*. Get down to her level and look at her so that she knows you are interested.
- Reduce the number of questions you ask – conversation should not be an interrogation!
- Have a special Small Talk Time everyday – aim for one ten-minute slot per day, when your child is not talking over others and the attention is wholly on her. Spend time together playing what your child wants to play and talking about what she wants to talk about – this will ensure a relaxed, unrushed environment. Don't forget to praise her when she says things smoothly and for the efforts she makes – this will boost her confidence.

For more help and support, contact your local speech and language therapist immediately and/or the British Stammering Association, who kindly gave me permission to reproduce their advice on what can help stammering, above.

BILINGUALISM

How a bilingual home affects speech development

My patch in Oxford is very multicultural and it is common for me to see a child who lives in a home where one or even two foreign languages are spoken, and who goes to an English-speaking school, so that the child is exposed to two or three different languages. This is something that speech and language therapists embrace rather than worry about. Imagine the long-term advantages this child will have if she can speak three languages fluently.

Until quite recently, experts thought that bringing up a child in a bilingual home could cause language confusion, which would lead to a delay in speech development.

However, research now tells us to encourage parents to make the most of young children's sponge-like knack for acquiring language and revel in their ability to switch between languages, potentially boosting the speed at which the brain works. And there are other benefits, too. Over the past decade, Ellen Bialystok, a research professor of psychology at York University in Toronto, has established that bilingual children develop crucial skills in addition to their double vocabularies, learning different ways to solve logic problems or to handle multi-tasking – skills that are often considered part of the brain's so-called executive function.

However, that doesn't mean that raising a bilingual or trilingual child is easy – it can be confusing and worrying for parents and many are desperate for more information about how to juggle all the languages their child is exposed to. Below, I share my best strategies for nurturing a happy, confident and chatty bilingual child:

- The general rule is 'one place, one language' and, if this is not possible, then 'one person, one language'. This is in an ideal world and, in reality, a lot of families switch from one language to another fairly frequently throughout the day and so do the children. If this is the case, try to ensure you don't mix two languages into one sentence, conversation or activity; it is definitely better to keep the languages apart if possible.
- Try to speak only one language at a time – so when reading a book, *don't* say 'ball' in English and then 'pel' in Welsh, for example.

Read the whole thing through in English and then again in Welsh. During mealtimes, try to stick to one language and not switch between two. This is not always possible, but we're talking about an ideal world!

- If your child is going to be bilingual, she needs a high level of exposure to two languages over a long period of time. All the same games and activities to encourage language development – nursery rhymes, books, play, discussions, word games and daily language-rich activities such as visits to the park or supermarket – should be carried out in both languages.

- It's very common for a child to go through a silent period, which can last a few months, when she is first immersed in a setting where a different language to her mother tongue is spoken. This is normal and allows the child an opportunity to hear and understand the language before she starts to speak it. If this silent period lasts longer than four months, speak to a speech and language therapist for advice.

- It is normal for a child to refuse to speak in a particular language for a short time and only answer in another language, and your child may even tell you that she hates talking in a particular language. Continue as you always have done – this is just a phase and it will pass. Remember – the long-term benefits far surpass a periodic disagreement.

Myth-busting

There are a couple of myths about raising bilingual child that should be laid to rest.

Myth: language delays in a child's mother tongue are caused by learning a second language

This is not true. Learning a second language neither increases nor decreases the chances of having a language delay, and delays in learning language are just as common in bilingual children as they are in a monolingual community. If your child is thought to have a speech or language problem, or an additional need of some sort, *don't* stop speaking to her in the language in which you have always spoken to her – this will only hinder her language development. It's amazing how many parents do this or are told to do this, thinking that

HOW BILINGUALISM SHAPES THE BRAIN

Researchers at the University of Washington compared the electrical brain responses in infants from homes in which one language was spoken (monolingual) with those of infants exposed to two languages at home.[1]

They found that, at six months, the monolingual infants could discriminate between speech sounds, whether they were uttered in the language they were used to hearing or in another language not spoken in their homes. By 10 to 12 months, however, monolingual babies were no longer detecting sounds in the other language, only in the language they usually heard. The researchers suggest that this represents a process of neural commitment, by which the infant's brain wires itself to understand one language and its sounds.

In contrast, the bilingual infants followed a different developmental trajectory. At six to nine months, they did not detect differences in phonetic sounds in either language, but when they were older — 10 to 12 months — they were able to discriminate sounds in both.

'What the study demonstrates is that the variability in bilingual babies' experiences keeps them open,' says Dr. Patricia Kuhl, co-director of the Institute for Learning and Brain Sciences at the University of Washington and one of the authors of the study. 'It's another piece of evidence that what you experience shapes the brain.'

if there is only one language, the child will learn faster so long as the two languages aren't mixed together in the same game conversation. There is no evidence to suggest that this is true. Just to reiterate, no one should ever tell you to give up talking in one language. Being bilingual is not bad for your child, will not hold her back, confuse her or make life difficult for her; on the contrary, the advantages are vast!

Myth: it's easier to learn a second language if you stop using your first or home language and concentrate on the new language

This is definitely *not* true. We say that the stronger the first language is, the easier it is to learn a second language, because the child has already been exposed to, and has a grasp of, all the vocabulary and grammatical structures needed to acquire a language. Some families get into muddy waters when they switch to English in order to prepare their child for school. *Please don't do this.* The child can get very confused, not knowing which language is which, so just leave English to school – it'll be so much easier for your child.

BILINGUALISM STARTS IN THE WOMB!

Janet Werker, a professor of psychology at the University of British Columbia, studies how babies perceive language and how that shapes their learning. Even in the womb, she says, babies are exposed to the rhythms and sounds of language, and newborns have been shown to prefer languages that are rhythmically similar to the one they've heard during foetal development.

In one recent study, Dr Werker and her collaborators showed that babies born to bilingual mothers not only prefer both of those languages over others, but are also able to register that the two languages are different.

If you are worried, instead of speaking to your child in English yourself (particularly if it's broken or pigeon English), take her to a toddler group, a childminder or the house of a friend who speaks English before she starts school. An old teacher colleague of mine says it takes about one academic year for a three to four-year-old attending nursery every morning to be fluent in English if she has not had any exposure to English prior to this. Clever stuff, hey?

GLUE EAR

Glue ear is a temporary hearing problem in which the middle ear fills up with fluid instead of air, which muffles sound. Having glue ear is is rather like trying to hear while wearing a huge pair of ear muffs. Glue ear can fluctuate, but during a 'gluey' phase, a child can't hear language and speech sounds consistently, which means she can fall behind and/or pick up bad speech sound habits.

Glue ear is very common in young children because they do not have robust immune systems and tend to catch many of the bugs going around, and they may be prone to congestion through lots of coughs and colds, ear infections or allergies such as hayfever. When a child gets bunged up, so does the small tube that connects the nasal cavity to the middle ear, consequently filling the middle ear with 'glue'.

The incidence levels of glue ear peak from about two to six years of age. In the two to five-year age range 15–20 per cent of children will have glue ear at any time. The prevalence in children older than this falls to less than 5 per cent by age seven. In the vast majority of cases, glue ear will not persist beyond early childhood.

Detecting glue ear

Your child may have glue ear if:

• she has lots of colds.

- she does not hear so well, for instance, if she turns up the volume on the TV frequently, or says 'What?' or 'uh?' a lot.
- her behaviour deteriorates.
- she becomes quieter than usual.
- her concentration is poor.
- she finds listening with background noise difficult.
- she is unable to hear the differences between some speech sounds, which can affect pronunciation.
- she 'tunes out' because listening is hard work and, therefore, she misses information.
- she appears clumsy with poor balance (my daugher Jess weirdly started falling over a lot at the age of 16 months and my mum insisted I took her to the doctor. I felt like a fool, but the doctor took it very seriously, partly because Jess went splat on his office floor, and sent her to a paediatrician and for a hearing test. Sure enough, she had glue ear and had to be retested in four months).

If you are worried that your child may have glue ear, see your GP, who will look in her ears and possibly refer her for a hearing test. The audiology clinic is likely to monitor her hearing over a two to three-month period in most cases. Consultants tend to give a child a grommet (a little tube that fits into her eardrum in order to drain the glue away) only if there is no improvement over time, as grommets permanently damage the ear drum. As an interim measure, your child may be offered hearing aids.

There are adjustments that you can make to help a child with glue ear. Firstly, keep background noise to a minimum – turn off the TV, move away from noises when talking to your child and, if you have a busy, bustling home, try and have some quiet times. Also, encourage your child to look at you when you are talking so she can watch your mouth to work out how you are making those tricky speech sounds.

Ensure you have your child's attention before you speak. Keep your voice clear and speak slightly louder than usual, without shouting.

Talk to her when she is near you so she has a better chance of hearing you. Be patient and explain things more than you usually would – your child may be mishearing or confusing similar sounding words. And make sure you spend some one-to-one time with her every day, doing the Small Talk Time activities described below.

Small Talk Time **Glue ear**

- Practise lots and lots of listening games (see pages 97 to 99). If your child's ears become used to not hearing, even when the hearing improves you might have to retrain her ears to listen to sounds.
- Focus on phonics (speech sounds) and ensure your child can discriminate one single speech sound from another, then see if she can determine which sound particular words start with. Take a selection of toys, animals, perhaps, and say, 'Find an animal that starts with "b".'

GLUE EAR AT NURSERY OR PRE-SCHOOL

If your child has had a glue ear diagnosis from your GP, let your child's teachers, childminders or nursery assistants know, and encourage them to take the following action:

- Ensure your child is sitting near the speaker during communal times, such as mealtimes, carpet time, story time or song time.
- Check whether your child has heard an instruction by encouraging her to repeat it back prior to carrying it out, for instance, 'What did Gill say? She said, "Everybody stand up, collect your lunch boxes and line up by the door".'
- Have a quiet time and practise listening games, as suggested above.

GIRLS AND BOYS – THE DIFFERENCES

We often treat boys and girls differently as we bring them up, without even realizing that this is the case. As a general rule, girls tend to get more cuddles and conversation, whereas for boys, it's all about rough and tumble and physical games.

Psychologists have shown that if someone is told that a baby is female (whether it is or not), that person will talk more to them and give them more gender-specific toys, such as a hairbrush versus a ball, than they will if they're told the baby is male.

This difference in upbringing probably accounts for many of the differences between boys and girls, but there are other key differences, too, that have nothing to do with upbringing. For example, at birth, the brains of girls are subtly different from those of boys – in particular, a girl's language centre is slightly larger than a boy's, making girls more likely to pick up language when they hear it. This is a fact.

Boys are generally born heavier and with a more muscular build than girls, whereas girls develop fine motor coordination more readily. These subtle physiological differences mean that boys and girls will usually choose to play in different ways and with different toys. You'll probably notice this at your mother-and-baby group – the girls will play happily with a set of stacking cups while the boys want to rush around.

You might also spot that the girls in the group seem to be more advanced than the boys. This is because they develop at different speeds, so girls are usually slightly more ahead when it comes to vision, hearing, memory, smell and touch than male infants. Girl babies also tend to be more socially attuned, too, responding more readily to human voices or faces, or crying more vigorously in response to another infant's cry – and they are generally ahead of boys in language skills.

Boys eventually catch up in many of these areas and, by the age of three, they tend to out-perform girls in one cognitive area – visual-spatial integration, which is involved in navigation, assembling jigsaw puzzles and certain types of hand–eye coordination. I am afraid I have to mention the cliché about men being better map readers than women here – amazing that this difference is evident from such a young age!

Obviously, these are just my thoughts and observations and, as usual, I want to emphasize that we should not expect all children to conform to these norms – they are all unique!

IT'S A FACT – GIRLS LIKE DOLLS AND BOYS LIKE CARS

Research suggests that girls play with dolls because they're programmed to, not because of any sexual stereotyping. Richard Wrangham of Harvard University found that young male and female chimpanzees in the wild both play with sticks, but that girl chimps treat sticks like dolls, copying their mothers as they care for infants.

Wrangham says, 'This is the first evidence of an animal species in the wild in which object play differs between males and females.' The findings, published in *Current Biology*, were the result of 14 years of observation of the Kanyawara chimpanzee community in Kibale National Park, Uganda.[2]

CASE STUDY: MY SON ONLY WANTS TO PLAY WITH CARS

A parent came to see me with the following concern. She said, 'I know that play is crucial to learning but my three-year-old son, Dev, only ever wants to play with cars. I try to expose him to a wide range of toys in order to broaden his experiences, but he totally refuses and goes back to the cars or dumpers. I feel like it's so boring for him and for me. What can I do?'

In a nutshell, I told Dev's mum that she must play with the toys that motivate her son and think laterally about how to elicit language from them. There are tons of language-related games to play. Below are the ones I suggested.

Ready, Steady, Go (to promote listening skills)

Sit on the floor opposite your child. Get a car and say, 'Ready, steady . . .' Wait for your child to say, 'Go!' and, once he says it, push the car to him and praise him, saying, 'Well done, you said "Go!".' Take turns to push the car to each other.

Listening to sounds outside the window (to promote listening skills)

Open the window and listen to the noises you can hear. Encourage your child to listen for the difference between the vehicle noises, such as loud and quiet noises – for instance, a bus is loud and a car is quiet.

Asking for more (to encourage expressive language)

Put all the cars into a box and sit with the box on your lap, or next to you on the floor. Give your child a car. When he reaches for another one, encourage him to say, 'More!' and do the sign for 'more' (see page 48). If your child can put two words together, encourage him to say 'More car!' or three words, 'More car, please', 'More big/little car, please' (you will need to show him a big and a little car so he can choose), 'More blue/red car' (you will need to show him a blue car and a red car so that he can see the difference).

Learning action words (to encourage understanding and expressive language)

When your child is playing, give a running commentary of what he is doing – yes, it's my Say What You See technique *again* (see page 17)! Hopefully, next time you play a similar game, he'll begin to use the words he has heard before. Use the following action words and phrases: 'going', 'stoping', 'driving', 'crashing/ bumping', 'waiting', 'opening the door', 'putting the seat belt on', 'playing the radio', 'looking out of the window' and 'beeping the horn'. You could even try some unrelated action words, such as 'car jumping', 'car sleeping', car looking', and so on.

Learning basic concepts (to promote understanding and expressive language)

Try to teach the following words while playing:

- up/down
- big/little
- fast/slow
- over/under
- in front/behind/in between

You could try playing hide and seek with the cars around the room, introducing these concepts into your game.

Sorting cars (to promote understanding and expressive language)

Sort the vehicles into different categories. For example:

- cars/lorries/buses
- big/little
- colours
- fast/slow
- those that have doors that open and those that don't

If you then pack the cars into different boxes according to how you have sorted them, when you go to play with them again you can ask your child specifically which cars he wants. 'Do you want the fast cars or the slow cars?' This game is a great way of cunningly testing your child's level of understanding!

Dev's mum visited my clinic a few weeks after she'd begun playing these games with him. She felt a sense of relief knowing that he was learning new words and skills through playing the games he loved. They were both enjoying their playtimes more and Dev's willingness to play with his mother had massively improved. She'd noticed small improvements in his concentration and language development and even bought him a new monster truck to celebrate!

HOW SIBLINGS AFFECT SPEECH AND LANGUAGE DEVELOPMENT

On page 225, we considered how the birth of a new baby might affect an older sibling's language, but let's consider other possibilities concerning siblings that might also have an impact.

We've learnt that boys need a little extra attention when it comes to certain aspects of learning, so imagine a scenario in which a new baby boy is born into a family where the older sibling – a very articulate, sociable and confident older sister – rules the roost. We must ensure the younger brother is included and that the amount of time spent in both one-to-one engagement with a parent and with the entire family is balanced. For example, during mealtimes when everybody is telling their news, allow the younger baby to tell his news, too – it might be a load of babble or gibberish, but allow him a chance to get a word in, in order for his language skills to develop.

In some of the families I visit at home, I have spotted that there's a bit of a habit of 'parking' a younger baby in a reclining baby bouncer seat or even a car seat, to the side of what's happening with the older children. Try to include your younger children in as much of the action as possible. Allow them to sit with you as you play together, or use a jumping baby bouncer, which allows them to feel much more included in whatever's going on.

HOW TO GET THE BEST OUT OF YOUR STORYBOOKS

Throughout this book I suggest using storybooks to help expand your child's language skills. This is because, besides yourselves, books and stories are the ultimate resource for helping your child to develop advanced language skills. There are many reasons for this and, below, I have listed a few. Sharing a book regularly with your child:

- provides a lovely opportunity to snuggle up, share a moment together and bond with each other. It gives you an opportunity to hear and watch your child as she communicates.
- helps to develop better attention and listening skills as your child learns to concentrate for the duration of the whole book, while she turns the pages, looks at the pictures and listens to familiar words in increasingly longer sentences.
- develops a child's understanding because looking at the same books over and over again allows her to hear a repetition of the same words while looking at corresponding pictures, and the repetition develops and cements her understanding of the words and the narrative.
- helps a child to learn new words, hear longer sentences and be exposed to grammatical structures to help develop her expressive language.
- provides an opportunity to work on making choices. Even with a very little baby, ensure you offer a choice of which book she would like to read.

- helps to develop fine motor control, by turning the pages and pointing to the pictures, so encourage your child to do so.
- provides older children with a format with which to retell their own stories.
- helps to develop many aspects of language development, such as use of tenses, prediction and narrative. Ask your child what happened on the previous page once you have turned it, what might happen next before you turn the page and what might happen at the end. Then ask her to retell the whole story when you've finished.
- encourages your child to get into a daily reading routine or an academic routine that will stand them in good stead for life!
- expands your child's thought and opens up and enriches her life as she enters a world of dragons, fairy princesses, faraway countries and other things that are not in her own daily experience.

Selecting books for your child

Choose books that are suitable for your child's age group. The tips below should help you make the right book choices for your child.

0–6 months

Very young babies love being snuggled and enjoy listening to the sound of a parent's voice and looking at pictures in high contrast (for instance, pictures in black and white or black and yellow) especially pictures of faces.

Then they move onto board books with simple but bold pictures and one or two words per page. Encourage your child to turn the pages by lifting one page up slightly with your right hand. Remember to always offer a choice of book and, at this age, your child will reach to the one they want.

Try books with familiar songs in them and cloth books, so that your child can give them a good chew.

6–12 months

Try fairly short books – about one sentence per page or less – with bright colours and sturdy pages. And if there's a repetitive line, even better. Try the *That's not my . . .* series by Fiona Watt and Rachel Wells or *Dear Zoo* by Rod Campbell. Try bath books and noisy books and also make a family book (an album) yourself with all your child's favourite people in it.

12–18 months

At this age, children still enjoy repetition, so I often add a repetitive line when there isn't one (for example, when reading *Where's Spot*, I will add the line 'Where's Spot?' each time I turn the page). Also, why not try a book with a rhythm or rhyme? Children will be more interested in the pictures than the story. Lift-the-flap books are good, but pop-up books are not so great because all the pictures get ripped out!

If possible, sit so that your child can see your face and the book, so she can watch your mouth move. Better still, if you can use your hands as you are talking, it'll really help the book to come alive – you'll need a cookbook stand! My favourite books for this age group include: *Big Red Bath* by Julia Jarman and Adrian Reynolds, *The Tickle Book* (with pop-up surprises) by Ian Whybrow and Axel Scheffler, *Tales from Acorn Wood: Rabbit's Nap* by Julia Donaldson and Axel Scheffler, *Brown Bear, Brown Bear, What Do You See?* by Bill Martin Jr. and Eric Carle and *Where's Spot?* by Eric Hill.

18–24 months

Children of this age group still like the types of books listed above but they are beginning to like a storyline running though. My favourite books for this age group include: *The Tiger Who Came to Tea* by Judith Kerr, *We're Going on a Bear Hunt* by Michael Rosen and Helen Oxenbury, *Handa's Surprise* by Eileen Browne, *The Very Hungry*

Caterpillar by Eric Carle and *Chocolate Mousse for Greedy Goose* by Julia Donaldson and Nick Sharratt.

Also seek out books that will extend your child's vocabulary, such as *First Thousand Words in English* by Heather Amery and Stephen Cartwright or *The Baby's Catalogue* by Allan Ahlberg and Janet Ahlberg.

Two to three years

When choosing books for two to three-year-olds, look for those with a basic story supported by quite busy pictures so that, if your child doesn't understand the words, she can see the pictures. Children love the detail in the pictures and when you point something out that they haven't yet noticed. A child will like a book that means something. For example, the mother of a friend of mine died, and when she broke the news to her son, she told him that her mother was now a star, and the book *How to Catch a Star* by Oliver Jeffers then went down really well.

Other books that are great for this age group include the *The Gruffalo* and *The Gruffalo's Child* by Julia Donaldson and Axel Scheffler, *Who Sank the Boat?* by Pamela Allen and *Where's Wally?* by Martin Handford. And for extending vocabulary, try *You Choose* by Pippa Goodhart and Nick Sharratt.

Three to four years

At this age, a child likes a good story, perhaps a fairy tale with longer paragraphs – probably five sentences or more per page. She also loves humour and expanding her thought and imagination. Good books for this age group include: *The Three Little Pigs* by Joan Stimson and Steve Smallman, *The Lamb Who Came for Dinner* by Steve Smallman and Joelle Dreidemy, *Charlie Cook's Favourite Book* and *A Squash and A Squeeze* by Julia Donaldson and Axel Scheffler, *Q Pootle 5* by Nick Butterworth, *Mixed-Up Fairy Tales* by Hilary Robinson and Nick Sharratt and *The Astonishing Secret of Awesome Man* by Michael Chabon and Jake Parker.

Another thing to try at this age is picture books without words to help your child to retell the story by herself. You could try *Window* by Jeannie Baker or *Hug* by Jez Alborough.

A FINAL WORD FROM ME

I've really enjoyed writing this book and sharing my expertise as a speech and language therapist with you. I hope you've found our journey from babbling baby to talking toddler entertaining and inspiring, too, and that I've filled you with confidence when it comes to communicating with your child. If my Small Talk Time games have given you lots of laughter and brought some fun to those afternoons when you just don't know how to entertain your little one, then I've achieved what I set out to do. I'd be even more delighted if I knew that every reader had used Say What You See, stayed one step ahead and ditched the dummy!

As I've said all along, you are your child's best resource for learning, so keep Small Talking and feel confident in the fact that you are giving your toddler the very best possible start in life. Good luck.

Appendix

Recognizing a problem*

You can have a gut feeling that there is something wrong with your child's speech or language development, but often it is difficult to know where the problem lies. Below are a few pointers that might help you to detect the main area in which your child needs support.

A child with attention and listening difficulties might:

- be easily distractible, unable to focus on an activity led by an adult, or even on something he has chosen, for long enough to gain information from it.
- have difficulty sitting still.
- appear to rush around and find it hard focusing on one activity.
- be unable to assimilate two pieces of information at the same time, for instance, if he is watching TV, he won't be able to listen to you calling his name and will seem as if he is ignoring you.
- be unable to complete a task.
- not recall information immediately after it has been given.
- daydream or appear to be 'away with the fairies'.
- not engage with group activities.
- need constant reminders from adults to look and listen.

---

* 'Recognising a problem' was adapted by Karen Fern (Oxfordshire Children's SLT) and Susie Fuller (EYSENIT), with kind permission from I CAN – www.ican. org.uk

A child with difficulty understanding might:

- repeat instructions rather then carry them out known as echolalia.
- follow part of an instruction rather than the whole thing.
- not appear to listen when spoken to.
- appear quiet and withdrawn.
- show a lack of interest when stories are read.
- be labelled as 'naughty' because he can't do what he is told.
- answer questions incorrectly and inappropriately.
- wait for others to move before following an instruction when in a group.
- generally copy other children.
- rely on the use of gestures and other non-verbal clues.
- look slightly vacant when you talk to him.
- prefer to stick to an established routine and get upset or agitated when it changes.
- be unable to understand complicated sentences and follow verbal instructions.

A child who has difficulty expressing himself might:

- use a limited amount of words, relying on a reduced vocabulary.
- say only the key words in a sentence and miss out the grammar.
- sound like a much younger child.
- repeat the same phrases over and over again.
- shorten long words and long sentences.
- frequently have trouble finding the right word and get stuck, or use a word that is closely related to the target word but not exact, for instance, using 'that one' or 'caravan' for 'tent'.
- be shy or withdrawn with other children or adults, especially if he perceives he will have to talk during an activity.
- use gestures, facial expressions and body language to communicate.
- be very physical to get attention, for instance, by tapping or hitting other children.

- be frequently frustrated.
- be reluctant or refuse to answer direct questions.
- have difficulty retelling a story or relaying information.

A child with speech sound problems might:

- sound like a younger child.
- talk, but be difficult to understand.
- have difficulty making himself understood to unfamiliar adults and look to his parents to interpret.
- use non-verbal communication, for instance, signs, gestures, facial expressions, pointing and so on to communicate.
- be frequently frustrated.
- use the same word or sound over and over again.

A child with social communication difficulties might:

- appear to be a loner and spend a lot of time playing alone.
- have limited or inappropriate social communication, e.g. be quite physical rather than verbal.
- have inappropriate volume, speak with a monotone or talk too fast.
- talk about one subject for much of the time.
- not give eye contact during communication.
- be unable to play imaginatively with toys.
- not be able to take turns in a conversation.
- talk continuously or find it difficult to take turns or shout out.
- make inappropriate comments which appear rude or obnoxious.
- be quiet or withdrawn.
- have difficulty sitting for group activities.
- prefer to follow a routine and may be anxious when routine is abandoned.

What to do if your child needs help

If you are concerned that your child may have a speech and/or language problem, get help early – the earlier the better. Talk to your

GP, health visitor or local speech and language therapist. There is a fairly long waiting list for an initial assessment on the NHS – usually around eighteen weeks, depending on your postcode – and you may have to wait again for individual or group therapy. Below is some advice to help you identify when a referral to a speech and language therapist should be made. If your child has a stammer, ask for a referral, whatever his age.

A child of less than 12 months of age

A child of this age should see a speech and language therapist if he:

- has difficulty with eating or drinking.
- is not responding to noises in the environment or your voice.
- is not looking at or interacting with familiar adults.
- is not babbling at 12 months.

A two-year-old child

A child of this age should see a speech and language therapist if he:

- cannot focus on an activity that he has chosen for more than a few seconds.
- cannot follow very simple instructions.
- cannot understand short phrases, for instance, 'Where's teddy?' or 'Get your coat.'
- is saying fewer than fifty words.

A two-and-a-half-year-old child

A child of this age should see a speech and language therapist if he:

- has difficulty concentrating on an activity for more than a few seconds.
- cannot understand two key words in a sentence, for example, 'Make the *baby sit*,' or 'Show me your nose and your *hair*.'

- is saying fewer than seventy-five words and not joining two words together.

(Note that, at this age, speech sounds are still inconsistently spoken, and it is common for a child to find the following speech sounds tricky: 's', 'sh', 'f', 'v', 'ch', 'j', 'th' and 'r'.)

A three-year-old child

A child of this age should see a speech and language therapist if he:

- is not able to concentrate on an activity led by an adult for a few seconds.
- has difficulty understanding three key words in a sentence, for example, 'Put teddy under the bed.'
- is still only using single words and learned phrases.
- only familiar adults can understand his speech.

A four-year-old child

A child of this age should see a speech and language therapist if he:

- seems vacant when you talk to him or repeats your sentence back.
- is not able to make a conversation and seems reluctant to communicate.
- seems to be still using only key words in a sentence and not using grammar, such as past and future tenses, and therefore sounds like a younger child.
- does not understand or use concepts such as big/little or in/on/under.
- is difficult to understand when he is talking.
- isn't mixing with peers.

What will a speech and language therapist do?

A speech and language therapist will see a child who has a difficulty in any of the areas listed below:

- attention and listening.
- language skills for comprehension and expression.
- social communication skills.
- speech skills.
- voice problems.
- oral skills (problems with strength, range and speed of oral movements).
- eating and drinking issues.

The therapist will assess your child's skills to establish where the problem lies. You will then be offered tailored advice, targets and a programme of exercises and training workshops designed in order to achieve the targets. Your child's speech and language therapist will include the whole family as far as possible, and will work together with other agencies, such as teachers, health visitors, occupational therapists, nursery nurses and so on to provide an integrated service for your child.

If you would like more information on children's speech and language difficulties, I recommend the book *Time to Talk: Parents' Accounts of Children's Speech Difficulties* by Margaret Glogowska.

Glossary

Anticipation game – a game in which the adult will expect the child to do something to take part in the game.

Articulators – the jaw, lips and tongue.

Attention/listening – the ability to focus attention on the person talking to receive an intricate message.

Auditory memory – the ability to process, analyse and recall orally presented information.

Babble – the stage where babies are experimenting with consonant sounds but not yet using recognizable words.

Blends or consonant clusters – when two consonant sounds appear together, e.g. train.

Comprehension – understanding what spoken words mean.

Concentration – the ability to focus on a given activity for an appropriate amount of time in order to complete a task.

Concept – an idea, a thought or a notion that corresponds to a class of entities, e.g. big, small, medium.

Container play – a game of transferring objects from one container to another, enjoyed by children of approximately two to two and a half years.

Conversational babble – when the babble becomes more elaborate, reaching four or five syllables, and varied tones are used, such as 'goo-eee-yah', 'bay-me-ooo-du', 'ka-da-bu-ba'. This usually appears by about ten months.

Delay – when a child's language is developing in the right sequence, but at a slower rate.

Difficulty/impairment – a difficulty is something which may be overcome; an impairment is something thought to be longer term.

Disorder – when language is not typical of normal language development. Children will have some language skills, but not others, or the way in which these skills develop will be different from usual.

Dysphagia – an inability or partial inability to swallow.

Expressive language – the use of words and sentences to communicate our needs, wants and thoughts.

Gesture – naturally using your hands or body to communicate in order to emphasise a point, e.g. palms facing upwards accompanied by a shoulder shrug for 'I don't know'.

Grammar – how words and their component parts combine to form sentences.

Information carrying words (ICW) – a word that carries a meaning, e.g. the table is dirty = two ICWs.

Jargon – speech therapy term for conversational babble.

Key word – this refers to a word that your child has to understand in order to carry out an instruction.

Language – the combination of sounds, words and sentences used to express meaning.

Minimal pair – pairs of words that only differ in one phonological element, e.g. Kate and gate.

Motherese/Parentese – a unique form of speech used by adults when talking to babies. Also known as child-directed/infant-directed speech and baby-talk.

OT – occupational therapist.

Phonics – a method of teaching letters using their speech sounds in preparation for reading and spelling, so the 's' sound would be 'sss' not 'suh' or 'ess'.

Phonology – the way a child uses individual speech sounds to formulate words.

Physio – physiotherapist.

Play-based learning – the method of using play to encourage learning.

Pragmatics – when a person had good language skills, but a problem with using language socially, e.g. using inappropriate or unrelated words in conversations.

Pre-babble – the sounds that are made unintentionally before babble appears including vowle sounds and experimental noises.

Pretend play – using props in an imaginative way like role play, e.g. the home corner or a shoe shop.

Pre-verbal stage – the stage before a child uses words to communicate. Infancy is, by definition, a pre-verbal phase in development. (The Latin word *infans* means 'without language'.)

Reduplicated babble – when the same sound is repeated in babble, for example, 'ba ba' or 'goo goo'.

Semantics – the meaning of words.

Sensory overload – when a child is bombarded with too much sensory information (visual, verbal or tactile), causing the child to feel overwhelmed or to shut down in response.

Sequencing skills – the ability to retell parts of a story or event in the correct order.

Signs – using your hands to convey meaning in a more formal way.

SLT – speech and language therapist.

Small World play – playing with miniature toys that represent real life, e.g. a doll's house and furniture.

Speech sound system – the range of sounds that are used within a given language.

Symbolic play – pretending that one object represents another, e.g. a colander as a helmet.

Symbols – pictures which represent meaning, e.g. a disabled toilet sign.

Syntax – the grammatical arrangement of words in sentences.

Tongue thrust – a reflex that causes tongue protrusion that prevents choking. This should disappear by four to six months.

Variegated babble – the second stage of babbling, which involves adding two different consonant sounds together, such as 'mu bu' or 'du wu'. This should appear by about eight to nine months.

Vocabulary – the total number of words a person knows and uses.

Word – a consistently spoken utterance that represents a particular object or person.

Support Groups and Charities

Afasic (UK-wide parent support group) – visit www.**afasic**england. org.uk for details of information and activities across the four countries

British Stammering Association – www.stammering.org

The Communication Trust (a coalition organization raising awareness, providing information, influencing policy and promoting best practise among the children's workforce) – www. thecommunicationtrust.org.uk

Hanen (programmes, resources and workshops for parents and professionals) – www.hanen.org

Help With Talking (independent speech and language therapy website) – www.helpwithtalking.com

I CAN (resources, information and training on children's communication development and SLCN for parents, carers and professionals) – www.ican.org.uk

National Autistic Society – www.autism.org.uk

Royal College of Speech and Language Therapists – www.rcslt.org

Talk To Your Baby – www.literacytrust.org.uk/talk_to_your_baby

Talking Point (information about children's communication including online progress checker) – www.talkingpoint.org.uk

Recommended Reading

Books for Parents

A First Language by Roger Brown

Baby-led Weaning by Gill Rapley

It Takes Two to Talk by Jan Pepper and Elaine Weitzman, published by the Hanen Centre

My First Signs by Annie Kubler

Raising Boys: Why Boys Are Different – and How to Help Them Become Happy and Well-Balanced Men by Steve Biddulph

Reasons to Communicate – adapted from the *Early Bird Programme Parent Book* by Jane Shields and Jo Stevens, published by the National Autistic Society

Time to Talk: Parents' Accounts of Children's Speech Difficulties by Margaret Glogowska

Why Love Matters by Sue Gerhardt

Books for Children

Big Red Bath by Julia Jarman and Adrian Reynolds

Brown Bear, Brown Bear, What Do You See? by Bill Martin Jr. and Eric Carle

Charlie Cook's Favourite Book and *A Squash and A Squeeze* by Julia Donaldson and Axel Scheffler

Chocolate Mousse for Greedy Goose by Julia Donaldson and Nick Sharratt

Dear Zoo by Rod Campbell

Farmyard Tales by Heather Amery and Stephen Cartwright

First Thousand Words in English by Heather Amery and Stephen Cartwright

Five Minutes' Peace by Jill Murphy

Funny Face by Nicola Smee

Handa's Surprise by Eileen Browne

How to Catch a Star by Oliver Jeffers

Hug by Jez Alborough

Mixed-up Fairy Tales by Hilary Robinson and Nick Sharratt

Opposites Peek-a-boo by Eric Hill

Owl Babies by Martin Waddell and Patrick Benson

Peace at Last by Jill Murphy

Q Pootle 5 by Nick Butterworth

Rosie's Walk by Pat Hutchins

Tales From Acorn Wood: Rabbit's Nap by Julia Donaldson and Axel Scheffler

That's Not My . . . series by Fiona Watt and Rachel Wells

The Astonishing Secret of Awesome Man by Michael Chabon and Jake Parker

The Baby's Catalogue by Janet and Allan Ahlberg

The Gruffalo by Julia Donaldson and Axel Scheffler

The Gruffalo's Child by Julia Donaldson and Axel Scheffler

The Lamb Who Came for Dinner by Steve Smallman and Joelle Dreidemy

The Red Book by Barbara Lehman

The Smartest Giant in Town by Julia Donaldson and Axel Scheffler

The Snowman by Raymond Briggs

The Three Little Pigs by Joan Stimson and Steve Smallman

The Tickle Book (with pop-up surprises) by Ian Whybrow and Axel Scheffler

The Tiger Who Came to Tea by Judith Kerr

The Very Hungry Caterpillar by Eric Carle

Thomas' Really Useful Word Book by Rev. W. Awdry

What's the Time Mr Wolf by Annie Kubler

We're Going on a Bear Hunt by Michael Rosen and Helen Oxenbury

Where's Spot? by Eric Hill
Where's Wally? by Martin Handford
Who Sank the Boat? by Pamela Allen
Window by Jeannie Baker
You Choose by Pippa Goodhart and Nick Sharratt

Resources

See our website for a range of resources: www.smalltalktime.com

- A doll, teddy, bricks, balls and cars
- Babble bag
- Big Mouth Sound Pack – Stass Publications
- *Baby Shapes 3*, The Children's Project Ltd, 1999 – one of a set of books for newborn babies
- Bubbles
- Bumbo seat
- Chewy tube – Amazon
- Doctor's kit
- Ella's Kitchen pouches
- Fishing game
- Flashcards of everyday objects, verbs and position words
- What's Next? puzzle by Galt Toys
- Photos of family members
- Sound sock

General games found in any speech and language clinic:

- Flash cards
- Jolly Phonics – Jolly Songs CD
- Leap frogs – Early Learning Centre
- Little furniture
- Mirror
- Monkey Business

- Mr Pop
- Opposites cards
- Oral motor toys – (see chapter Four)
- Pop-up Pirate
- Post box made from an old shoe box
- Pretend food and tea set
- Puppets
- Sequencing cards
- Shark attack
- Shopping game
- Skittles
- Small world people and animals
- Springy spiders
- Story-building jigsaw puzzle
- Z-vibe – a tool for desensitizing the mouth

The following websites are useful for the resources listed above:

- www.earlyyearsresources.co.uk – for 4-scene sequencing cards
- www.stasspublications.co.uk – for the Bigmouth Sound Pack
- www.makaton.org – for books, resources, DVDs and an overview of research into language development

Endnotes

Introduction

1 Sue Roulstone, James Law, Robert Rush, Judy Clegg, Tim Peters, *Investigating the Role of Language in Children's Early Educational Outcomes*, commissioned by the Department for Education, June 2011.

Chapter Two: What is Language and How Does it Develop?

1 J. Coupe O'Kane and J. Goldbart, *Communication Before Speech – Development and Assessment* (London: David Fulton, 1998, 2nd edition).

2 Judith Coupe O'Kane, Headteacher of Melland High School, Manchester, and Juliet Goldbart, Department of Psychology and Speech Pathology, Manchester Metropolitan University.

Chapter Three: The Pre-Babble Phase (0–6 Months)

1 Kathleen Wermke, 'Newborns' Cry Melody Is Shaped by Their Native Language', *Current Biology*, Vol. 19, Issue 23, 5 November 2009.

2 Blasi and Mecire et al., *Current Biology*, Vol. 21, Issue 14, 1220–1224, 30 June 2011.

3 M. S. Zeedyk, in collaboration with the National Literacy Trust and the Sutton Trust, 'The Impact of Buggy Orientation on Parent–Infant Interaction and Infant Stress', 2007.

4 E. D. Thiessen, E. A. Hill and J. R. Saffran, 'Infant-Directed Speech Facilitates Word Segmentation', *Infancy*, 7, pp. 49–67, 1 January 2005.

Chapter Five: The Babble Phase (6–12 Months)

1 David Lewkowicz,'Babies Lip-read Before Talking', *Science News*, Vol. 181, 3, p. 9, February 2012.

2 K. J. Topping, R. Dekhinet and S. Zeedyk, 'Hindrances for Parents in Enhancing Child Language', *Educational Psychology Review*, Vol. 23, No. 3, September 2011, pp. 413–455.

3 Luigia Camaioni, Francesca Bellagamba and Alan Fogel, 'A Longitudinal Examination of the Transition to Symbolic Communication in the Second Year of Life', *Infant and Child Development*, Vol. 12, Issue 2, pp.177–195, June 2003.

Chapter Six: Single-word Phase (12–18 Months)

1 Lewis, B. A. & Thompson, L. A., 'A Study of Developmental Speech and Language Disorders in Twins'. *Journal of Speech and Hearing Research*, 35, 1086–1094, 1992.
2 Bill Wells and Joy Stackhouse, *Children's Speech and Literacy Difficulties: A Psycholinguistic Framework* (Chichester: Wiley Blackwell, 1997).

Chapter Seven: Combining Words Phase (18–24 Months)

1 L. Rescorla, A. Alley and J. B. Christine, 'Word Frequencies in Toddlers' Lexicons', *Journal of Speech, Language, and Hearing Research*, 44, pp. 598–609, 2001.
2 'The Human Speechome Project', Deb Roy, Rupal Patel, Philip DeCamp, Rony Kubat, Michael Fleischman, Brandon Roy, Nikolaos Mavridis, Stefanie Tellex, Alexia Salata, Jethran Guinness, Michael Levit, Peter Gorniak – Cognitive Machines Group, MIT Media Laboratory. Presented at the 28th annual conference of the Cognitive Science Society, July 2006.
3 J. Berko and R. Brown, 'Psycholinguistic Research Methods', reported in *Handbook of Research Methods in Child Development*, edited by P. Mussen (New York: John Wiley, 1960).

Chapter Eight: Language Expansion (24–36 months)

1 The reflections in 'Two Years On: final report of the Communication Champion for children' are based on findings from an extensive programme of meetings with local commissioners and service providers across England, undertaken between January 2010 and December 2011. Jean Gross has met with 105 out of the 152 local authority/NHS Primary Care Trust pairings in England.

Chapter Ten: Common Parental Concerns

1 Adrian Garcia-Sierra, Maritza Rivera-Gaxiola, Cherie R. Percaccio, Barbara T. Conboy, Harriett Romo, Lindsay Klarman, Sophia Ortiz and Patricia K. Kuhl, 'Bilingual Language Learning: An ERP Study Relating Early Brain Responses To Speech, Language Input, and Later Word Production', *Journal of Phonetics*, DOI: 10.1016/j.wocn.2011.07.002, 2011.
2 *Sex differences in Chimpanzees' Use of Sticks As Play Objects Resemble Those of Children*, Sonya M. Kahlenberg, Richard W. Wrangham, 21 December, 2010, *Current Biology*, 20 (24) pp. R1067–R1068.

Index